ADMIRAL GORSHKOV

ADMIRAL GORSHKOV

The Man Who Challenged the U.S. Navy

Norman Polmar
Thomas A. Brooks
George Fedoroff

Naval Institute Press
Annapolis, Maryland

Naval Institute Press
291 Wood Road
Annapolis, MD 21402

Library of Congress Cataloging-in-Publication Data

Names: Polmar, Norman, author. | Brooks, Thomas A., author. | Fedoroff,
    George (George E.), author.
Title: Admiral Gorshkov : the man who challenged the U.S. Navy / Norman
    Polmar, Rear Admiral Thomas A. Brooks, U.S. Navy (Ret.), George Fedoroff.
Description: Annapolis, Maryland : Naval Institute Press, 2019. | Includes
    bibliographical references and indexes.
Identifiers: LCCN 2018042638 (print) | LCCN 2018043734 (ebook) | ISBN
    9781682473320 (ePDF) | ISBN 9781682473320 (ePub) | ISBN 9781682473306
    (hardback) | ISBN 9781682473320 (ebook)
Subjects: LCSH: Gorshkov, Sergei Georgievich, 1910–1988. | Soviet Union.
    Voenno-Morskoi Flot—Biography. | Soviet Union. Voenno-Morskoi
    Flot—History. | Admirals—Soviet Union—Biography. | Sea-power—Soviet
    Union—History. | Soviet Union—History, Naval. | BISAC: BIOGRAPHY &
    AUTOBIOGRAPHY / Military. | HISTORY / Military / Naval. | HISTORY / Europe
    / Russia & the Former Soviet Union.
Classification: LCC V64.S65 (ebook) | LCC V64.S65 P65 2019 (print) | DDC
    359.0092 [B] —dc23
LC record available at https://lccn.loc.gov/2018042638

♾ Print editions meet the requirements of ANSI/NISO z39.48-1992 (Permanence of Paper).
Printed in the United States of America.

27 26 25 24 23 22 21 20 19   9 8 7 6 5 4 3 2 1
First printing

Maps created by Chris Robinson.

Modern naval battle consists of the inter-weaving of complex phenomena. The arena of this battle is the many miles of expanse in the depths of the seas and oceans, their surface, and the air which extends above them. The mightiest power engineering and radio-electronics and effective means of struggle compete here. But it is primarily the contest of people, the contest of minds.

—Editorial, *Krasnaya Zvezda* [Red Star], 14 April 1970

CONTENTS

Appendixes

FOREWORD

Greatness in a leader moves history. That view is not accepted by economic determinists, communists or geopoliticians, who believe massive tides and forces, not individuals, determine outcomes. The life of Sergey Gorshkov refutes the latter view.

Joining the Navy at age 17, a decision opposed by his distinctly academic family, Gorshkov rose and survived amidst revolutions, two world wars, repeated purges, plots, and endless intrigues to build and lead one of the great navies of the 20th Century.

As a non-political junior officer serving in surface combat, he was a disciplined, professional, and natural leader who rose quickly to command destroyers, cruisers, squadrons, and then fleets. During World War II, he was almost always in combat, alternating with staff positions where he made crucial decisions. With seemingly flawless political instincts, he realized that to succeed and survive in the Navy that he loved, he had to join the Communist party and be "politically reliable." In this, he proved to be quite adept, impressing future leaders like Nikita Khrushchev while avoiding making enemies. During the Stalin purges of the late 1930s he saw many of his naval superiors executed or sent to the gulags.

Admiral Gorshkov had a vision of what kind of navy his country needed to be a great power, and he had the grasp of technology and its rapid development that was needed to guide weapons and warship procurement. At first the Soviet Navy benefited from Josef Stalin's pursuit of naval superiority over the "imperialists" and the plans to build a massive conventional fleet. However, when Stalin was succeeded by Nikita Khrushchev—not unlike Harry S. Truman succeeding Franklin D. Roosevelt—a navalist replaced

by a landsman, the Soviet Navy's budget was decimated and warship construction virtually halted. Gorshkov, now appointed
Commander-in-Chief of the Soviet Navy, was wise enough to
hold his tongue and bide his time.

That time soon came with the Cuban Missile Crisis during
which Khrushchev was humiliated by the American naval blockade.
Soon, with Khrushchev succeeded as head of the party and government, the successors to the leader realized that as a super-power the
Soviet Union must pursue naval parity if not superiority. Admiral
Gorshkov was the man to move things in that direction. The Soviet
Government soon embarked on a building program developed by
the admiral and his highly capable aircraft, warship, and submarine
design bureaus.

Under his firm leadership the Gorshkov navy emerged. In 1970
he directed a massive, multi-ocean naval exercise called *Okean-70*
that created global shockwaves, ending any doubt that the Soviets
were determined to challenge the naval supremacy of the United
States. It was the largest peacetime naval exercise ever conducted
with more than 200 surface ships and submarines, plus land-based
naval aviation, carried out in multiple theaters of operations.

In little more than a decade after the Cuban Missile Crisis,
with the U.S. Navy depleted and demoralized by Vietnam, in 1974
the just-retired Chief of Naval Operations, Admiral Elmo Zumwalt,
declared that the U.S. could lose a war at sea against Admiral
Gorshkov's larger fleet.

Despite these forebodings, the post-Vietnam military reductions and Watergate scandal prevented any American reaction, and
American and NATO naval policy became defensive and reactive.

This situation began to change with a new administration in
Washington in 1981: a new, bipartisan forward-thinking naval strategy was funded and enacted which resulted in a rapid rebuilding of
U.S. naval strength and a new strategy that undertook offensive naval
exercises around the Soviet periphery. The U.S. Navy demonstrated

that geography and superior NATO technology would give the West the capability of defeating the Soviet fleet and neutralize their conventional superiority in Europe. With the declining Soviet economy, hastened by the collapse of oil prices, it became clear to President Mikhail Gorbachev that the Soviet regime was nearing bankruptcy. Thus, when Admiral Gorshkov's reaction to the new U.S. naval strategy was to call for major increases in spending for the Soviet Navy, Gorbachev decided to send him ashore. The Admiral was retired in December 1985, one month short of the 30th anniversary of his appointment as Commander in Chief.

This riveting account by Messrs. Polmar, Brooks, and Fedoroff will be the definitive source on this great naval figure for decades to come.

John Lehman
U.S. Secretary of the Navy
(1981–1987)

PERSPECTIVE

This is a book about a man and his ability to change a culture and to create a powerful navy that was radically different from traditional navies. And, he accomplished this despite strong opposition from the nation's army-dominated power structure. The Russian Navy that is at sea in the 21st Century is, to a significant degree, based on the fleet that this man built. This Russian Navy that sent a nuclear-propelled battle cruiser into the Caribbean in 2008, supported the Soviet combat actions in Syria beginning in 2015, and fired missiles from surface ships and a submarine into ISIS areas in Syria can trace its "roots" directly to Admiral of the Fleet of the Soviet Union Sergei G. Gorshkov.

This officer was the product of a tradition very different from that of his Western contemporaries—and a decidedly non-naval one. He had a unique background of revolution, civil war, world wars, and the forcible implementation of an all-controlling communist dictatorship. Out of this background of violence and overwhelming transformation came a man with a vivid appreciation of the role and value of navies but with his own, unique ideas about the kind of navy the Soviet Union required and the role that navy should play in Soviet military and national strategy.

Western naval observers have persisted in attempting to define Admiral Gorshkov in Western naval terms and often have been baffled when they found that the man and his actions simply "didn't fit." This book lays out the tradition, background, experiences, and thinking of the man as they relate to the development of the Soviet Navy he commanded for almost three decades and that was able to challenge directly the maritime dominance of the United States—a traditional sea power.

Some of the content of this book is derived from interviews with men who knew, or at least had met, Admiral Gorshkov, as well as with some of his colleagues. (One of the authors of this book had extensive discussions with Fleet Admiral Vladimir N. Chernavin, Gorshkov's successor.)[1]

Much of the content is derived from information and writings publicly available during Admiral Gorshkov's time in office—particularly the writings of Gorshkov himself. But it was the recent availability of three books, published only in Russian, relating to Gorshkov and the Soviet Navy during his period and the new and more detailed insights into the man they have provided that made this book not only possible but necessary.

The first of these books is an autobiography-memoir by Admiral Gorshkov.[2] The second is a book about Gorshkov by an officer who appears in several respects to be the official historian of the Soviet/Russian Navy.[3] The third, by two Soviet naval engineering officers, details the history of Soviet Navy developments from World War II to 1991.[4] All three offer detailed information on Gorshkov and on the Soviet Navy of his time not found in open sources previously available in the West.

Also, two of the authors of this book have had extensive personal contact with Soviet/Russian officials, naval officers, and surface ship and submarine design bureaus both during the Cold War and in the post–Cold War years. The third author observed and scrutinized Admiral Gorshkov and the Soviet Navy from the "other side" while serving as a U.S. naval intelligence officer and, ultimately, as Director of Naval Intelligence.[5]

And, one of the authors had extensive, private discussions about Admiral Gorshkov and the Soviet Navy with Paul H. Nitze (Secretary of the Navy, November 1963–June 1967, and Deputy Secretary of

Defense, July 1967–January 1969) and Admiral Elmo R. Zumwalt (Chief of Naval Operations, July 1970–July 1974).

Admiral Gorshkov has been gone from the senior leadership of the Soviet (now Russian) Navy for three decades. Today we can go back and better interpret the debates over the evolution of the roles and missions of the Soviet Navy that Gorshkov led. Much that had been obscure in the 1970s and 1980s is now better—although not always completely—understood. Yet, despite the availability of the new information and books cited above, no one in the West has published an appreciation of the man, his mission, what he accomplished, or of how he accomplished it. That is the purpose of this book.

This book contains little of the private life of Admiral Gorshkov—his health, parents, wife, and children. Like most Soviet/Russian officials, such details were carefully guarded; within the Soviet system, revelations of such details—or exposés—were severely punished.

Also, because the development and the operations of the Russian and Soviet Navies in World Wars I and II were so radically different from those of Western fleets, an understanding of those periods of naval history is critical to an understanding of Admiral Gorshkov—the man, the sailor, the commander-in-chief, and the innovator.

Norman Polmar
Thomas A. Brooks
George Fedoroff

ACKNOWLEDGMENTS

The authors are especially indebted to Dr. N. F. (Fred) Wikner, who, as the Department of Defense Special Assistant for Net Technical Assessment in the early 1970s, sponsored several studies of the Soviet Navy and of Admiral Gorshkov's role in its development. Much of the material in this book was derived from research undertaken in support of those studies.

We are particularly in debt to a small group of remarkably talented scholars who worked at the Center for Naval Analyses and pioneered the effort to understand the direction in which Gorshkov was seeking to take the Soviet Navy and the evolution of the Navy's missions. These individuals included James M. McConnell, Bradford Dismukes, Robert Weinland, and Commander Robert W. Herrick, USN (Ret.), a former assistant naval attaché in Moscow. Other scholars of the period to whom we are indebted are Thomas Wolfe, Harriet Fast Scott, and Commander Michael MccGwire, RN (Ret.), then at Dalhousie University in Canada. We have borrowed heavily from them and believe that most of their work has stood the test of time.

A small number of British and U.S. naval intelligence officers followed Admiral Gorshkov's writings, as did a handful of analysts at the Central Intelligence Agency; among the latter Raymond Robinson deserves special credit.

The contribution to understanding Admiral Gorshkov's impact of Theodore Neeley of the Office of Naval Intelligence cannot be over-estimated. Without the dedicated effort of Mr. Neeley in translating both the admiral's *Morskoy Sbornik* articles and his seminal book *Seapower of the State,* the work of non–Russian fluent analysts would not have been possible.

A large debt is owed to the late Rear Admiral Sumner Shapiro, the Director of Naval Intelligence from 1978 to 1982. A former naval attaché in Moscow, "Shap" Shapiro saw the importance of understanding the development of Soviet Navy missions and strategy, and he dedicated a small cadre of very talented naval intelligence officers to its study. They were able to integrate the analysis of Soviet writings with classified information from highly reliable sources and to support major portions of the conclusions that had been reached by scholarly research. This information was used to persuade senior naval leadership of the validity of that research. It had a direct impact on the development of U.S. Navy counterstrategies.

Two of the authors are grateful to the many Soviet and, subsequent, Russian Navy officials, political scientists, and, especially, submarine designers who assisted them in better understanding the background and culture of the Navy. In addition, Jessica Huckabey, and Dr. David A. Rosenberg of the Institute for Defense Analyses, and K. J. Moore of the Cortana Corp., helped the authors better understand some of the nuances of Soviet/Russian naval matters.

A final acknowledgment is due to "Nick Shadrin"—Nikolay Fedorovich Artamonov—the commanding officer of a Soviet Navy destroyer who defected to the United States in 1959. He reviewed portions of the Wikner projects and worked closely with one of the authors of this book in helping him develop an understanding of Admiral Gorshkov's navy.

Several members of the staff of the U.S. Naval Institute had key roles in bringing this work to fruition, most especially Ms. Janis Jorgensen, Glenn Griffith, Rachel Crawford, and, of course, Richard Russell, Director of the Naval Institute Press.

ABBREVIATIONS

The ship designations used in this volume are listed at the beginning of the Ship and Submarine Index.

ASW	Anti-Submarine Warfare
bis	modification
BPK	Bolshoy Protivolodochnyy Korabl (large anti-submarine ship)
CinC	Commander-in-Chief
DOSAAF	Dobrovol'cheskoye Obshchestvo po Sotrudnichestvu s Armiyey, Aviatsiyey i Flotom (Voluntary Society for Cooperation with the Army, Aviation, and Fleet)
GLCM	Ground-Launched Cruise Missile
ICBM	Intercontinental Ballistic Missile
IRBM	Intermediate-Range Ballistic Missile
KGB	Komitet Gosudarstvennoy Bezopasnosti (Committee for State Security; 1954–1991)
MGB	motor gunboat
MPA	Main Political Administration
MTB	motor torpedo boat
NATO	North Atlantic Treaty Organization
NKVD	Narodnyy Komisariat Vnutrennikh Del (People's Commissariat for Internal Affairs; 1934–1953)
PVO-*Strany*	Protivovozdushnoy Oborony Strany (Air Defense of the Country)

SLBM	Submarine-Launched Ballistic Missile
SRF	Strategic Rocket Forces (i.e., Troops)
SS	Schutzstaffel (Protection Squadron)
VSTOL	Vertical/Short Takeoff and Landing
WIG	Wing-In-Ground (effect)

CHAPTER 1

Genesis

Russia, possessing a sixth of the land of the world, was undoubtedly the biggest continental power of the world. But at the same time, she had always been a great sea power.

—Admiral S. G. Gorshkov, *The Seapower of the State* (1976)

When Admiral S. G. Gorshkov took command of the Soviet Navy in 1956—at age 45—Russia had little tradition of being a high-seas naval power and no political support to build a major, ocean-going fleet. Accordingly, there was no reason to believe that Gorshkov would attempt to build such a navy and far less reason to believe that he could succeed in doing so under an Army and strategic missile–oriented political-military leadership. Yet during his 29 years as commander-in-chief of the Soviet Navy, Gorshkov demonstrated a single-minded drive and dedication, exploiting new technologies to the benefit of the fleet, and taking advantage of the political contacts that he had made during World War II. He thus was able to design and build a potent high-seas fleet that could in many respects challenge the U.S. Navy. In fact, some naval experts—including American naval leaders—have said that under some conflict scenarios the Gorshkov fleet could have been more effective than that of the United States!

Several decades after Gorshkov left command of the Soviet Navy, the impact of his actions and views still is evident in the Russian

Navy; it is visible in the deployment of a nuclear-propelled battle cruiser to the Caribbean—the "backyard" of the United States; the brief but politically significant deployment of an aircraft carrier to the eastern Mediterranean to carry out air strikes in Syria; and the firing by surface ships and submarines of cruise missiles at targets in war-torn Syria. These are surviving manifestations of the Navy that Gorshkov built.

To the Western observer the term "sea power" is virtually synonymous with "naval power." But Admiral Gorshkov's assertion that Russia "had always been a great sea power" almost invariably has been taken in the West as a claim that Russia has always been a great *naval power*—a statement that would be false. There were several periods when Russia could have been considered a great naval power, but they were typically brief, often restricted to regional seas, while there were other, much longer periods when the ocean-going Russian Navy virtually ceased to exist.

In his book *The Seapower of the State,* Admiral Gorshkov takes great pains to point out that sea power comprises not only naval fleets but also merchant marine, fishing, and oceanographic research fleets. The Russian language title of the book could have been read in English as *The Maritime Power of the State;* that translation would have been equally accurate, and had it been used Gorshkov's true meaning would have been more apparent to readers who are not familiar with the Russian language.

Still, Russia has the longest coastline of any nation. Although most of its foreign trade is by land, Russia has a substantial merchant fleet and its ocean-going fishing and research fleets are among the world's largest. Russia also has a vast system of rivers and canals that are highways for internal trade and communications. It is—and always has been—a *maritime* nation, although not a nation consistently having a high-seas naval fleet.

The difference between Russian/Soviet naval history and that of the United States is predominantly one of *focus*. While the U.S. Navy from the start of the 20th Century was built primarily for distant, high-seas operations, the focus of the Russian/Soviet Navy has primarily been on defending ports and coastlines and supporting the seaward flanks of ground forces, its operations centered on regional seas. High-seas operations before the "Gorshkov era" generally were limited to naval engagements—primarily with Sweden and the Ottoman Empire—to gain access to and passage through the Baltic and Black Seas, respectively. Tsar Peter the Great founded the Imperial Russian Navy in October 1696 with the immediate goal of attaining unimpeded access to the Baltic Sea and ultimately of making Russia a maritime power for trading with Western Europe. His task was not simple.

The only port that Russia had on the open ocean at that time was Arkhangelsk, on the White Sea, and even that Arctic outlet was closed by ice at least one-half of the year. Russia had no access to the Baltic Sea, which was then controlled by Sweden, and no useful access to the Black Sea, which was controlled by the Ottoman sultan and his allies. By 1703, Peter had seized a narrow outlet to the Baltic where the Neva River enters the Gulf of Finland. There he established his capital city of St. Petersburg. By 1721, Russia had acquired today's Latvia, Lithuania, Estonia, and part of Finland and had secured unimpeded access to the Baltic Sea and thence to the open ocean. In the words of historian Donald W. Mitchell, "There are in all history, few greater maritime achievements than this accomplishment of Peter the Great."

In the 37 years following Peter's death in 1725 there were seven rulers; they paid little attention to the Russian Navy, and the fleet decayed at its anchorages. It was not until the rule of Catherine the Great (1762–1796) that the fleet was rebuilt and access to the Black Sea was assured by, first, the defeat of the Ottoman fleet at the Battle of Chesme in the Mediterranean in 1770 and, second, the successful seizure of the Crimea by the Russian Army. (Among Catherine's admirals was American naval hero John Paul Jones, who had been denied promotion in the fledgling U.S. Navy.)

Russia thereafter and then the Soviet Union periodically built high-seas fleets, but there was little continuity in this regard. As Russian naval strategist and historian Nikolay Klado observed in 1905 when the Duma (parliament) was debating what to do with the Russian Navy after its devastating defeat by the Japanese at Tsushima in 1905, "In more than two centuries of Russian naval history, we have not shown ourselves capable of firmly deciding not only what kind of fleet we need, but absolutely whether we need one at all."

The performances of the Russian Navy in World War I (1914–1917) and the Soviet Navy in World War II (1941–1945) are considered in the West to have been lackluster at best. Neither fought decisive high-seas engagements, as had Western navies at Jutland (1916), Coral Sea (1942), Midway (1942), the Marianas (1944), and Leyte Gulf (1944). For most of World War I the Russian fleet was largely bottled up in port, its ships serving as floating artillery batteries and sortieing for only limited operations in the Baltic. World War II witnessed a continuation of the traditional Russian naval mission of protecting the seaward flanks of ground forces, with few successes in the Baltic, where the German armies were defeated on land by the Red Army.

To the post–World War II political leaders of the Soviet Union, most of whom had served in the Red Army, *the* appropriate role of the Navy was to provide support to the ground forces, and they believed that the Navy had performed this role quite well in the 1941–1945 conflict. The only high-seas fleet within their memory had gone down to defeat by the Japanese at Tsushima in 1905. They had no experience or "corporate memory" to suggest that the Soviet Union should have a high-seas fleet.

Midway through the 20th Century, Admiral S. G. Gorshkov was promoted to the position of commander-in-chief of the Soviet Navy. During World War II he had commanded naval forces in the

Black Sea area that were devoted almost exclusively to supporting the Army. In fact, he had served briefly as the commander of Soviet ground forces fighting near the Sea of Azov: in addition to Naval Infantry (marine) units under his command, many of his sailors were given rudimentary infantry training and assigned to reinforce ground units. Although he had earlier commanded a patrol ship and a destroyer in the Far East and surface forces in the Black Sea, he was a man with no significant experience in major naval operations.

Still, upon becoming its commander-in-chief he put the Soviet Navy on the path to developing a powerful, large, and innovative high-seas fleet—a purpose that continues to influence today's Russian Navy.

CHAPTER 2

Growing Up in the New World Order, 1910–1927

Sergey Georgiyevich Gorshkov was born on 26 February 1910, in Kamenets-Podolskiy in what is now the western Ukraine. Both of his parents were schoolteachers, holding government positions within the imperial civil service. His mother, Elena Feodosiyevna, was the daughter of an Orthodox priest, a circumstance that greatly influenced her views on life and her moral principles; she was soft-spoken and instilled a love of books in her children. His father, Georgiy Mikhailovich, was a well-known and respected member of the city's educational community; he was known as strict and demanding with his children.[1]

When Sergey was two years old the family moved from the Ukraine to Kolomna, then a provincial Russian city of about 40,000 inhabitants located some 75 miles southeast of Moscow. The reason for the move was the promotion of Gorshkov's father to a new post, effectively the superintendent of schools in Kolomna. The fortunes of the family were on the rise, and the senior Gorshkov was a prominent and respected member of the new community as well.

Young Sergey was born, however, into a Russia in turmoil. The 20th Century had begun with economic depression and continued with war and insurrection. By 1910, the government was seriously weakened and the Romanov dynasty—enhanced by Peter the Great—was shaken by domestic turmoil, caused in part by staggering defeats on land and, especially, at sea at the hands of the Japanese in the 1904–1905 conflict. But by the time he was a teenager Gorshkov would come to view the Russia of 1910 as a time of relative peace and tranquility. The events of the next decade would bring dramatic and costly change to Russia and to much of the rest of the world, and they would create the conditions that make the young Gorshkov one of history's most influential naval commanders.

Russia had been humiliated by Japan in the Russo-Japanese War, and her fleet had been decimated. Mutinies and rebellions had followed, encouraged and supported by revolutionaries both in Russia and abroad. Most notable among these radicals was Vladimir Ilyich Ulyanov, better known by his alias "Lenin." Although living in exile in Switzerland, Lenin was actively encouraging and supporting revolution and assassination inside Russia.

Tsar Nicholas II reacted to the on-going acts of rebellion and sedition with increasing brutality. He had granted the country a representative assembly known as the Duma in 1905, but two successive Dumas had been dissolved, their members finding themselves unable to work with the tsarist government. The Russian prime minister was assassinated in 1911, and a new, third Duma was elected in 1912. Although its majority was from the pro-government Kadet Party, other members were outspoken in their criticism of the government and of the tsar's court. The mood of revolution continued among the people, protesting the horrible working and living conditions, accompanied by the continuation of violent pogroms against Jews and Armenians that swept the country in this period.

The year 1913 also marked the 300th anniversary of the Romanov dynasty, and great celebrations were staged across Russia. The Romanovs had produced outstanding and notable rulers— Peter the Great and, through marriage, Catherine; good, strong, and effective tsars, such as Alexander II; but also several weak, ineffective ones. Nicholas II, who had come to the throne in November 1894, was not a strong tsar. He was sensitive, rather retiring, and very

much devoted to his family. He tended to temporize and procrasti-
nate; he was characterized by contemporaries as a man who would
have made an excellent constitutional monarch. However, there was
no constitutional monarchy in Russia. As Nicholas celebrated the
dynasty's 300th anniversary, he little suspected that it had less than
four more years to reign.

★ ★ ★

Gorshkov was four years old when World War I erupted in the summer of 1914. The conflict destroyed imperial Russia and caused massive change in Europe's political and economic structures.[2] The tsar,
recognizing that Russia was not prepared for war and would not be
for at least another year, attempted to prevent—or at least delay—
hostilities, but events moved too quickly. Following the assassination
of Archduke Franz Ferdinand of Austria-Hungary, that empire, with
the backing of Germany, declared war on Serbia on 28 July, initiating counter-declarations by England, France, Belgium, and Serbia.
Russia, in support of Serbia, began mobilization; Germany declared
war against Russia on 1 August—the "Great War" had begun.

    The Russian government was consumed by graft and corrup-
tion, and its military leadership was generally incompetent—as had
been displayed during the Russo-Japanese War. The Russian armies
now suffered horrific defeats and massive casualties. During the
three years of its participation in the war Russia mobilized some
15 million men. By the end of 1914 it had already lost 1 million:
dead, wounded, or taken prisoner. In 1915 and again in 1916 the
Russian forces achieved successes against the Austrians in Galicia
but were unable to defeat or significantly slow the German armies
to their west. By the fall of 1915 Russia had lost all of Poland and
most of her Baltic provinces adjoining East Prussia. By the end of
that year Russia had suffered another 2.5 million casualties. The
Russian Army was now in extremis, fighting to defend the soil of
Mother Russia.

In August 1915, the tsar made the fateful decision to relieve Grand Duke Nikolai (his cousin) as the head of the Army and go to the front to assume personal command. The tsar, however, could not both be at the front commanding the Army and be in the capital of Petrograd—as St. Petersburg was renamed in September 1914—conducting the daily affairs of state. There the massive problems plaguing the government were exacerbated: despite the objections of government ministers and Duma members, the tsar did nothing to stop his German-born wife, Empress Alexandra, from stepping into government affairs and, under the sway of a mystic—the "mad monk" Gregory Rasputin—attempting to rule the country. With guidance from Rasputin, she replaced ministers with men of her (or often his) choosing and generally interfered with both the government and the war effort. On two occasions, at the behest of Rasputin, she cabled the tsar urging him to stop successful Russian offensives into Austria-Hungary; in both cases he complied.

The government became totally ineffective. Supplies, weapons, and munitions failed to reach the troops, and foodstuffs failed to reach the capital. In the Duma, parties of both the right and the left united against the government. Resentment especially mounted against Alexandra and Rasputin. By November the government—such as it was—had disintegrated. A new government was formed, but the new appointees were no more capable. The May–October 1916 Russian offensive in the west cost another 200,000 lives and was ultimately stopped and turned around by a German counteroffensive. The morale of the Army was disintegrating rapidly.

Young Gorshkov's city of Kolomna began seeing the effects of the war as contingents of soldiers passed through on their way to the front and as refugees and the wounded fled from the advancing German armies. The war environment also manifested itself by a severe deterioration of living conditions, with increasing shortages of food and other goods.

The Navy Situation

Conditions in the Russian Navy were little better. In 1912 a 15-year shipbuilding program had been approved that was to have produced 20 battleships and 12 battle cruisers, but only 2 of these ships were complete at the outbreak of World War I. Thus Nicholas was able to replace only one-third of the battleship losses of the Russo-Japanese War before Russia was again at war. He was able to construct a substantial number of torpedo boats, destroyers, mine craft, and submarines. But the newer ships had not had time to work up adequately, overall readiness of the fleet was low, and morale and discipline among the sailors was problematic: a number of Baltic Fleet sailors had been heavily influenced by revolutionary activists during their long periods of inactivity in port.

When hostilities began Russia's premier Baltic Fleet had only four pre-dreadnought battleships against almost five times that many German dreadnought battleships and battle cruisers.[3] Obviously, however, most of the German fleet would be engaged with the superior British fleet, mainly in the North Sea. The Russian fleet accordingly assumed a defensive posture focused on mining, commerce raiding, submarine attacks (augmented by British submarines sailing from Russian ports), and small-scale sorties to deny the Germans access to the eastern Baltic and the approaches to Petrograd. With the exception of two German attacks on Riga, in Latvia, in 1915 and late 1917—when the Germans deployed battleships and other naval forces and were briefly challenged by the Russian fleet—there were no noteworthy engagements in the Baltic. Thus, the major units of the Russian Baltic Fleet spent most of the war in port, subordinated to Russian Army commanders who had little understanding of how to employ naval forces. There were mutinies on several Baltic Fleet ships, which continued to be hotbeds of revolutionary sentiment.

In the northern theater, in the White Sea, Russian naval activity was limited to minor skirmishing with German and Finnish forces and the escorting of convoys delivering arms and ammunition from Britain and then the United States. In the Pacific there was no significant naval activity other than the German cruiser *Emden's* surprising and sinking the Russian cruiser *Zhemchug* in the harbor of Penang on the Malay Peninsula in October 1914.

At the beginning of the war Russia's Black Sea Fleet was vastly superior to that of the Ottoman Turkish forces and dominated early engagements, in which the Russians strove to interdict Turkish seaborne supply lines critical to the land war in the Transcaucasus. Both the Allies and the Germans had been courting the Ottoman sultan, but when the British refused to deliver two battleships that the Turks had ordered from a yard in Britain, the Germans, already having great influence in the Ottoman court, quickly stepped in and offered the battle cruiser *Göben* and the light cruiser *Breslau*, both already in the Mediterranean. The sultan accepted those ships, as well as German military advisors, and entered the war on the Austrian-German side.

The *Göben* and *Breslau* transferred but retained their German crews—now wearing fezzes—and a German admiral was put in charge of the Ottoman Navy. The Ottomans and the Russians began a war of attrition in which they shelled each other's ports and interdicted the other's merchant shipping. By mid-1915 German U-boats were operating in the Black Sea and had sunk several Russian cargo ships. Russian minelayers and submarines (some laying mines) accounted for an equivalent number of Ottoman ships. Vice Admiral Aleksandr V. Kolchak, in command of the Black Sea Fleet, was an effective commander, and the revolutionary activity and sentiment found in the Baltic Fleet had not yet reached the Black Sea.[4] Kolchak's fleet acquitted itself creditably against German and Turkish forces.

The End of an Empire

By the end of 1916, the military-naval situation was critical for Russia. In December, Rasputin was brutally murdered by aristocrats in conspiracy with several members of the Duma. Food riots broke out in Petrograd in early March 1917. The imperial troops sent to restore order mutinied against their officers. The entire city garrison rose in rebellion. On 12 March the Duma formed a "Provisional Committee" to govern; almost simultaneously strikers, revolutionaries, and mutinous soldiers formed the Petrograd Soviet of Workers' and Soldiers' Deputies. On the 15th the tsar abdicated in favor of his younger brother, Grand Duke Michael, but Michael refused the crown unless a Constituent Assembly invested him with it. Neither the Provisional Government nor the Duma had any inclination to make such an offer. The ex-tsar and family became prisoners at their palace in Tsarskoe Selo, on the outskirts of Petrograd. The Romanov dynasty thus came to an end.

But the war did not come to an end. The majority of the Duma favored continuing the war, while the Petrograd Soviet was violently opposed. The war with its staggering casualties and privations continued.

Meanwhile, Lenin, still in Switzerland and despairing of ever bringing about a revolutionary socialist government in Russia, was amazed at how quickly the situation in his homeland had changed. The German leadership, seeing in him an opportunity to drive Russia out of the war, smuggled him there in a sealed railcar and provided him with funds and support with which to agitate to overthrow the Provisional Government and make peace. Lenin arrived in Petrograd on 16 April 1917. The general populace and, most importantly, the mutinous army wanted "food, land, and peace"—no more fighting. Lenin successfully played to the public mood. With the slogan "All Power to the *Soviets*," he waged an incessant campaign against the Provisional Government. A series of riots in May 1917, presented Lenin with an opportunity to attempt to seize power, but Alexander Kerensky, now the prime minister of the Provisional Government, outmaneuvered him and disarmed his Red Guard. Lenin fled into hiding in nearby Finland.

In August 1917, General Lavrentiy Kornilov, recently appointed by Kerensky as the commander of what remained of the Russian Army, marched on Petrograd to preempt what he feared was a deal Kerensky was about to make with the Bolsheviks. At first Kerensky did not object, but he changed his mind when he learned that Kornilov—encouraged and supported by the British—intended a military coup. Kerensky's counter-move was to rearm the Red Guard. To the great surprise of most observers, Kerensky prevailed; Kornilov and a number of other generals were arrested. But when Kerensky then ordered the Red Guards to return their weapons to the Petrograd arsenal, they refused. At that point the Soldiers' and Workers' Soviet possessed the balance of military force in the capital—and was supported by the guns of several Baltic Fleet warships anchored in the Neva River.

Despite the fact that the Bolsheviks did not constitute a majority in most of the *soviets*, or "councils," their organization and discipline, plus the brilliant leadership of one of Lenin's commissars, Leon Trotsky, enabled them to outmaneuver and neutralize all opposition.[5] On 6 November (24 October by the older Julian calendar still in use there), the All-Russian Congress of Soviets voted to create an all-Bolshevik Council of People's Commissars, headed by Lenin, and to seize power from the Provisional Government.[6] The Petrograd garrison's soldiers immediately went over to the Soviets. The next day the troops of the Peter and Paul Fortress joined the Bolsheviks, and that evening, after the cruiser *Aurora*, moored in the Neva River, fired a single blank shot—the signal for the assault on the Provisional Government's offices. Kerensky and the Provisional Government fled. The "Glorious October Revolution" of 7 November (25 October by the old calendar) had taken power with virtually no loss of life. The Soviet era had begun.

The Soviet Era

A new government led by Lenin immediately began negotiations with the Germans to end the war. On 17 December 1917, a cease-fire was declared, roughly along the lines then held by each side. The Germans, however, returned to the offensive in February 1918, seizing vast amounts of territory against little Russian resistance. By 2 March 1918, Kiev in the Ukraine was captured, bringing German forces some 750 miles from Petrograd.

The next day Lenin was forced to sign the Treaty of Brest-Litovsk, making huge concessions of land to Germany and Austria-Hungary. Russia ceded its Baltic provinces of Latvia, Lithuania, and Estonia and renounced all claims to Poland and Finland; independence was granted to the Ukraine under a German-Austrian protectorate. Additional concessions were made in the Caucasus. Lenin had effectively surrendered all of the European territory that the Russian Empire had acquired since the time of Peter the Great.

★ ★ ★

As soon as it became apparent that Russia would seek a separate peace with Germany, the Allies began landing troops at key Russian ports. Ostensibly the troops were to prevent the capture of military stores by the Germans. Beyond that, their purpose was to buttress and support anti-Bolshevik Russian troops that might be willing to continue the war and reconstitute an "Eastern Front," thus requiring Germany to maintain forces in the east that otherwise could be moved west.

A total of 14 Allied nations provided troops for the intervention: British and American forces, landed at Murmansk and Arkhangelsk, respectively, in the north, took control of the ports and railways and then moved inland to seize the rail lines that ran south from the Arctic ports to Petrograd and Moscow.[7] Japanese, Canadian, Italian, and American forces occupied the Far Eastern port city of Vladivostok; French, Greek, and Polish troops occupied Odessa, Kherson, and adjacent areas of the Ukraine. The Czech Legion, a contingent of almost 40,000 Czech soldiers who were trapped in Russia and were making their way by train to Vladivostok, effectively controlled the vital Trans-Siberian rail line. The Czechs were the best organized and most capable force in Russia at that time. In all, more than a quarter of a million foreign troops were in Russia at one time or another during the 1918–1920 intervention. The intervention, however, did little to shore up the "White"—anti-Bolshevik—forces, and the presence of foreign troops gave a propaganda boost to the Bolsheviks, who quickly branded the Whites as unpatriotic stooges of foreigners.

The Allied armistice with Germany in November 1918, enabled Lenin to turn his attention to seizing other Russian cities and the heartland. While the majority of the Russian people favored Lenin's slogan "Food, Land, and Peace," the Bolsheviks did not by any means enjoy the support of a majority of the people. Units of Red Guards and former army units from which Leon Trotsky formed the "Red Army" set about establishing and enforcing Bolshevik control. They immediately met opposition from White Guards—units loyal to the now-defunct Provisional Government, plus other groups led by monarchists, landed aristocrats seeking the preservation (or restoration) of privileges, separatists of one stripe or another, or simply anti-Bolshevik elements. Foreign governments—primarily British—provided financing to these various anti-Bolshevik groups, and foreign intervention forces supplied military training and support. A vicious and deadly civil war began to rage across Russia. It would not end until 1920 in the west and 1922 in Siberia and in the Far East.

Under the terms of Brest-Litovsk Treaty, Germany occupied the Ukraine and, in combination with Ukrainian troops, seized the Crimea with its ports and naval support facilities, a position vital for operations in the Black Sea. Some of the Russian Black Sea Fleet escaped, and some ships surrendered to the local forces. After the armistice of November 1918, both French and British troops landed in the Crimea. Only the Russian ships that had managed to escape to Novorossiysk could be considered as at all operational: one old and one new (dreadnought) battleship, a cruiser, ten destroyers, and some torpedo boats. They were short of fuel and ammunition, and generally in poor repair. They supported the White Army with gunfire and limited transport.

★ ★ ★

By the end of the summer of 1918 a foreign observer would have concluded that the days of the Bolshevik "Reds" were numbered. In many respects the bands of workers and demobilized soldiers that constituted the Red Guards were little more than armed mobs and terrorists. Many of the Army units that had gone over to the Bolshevik side had suffered massive desertion rates and were now of little military value. Most of the Russian countryside and a number of major cities soon were under White control. Many nationality groups—such as Cossacks, Poles, and Ukrainians—were seeking some form of independence and were willing to supply troops to fight in the anti-Bolshevik cause. American historian W. Bruce Lincoln pointed out that by the summer of 1918 some 30 different governments functioned in the lands that had been the Russian Empire, with 29 of them anti-Bolshevik.[8] Additionally, there were masses of foreign troops on Russian soil, almost all of whom were committed in some degree to supporting the White cause. Against such overwhelming odds, how could the rag-tag forces of the Reds survive, let alone prevail?

Leon Trotsky, put in charge of the Bolshevik armed forces, was able to forge, little by little, an effective Red Army out of the Red Guards and the remnants of the Russian Army units that had gone over to the revolutionaries. Trotsky imposed a strict discipline. He drafted former tsarist officers back into service, often holding their families hostage to their loyal performance, until some 70 percent of his leadership consisted of former Imperial Army officers. The junior and field grade officers came from the ranks of former tsarist noncommissioned officers and of officers from proletarian families.

In contrast, at no time were the Whites a monolithic entity. The White Guards comprised a half-dozen major fighting forces and a number of minor ones, widely dispersed, under different leaders, and pursuing different goals and philosophies. The only thing that united them was their anti-Bolshevism. Some, like most of the Cossacks, fought the Reds to keep them out of their homelands. Others, like the Ukrainians, fought to create an independent nation. Some fought simply to "save Russia." Also, many fought because they had been forcibly conscripted. The Red Army conscripted soldiers too, but the Reds fought for their well-defined ideal of a new Russia as articulated by Lenin, whereas the Whites had no such unifying vision.

The situation in Siberia in 1918 was extremely complex, with no fewer than 19 different anti-Bolshevik administrations stretching across the length of the Trans-Siberian Railway, the only credible military force among them the Czech Legion. The Czech troops effectively controlled Siberia and held off Red attacks until the squabbling Siberian governments could agree on consolidated leadership in the form of a General Directorate. In November 1918, Vice Admiral Kolchak, the former commander of the Black Sea Fleet and a noted Arctic explorer, took over as the Supreme Ruler of the Russian Provisional Government. Ostensibly his rule was to extend to the forces in the north and the south, but coordination was seldom effective—when it took place at all.

Battles raged across the length and breadth of Russia during 1918. The Siberian armies marched westward, reaching their farthest point of advance at Kazan—500 miles east of Moscow—in September 1918, only to be forced to retreat the following month in the face of the major Red counteroffensive. The summer and fall of 1919 marked the high point of White fortunes. While Vice Admiral Alexander Kolchak stabilized the Siberian front and launched an offensive that almost reached the Volga River, General Anton Denikin led his White forces out of the Don and Kuban areas to the south and drove to Tula, only 100 miles south of Moscow. Other

White forces moved on Petrograd, reaching the heights overlooking the city.

But time had run out for the Whites. In mid-1919 the Red Army numbered two million men; in its unified control and central geographic position it had important advantages over the Whites. By the end of the year it was three million men strong and by the end of 1920 more than five million. The White forces increased as well but could not match the size or improving weapons of the Reds. More importantly, the White forces suffered from internal dissension and insecurity in their rear areas, to which White generals increasingly had to divert troops to maintain order. General Denikin tended to look on the areas that he occupied as "conquered" rather than "liberated" and treated the populations accordingly. Also, the Whites used conscription methods that generated among the peasant population not only resentment but also mass desertion, often followed by defection to the Reds. Corruption was rampant in the rear areas; entire trainloads of Allied equipment "disappeared," immediately finding its way onto the flourishing black market. To the previously anti-Bolshevik populations of the south the Whites came to represent a return to the worst aspects of tsarist rule.

When the fall 1919 Red counteroffensive began the Whites had no reserves to throw into the battle. During the period November 1919, to February 1920 the Reds advanced on almost all fronts. In January 1920 Admiral Kolchak was captured and executed; the collapse of the Siberian front followed. General Denikin, also fighting off attacks from Ukrainian anarchist forces, was forced back. On 3 April 1920, he turned over command of the south to General Baron Petr Wrangel and departed Russia to live out his life in exile.

The Allied forces in western Russia began to withdraw that spring. General Wrangel, totally abandoned by the British and getting little support from the French, worked near-miracles in restoring the morale and fighting abilities of the shrunken White forces in the south. In June 1920 he broke out of his Crimean stronghold and recaptured large portions of the eastern Ukraine and Don–Kuban areas, doubling the territory he held in less than a fortnight and gaining access to rich reserves of wheat, cattle, and horses. But the Reds had been obliged to concentrate on an invading Polish force; once they neutralized that threat they turned against Wrangel and drove him back to the Crimea. He held off continued Red assaults until November 1920, when the Bolshevik forces broke through his defenses and swept into the Crimea. It is a testimony to the effectiveness of his leadership and the efficiency of his planning that Wrangel was able to evacuate all of his followers—some 145,000 men, women, and children—on board 126 ships, which included the remnants of what had been the Russian Black Sea Fleet. On 16 November 1920, the last of the ships weighed anchor and headed for Constantinople. The White Russian émigrés entered lives of exile.

The White Russian warships were interned in French North African ports, where, until the French recognized the Soviet Union in 1924, the exiles continued to fly the Russian naval ensign of the St. Andrew's cross and proclaim themselves the Provisional Government of Russia. The new Soviet government repeatedly requested that the ships be returned, but the French ignored those requests. Most of the ships were scrapped in the 1930s, the money realized by their sale distributed among the émigrés.

The role of the Russian Navy during the Civil War was mixed. On one hand, most of the surviving ships of the Black Sea Fleet defected to the Whites, and those in the Pacific and the Arctic played only minor roles; on the other, the sailors of the Baltic Fleet were very active in supporting the revolution. The Baltic Fleet sailors and the garrison of the Kronshtadt naval fortress on Kotlin Island in the approaches to Petrograd were among the most fervent revolutionaries of the time. Placing themselves firmly in the Bolshevik camp, they became the "shock troops" of the revolution. These sailors dispersed the freely elected Constituent Assembly in January 1918 and soon became familiar throughout the country as commissars and local committee organizers. They also held key positions in the Cheka (Russian initialism for "Emergency Committee")—the secret police, established primarily to liquidate enemies of the Bolsheviks, and precursor of the NKVD and KGB.

In the eyes of the new Bolshevik government this revolutionary performance was the finest hour of the Russian Navy. Political-military leader Trotsky called the Baltic Fleet sailors the "glory and pride of the revolution." Admiral Gorshkov, later reflecting Party dogma, referred to the accomplishments of the Navy during the civil war in the most glowing terms: "The naval seamen defending the gains of the Great October Revolution performed wonders of heroism not only aboard ship but also on the land fronts where some 75,000 seamen fought. . . . The events of the Civil War once again confirmed the need to have as part of the armed forces of our country a powerful and comprehensively developed navy."[9] Red forces continued to suppress rebellions and impose their rule in the Ukraine and Transcaucasus through 1921. The last foreign troops left, through Vladivostok, in 1922. The "White Crusade" had lasted three years. It had been accompanied by widespread terror on both sides and a level of hatred and atrocity not seen since the Middle Ages.

While the armies fought, the people starved. Armed Bolshevik teams sent to the countryside requisitioned grain and foodstuffs. The peasants—particularly peasant landowners, known as *kulaks*–would not sell, and so the food was taken by force, often with considerable bloodshed. Frequently the land was appropriated as well. Resistance and uprisings by the kulaks were met with bloody reprisals. (The subjugation of the kulaks was to continue through the next decade, with great loss of life.) In Petrograd there was neither sufficient food nor coal for heat during the winter of 1920–1921. People were fleeing the cities, seeking food in the countryside. That winter some 800,000 people remained in Petrograd—about 31 percent of the capital's 1915 population. Factories were abandoned. To control strikes and uprisings, the Bolshevik government outlawed meetings and imposed martial law.

Sailors at the huge naval base and fortress of Kronshtadt, who had fought on the side of "the people" against the government in 1905 and again during the revolution of October 1917, spoke out against the new "dictatorship." Many of the sailors were of countryside peasant origin and had seen the wretched conditions of their villages under Bolshevik rule when home on leave. The sailors elected as their leader and principal spokesman a sailor named Stepan Petrichenko, who led them in establishing a Provisional Revolutionary Council to govern Kronshtadt and to demand the election of a new Petrograd Soviet that would be truly representative of the sailors and workers. On 2 March 1921, these sailors took control of Kronshtadt. A headline in their base newspaper best proclaimed their purpose: "All Power to the Soviets. Not to Political Parties."

The Bolshevik regime soon responded, sending General Mikhail Tukhachevskiy, its best and so far most successful military leader, to put down the "rebellion." On 7 March, Tukhachevskiy's artillery began a bombardment of Kronshtadt that was answered by the guns of the fortress and of warships anchored nearby. Repeated attempts to attack the island base over the ice-covered water between Petrograd and the fortress resulted in huge casualties for Tukhachevskiy's forces. Finally, on 18 March, his troops reached Kronshtadt and—with savage brutality—destroyed the rebellion. The leaders of the rebellion fled to nearby Finland, along with some 8,000 of their comrades. The Bolsheviks shot approximately 500 of the rebels and sent several thousand to the prison camps of the Gulag. The remaining sailors were dispersed among the fleets. The Red forces, according to Soviet figures, suffered 600 men killed and 1,000 wounded. Thus, in Soviet accounts a glorious page in the history of the Russian Navy, when it had been at the forefront of the revolution, was ripped out and burned.

The Kronshtadt uprising was not an extension of the Civil War. Kronshtadt sailors were dedicated socialists and revolutionaries. This was a "Red-on-Red" battle. It did have some positive results: in the midst of the attacks on Kronshtadt, Lenin declared an end to the hated forced requisitioning of grain that had been the reason for much of the resentment against the Bolsheviks.

Lenin suffered his first stroke in May 1922. A month earlier, in April, Josef Dzhugashvili—alias "Stalin"—had become the General Secretary of the Communist Party. Lenin died in January 1924, and Stalin rapidly consolidated his power. Stalin then redoubled the Party's efforts against the 100 million peasants of the country to force the collectivization of farmland. These policies cost millions of lives and inflicted massive harm to Soviet agriculture.

Bottom Lines

No one really knows how many Russians died in World War I, the Civil War, the "Red Terror," the equally appalling "White Terror," or the forced collectivization of farms. Probably more died of disease and starvation than from bullets, and more civilians died than soldiers. The total numbers can only be estimated: Russian World War I casualties are conservatively placed at eight and one-third million, about two-thirds of whom died. Military casualties on both sides during the Civil War added another million, and the Red campaign against the Cossacks produced another one-half million. Add 3 million people known to have died from the typhus epidemic in 1920–1921, and one reaches the staggering total of almost 15 million deaths in less than a decade.

This number does not include the people who died during the suppression of the kulaks or of starvation and disease during the various postwar upheavals. Estimates of total deaths of the period appear to center on the number 25 million. This total must be viewed in the context of a Russian population at the outbreak of World War I of 175 million, a figure that includes Poland and the Baltic States, which by 1918 were no longer part of Russia. Thus, "casualties" amounted to about one in seven Russians during the eight-year period.

This was the basis of the world of 1927—the year that Sergey Gorshkov entered the Navy and arrived at the Frunze Higher Naval School in Leningrad (as Petrograd was renamed in 1924). The first 17 years of his life had been characterized by continuous violence: rebellion, mutiny, revolution, world war, civil war, foreign occupation, dictatorships of various hues, and terror as a principal instrument of governing. A half-dozen armies had marched through the city of his birth in the Ukraine. He had experienced hunger in the great famines of 1918 and 1921, probably during later years as well. As he was finishing grammar school he probably learned of the thousands of American, British, Czech, French, and Japanese troops who were occupying Russian soil. Surely that would have affected his view of the world. Perhaps it is understandable that he would want to join the armed forces to defend his homeland against such foreign "interventionists" and threats from the capitalist world.

Gorshkov later wrote that one year in Leningrad taking courses at the university, part-time work in the port, and long talks with a friend from home who had recently joined the Navy strongly influenced his decision to enter that service. This fateful choice definitely did not fit his parents' vision for his future. They had anticipated that he would follow them into the teaching profession and become a mathematician or perhaps physicist. His parents were not at all assured that joining the Navy would further their son's education, but they acquiesced when young Gorshkov convinced them that he was serious, even adamant, about his choice.[10]

CHAPTER 3

The Education of an Admiral, 1927–1941

I will be more useful serving in the
Navy than doing anything else.

—Admiral S. G. Gorshkov, *Vo Flotskom Stroyu* (1996)

Sergey Gorshkov graduated with honors from Kolomna High School in the spring of 1926.[1] In the late summer he entered university in Leningrad. The city's maritime and naval character seeped into his consciousness: when home on holiday he was enthralled and impressed by the uniform, bearing, and the stories of a longtime friend who had entered the Frunze Higher Naval School.[2]

When asked at the Party screening commission why he was giving up university for the Frunze Naval School, Gorshkov confidently said, as he later recalled, "I will be more useful serving in the Navy than doing anything else."[3] Obtaining the panel's required endorsement was not easy. In the politically charged post-revolution atmosphere a candidate's family background was as important as academic accomplishments and standing. Gorshkov's parents had been civil servants of the imperial government. Also, an uncle—his mother's brother Aleksey—was a tsarist general and had been forced to emigrate from Russia at the end of the Civil War. Still, the necessary approval was forthcoming, thanks to a combination of Gorshkov's demeanor and his father's demonstrated apolitical dedication to his profession.

Among Gorshkov's classmates at Frunze were Vladimir A. Kasatonov, Andrey T. Chabanenko, and Valentin A. Chekurov. Graduating the year before Gorshkov entered the school was Nikolay G. Kuznetsov. All of these men would become senior flag officers, and together they would shape the composition and the strategy of the Soviet Navy for more than half a century—from the late 1930s until the end of the Cold War.

At the time that Gorshkov entered Frunze the Bolshevik political-military leader Leon Trotsky had afforded the Navy a degree of protection from the excesses of proletarian military doctrine and attempts to define the role of the Navy in terms of Marxist doctrine and the experiences of the recent Civil War. But Mikhail V. Frunze replaced Trotsky as Commissar for Military and Naval Affairs in 1925. (Trotsky would be expelled from the Communist Party in 1927, exiled, and in 1940 murdered on Stalin's orders.) The Navy thus lost its "protector," and the future navy would have to develop within the parameters of communist doctrine as defined by the Communist Academy, whose military section was headed by Army officers. There would be minimal or no tolerance for deviation from the Communist Party line.

This change in leadership had an almost immediate impact on the faculties of the higher naval schools: former tsarist naval officers and advocates of "Old School" battleship naval theory would have to adhere to the new Party doctrine or be purged. In several noteworthy instances, heavy fines were imposed for expounding incorrect theories. Curriculum was changed to reflect the new thinking, which was essentially the thinking of the "Young School"—the irrelevance of high-sea fleets and the centrality of small warships, submarines, torpedo warfare, naval aircraft, and—of course—support to the army's seaward flanks. This change in doctrine came during the four years that Gorshkov was at Frunze and continued during his first years as a junior officer in the fleet.

Gorshkov's early years at Frunze also saw the implementation of the first Soviet Five-Year Plan, for the period beginning in 1929; it provided for the completion of a few ships already on the building ways—three light cruisers and a number of small submarines and coastal combatants. A force of 17 destroyers was authorized. Emphasis was given to the erection of new shipbuilding facilities and the rehabilitation of existing shipyards. There was no mention— none was allowed—of battleships, heavy cruisers, or other ships of the Old School philosophy.

A Naval Officer

When commissioned in February 1931, Gorshkov and his classmates became part of a navy just beginning to rise from its own ashes. If they "kept their noses clean" the newly fledged officers could look forward to rapid promotion in a navy being rehabilitated. Old School–versus–Young School debates would continue in one form or another for most of their careers. Career-oriented officers would have to steer carefully as Soviet policy periodically swung from one school to the other during the decade of the 1930s.

Gorshkov was commissioned as the equivalent of a junior lieutenant—personal ranks were not in use in 1931 (they would be restored by Stalin in 1933). He was assigned to a brief tour as navigation officer of the Black Sea Fleet destroyer *Frunze*. The next year he was transferred to the Pacific and assigned as navigator on a minelayer in what was then called the Far East Naval Forces.

In 1934 he was given his first command, the new patrol ship *Burun*. A 530-ton, 235-foot ship, Gorshkov's first command was armed with two 102-mm guns, lighter weapons, three torpedo tubes, and depth charges. The ship had been built in Leningrad, transported in sections across the country by railroad, and reassembled at Vladivostok, the largest city and port in the Soviet Far East. Thus, at age 24, Gorshkov attained a mid-career goal of every naval officer—the command of a warship. He obviously performed well, because in 1936, two years after taking command, his ship was officially honored as the "best in the Navy," gaining him widespread recognition.

During this period of Gorshkov's career the Second Five-Year Plan (1933–1937) was promulgated. It called for the first major surface warships constructed by the Soviet regime, the *Leningrad*-class large destroyers or flotilla leaders, followed by the Italian-designed *Kirov*-class heavy cruisers. These 9,287-ton cruisers, with a main battery of nine 7.1-inch (180-mm) guns, were out of context with the Young School concept—an early indication of Stalin's duplicity in directing naval strategy.[4] This Second Five-Year Plan also provided for the extensive modernization of the three surviving, tsarist-era battleships.

Although ostensibly Stalin supported the Young School strategy of coastal craft, submarines, and aircraft, his planning decisions were now more in line with that of the Old School: development of a major, ocean-going fleet. It now became apparent that Stalin had never been truly a supporter of the Young School strategy but had embraced it publicly in the late 1920s because the Soviet Union lacked the resources to construct major warships. By the mid-1930s Stalin's massive industrialization program had begun to take hold, and the nation's economy had recovered to the point that the construction of larger warships was possible.

On 11 January 1935, in light of the command's growing strength, the Far East Naval Forces were renamed the Pacific Fleet. Soon after, Stalin brought several of its officers to Moscow for meetings. (The delegation included some junior officers, but Gorshkov's memoirs and surviving records give no indication that he was one of them.) At these meetings the decision was made to send additional warships to the Pacific. Stalin apparently considered the Pacific naval

commanders to be the most "progressive" of the era, although at that time theirs was the smallest of the Soviet fleets.

A further indication of Stalin's naval preferences occurred in August 1935, when the Pacific Fleet commander, Mikhail V. Viktorov, was brought to Moscow to become the People's Commissar of the Navy (the position would later be renamed Commander-in-Chief of the Navy). His career had been rather bizarre. A submarine specialist with a reputation as a very capable officer, he had commanded the Baltic Fleet from 1921 until 1924, when he was relieved when his wife became involved in an espionage case. She had been cleared of suspicion, and Viktorov had been transferred to the Far East, where he had quickly regained Stalin's good graces; he was again appointed commander of the Baltic Fleet from 1925 to 1931. It was the following year that he had become the commander of the Far East Naval Forces.[5]

The period was a tense one in the Soviet Navy, in part because of confrontations with Japan over Manchuria. Open combat erupted between the two nations in 1938: aircraft and sizeable ground forces were engaged in the vicinity of Lake Khasan, at the junction of northeast Korea and southwest Manchuria.

A Big-Ship Navy

While Gorshkov, in command of the *Burun*, was gaining insight into small-ship operations, Stalin, far away in Moscow, was making further decisions that would re-direct the course of the Navy. The most dramatic evidence that Stalin was planning to build a first-class, high-seas fleet came following a decree of the government on 3 December 1936, when contracts were signed to build eight battleships in Soviet shipyards, all to be completed by 1941—the *Sovetskiy Soyuz* (Soviet Union) class. These would be 64,000-ton ships with main batteries of nine 16-inch (406-mm) guns.[6] Also, at Stalin's direction, massive, covered battleship construction halls were

Map 3-1. Soviet Far East

being erected at Molotovsk (later Severodvinsk) in the north and at Komsomol'sk-on-Amur in the Far East. In these vast facilities and the Baltic shipyard in Leningrad were to be constructed the new capital ships of the Red Navy.

The Third Five-Year Plan (1937–1942), in its turn, provided for at least one aircraft carrier to be laid down in 1942, plus large numbers of cruisers and destroyers. An emphasis on submarine construction would continue; at least 65 new submarines were scheduled to be delivered by 1940, albeit most for operations in coastal waters. If all went according to plan, the Soviet Union would have an impressive high-seas fleet by the mid-1940s. Without any doubt, Stalin had shifted the pendulum of naval strategy back in the direction of the Old School—"big ship"—strategy.[7]

All did not go according to plan. As the first step, as early as 1936 Stalin had begun negotiations with the United States for plans for battleships and aircraft carriers, quantities of armor plate, and miscellaneous naval armament. Although the Franklin D. Roosevelt administration was openly in favor of providing this support, the U.S. Navy's leadership would not cooperate.[8] Stalin's efforts were rebuffed after more than two years of negotiations; he then turned to Germany for assistance.

Beginning in the 1920s there had been extensive cooperation between the Soviet Union and Germany on a large number of military programs, especially aircraft and tank development, leadership training, and even chemical weapons production. After World War I Germany and the Soviet Union had been the world's pariahs—Germany had been defeated, disarmed, and put hopelessly in debt to the Allied nations; the Soviet Union was under the control of the "godless Bolsheviks," and communist infiltration threatened many European countries and the United States. Thus, military cooperation was beneficial to both. While naval cooperation lagged behind the other military areas, the two navies did assist one another until the eve of the German invasion of the Soviet Union in June 1941. The Germans provided the Soviets a few naval advisors, some warship construction plans, and miscellaneous hardware and sold them an unfinished heavy cruiser.[9] But Stalin would have to build his own battleships. This would delay the naval buildup and slow the realization of his vision of creating "the most powerful navy in the world." This vision focused primarily on battleships and heavy cruisers with their supporting ships and aircraft. Stalin was not, however, a strong supporter of aircraft carriers and even the one carrier slated to be started in 1942 was never begun.

The Great Purge

Another problem, a massive one, that would seriously interfere with Stalin's plan for a high-seas fleet would be the shortage of qualified senior officers that would exist after Stalin had completed his "Great Purge" of 1936–1939. Almost all Army and Navy officers with a history of tsarist service, as well as most of the senior services leaders, were removed; many of them were tried and either executed or sent to the labor camps of the Gulag, where most perished. It has been estimated that some seven million people were arrested and about half a million shot in the Great Purge. Often there were no trials; the charges generally were treason against the state, spying, sabotage, and simply of helping the enemies of the Soviet Union.[10]

The purges meant rapid promotion for the survivors, Sergey Gorshkov among them. In retrospect, it is difficult to ascertain the impact of the purges on young officers like Gorshkov; his later writings make no mention of the purges. Some insight, however, can be found in contemporary writings. Then-Colonel I. T. Starinov agonized over the purges: "How can it be that men should have served Soviet power for twenty years and then suddenly sold themselves? And what men! Men who received everything, absolutely everything from the state. And now they are enemies of the

people. Who are they? Bourgeois? Not at all. They are the first Red
Guards, the first Red Army commanders. What did they count on
when they sold themselves?"[11]

Professor Seweryn Bialer has written of the impact of the purges
on the military: "The level of military training for professional officers fell disastrously. As of summer 1941, only 7 percent of Soviet
officers had received higher military education and 37 percent had
not even completed intermediate military training; 75 percent of
all Soviet officers had occupied their posts for less than one year."[12]
Within the Soviet Navy, all the most senior officers at the beginning
of the purge—men who held the rank of *flagman*—were arrested
and executed before the purges ended: Vladimir M. Orlov, a former tsarist officer who had commanded the Soviet Navy from 1931
to 1937; the commanders of the Baltic, Black Sea, and Northern
Fleets; the commanders of the Amur River and Caspian Sea Flotillas;
and the head of the Naval Construction Department. Altogether
the Soviet Navy suffered the loss of some 3,500 men, most of them
officers, who were executed, sent to the Gulag as slave labor, or dismissed from the service on trumped-up charges.[13] One of the few
senior officers to survive the massive purge of the Navy—for a while
at least—was Mikhail Viktorov, the commander of the Pacific Fleet.

Stalin had brought Viktorov to Moscow in June 1937 to take
command of the Soviet Navy. He held the top post for less than six
months; Viktorov was arrested on 22 April 1938 and executed that
August. His successor was Petr A. Smirnov, who had limited naval
experience, having served only as political officer of the Baltic Fleet
in the late 1920s and, ashore, as head of the military's political administration and, from 1937, as deputy commissar of defense. He was at
least familiar with the structure and some of the personalities of the
Navy. Smirnov served as the People's Commissar of the Navy only
until August 1938, after which he was retained briefly as first deputy commissar. He, too, was arrested and, reportedly, died in prison
in March 1940.

The next People's Commissar of the Navy was Mikhail P. Frinovskiy, a secret police (NKVD) official with absolutely no naval experience. At the time of his appointment Frinovskiy held NKVD rank equivalent to a colonel-general (three stars) in the Army and is believed to have been in charge of the secret police organization within the Army. He was hardly the man to direct the Soviet Navy that Stalin sought to develop into an ocean-going fleet.

During this turmoil there was, nevertheless, considerable continuity in Soviet naval programs, because significant control was vested in the Main Naval Council, chaired by Andrey A. Zhdanov, a key lieutenant of Stalin. Coming from Leningrad and long associated with shipbuilding, Zhdanov reported directly to the ruling Politburo (of which Zhdanov was a full, voting member) and had direct supervision of the shipbuilding industry.

The next head of the Soviet Navy would be its most significant commander prior to Gorshkov. When Viktorov came to Moscow in 1937, his Pacific Fleet command eventually went to Nikolay G. Kuznetsov, a 34-year-old officer who had just returned to the Soviet Union after serving as naval advisor to the Republican forces in the Spanish Civil War. Kuznetsov commanded the Pacific Fleet from January 1938 until March 1939, having been assigned to that position over several more senior officers.

In December 1938, Kuznetsov, as a fleet commander, was summoned to Moscow for a meeting of the Main Naval Council. Upon his arrival in Moscow it immediately became obvious to him that Frinovskiy was in trouble. Most meetings were held at night: Stalin preferred to work at night, and his subordinates followed suit. Thus, Kuznetsov was awakened one night and told that a car was waiting to carry him to the Kremlin for a meeting with Stalin. Kuznetsov entered Stalin's office, where the Soviet dictator and several members of the Politburo sat at a long table. Kuznetsov was asked to take a chair.

And now I was in his office. I was not reporting to him. He was asking me questions and I was answering them. About my tour of duty in the Pacific, about our fleet. He wanted to know what I thought about the performance of the People's Commissariat of the Navy. For some reason Stalin displayed particular interest in my opinion of [Lev Mikhailovich] Galler and [Ivan Stepanovich] Isakov. I respected both of them. They were experienced leaders and enjoyed prestige among the sailors. And that was what I told him.

"What do you think about working in Moscow?" he asked at the end of the interview.

"I have never worked in the centre [i.e., the capital] and have never wished to."

"You may go," Stalin said.

I returned to my room at the hotel about three o'clock in the morning.[14]

Meanwhile, Frinovskiy had in fact been "unofficially" relieved as naval commissar, and P. I. Smirnov-Svetlovskiy was acting in his place. At the meeting of the council the day following Kuznetsov's "interview" with Stalin, Zhdanov took the floor and named him first deputy commissar for the Navy. No one had yet been appointed as commissar, thus as he was getting briefed as deputy commissar he was acting as commissar. (Frinovskiy was executed in 1939.)

Subsequently, Kuznetsov was able to return to his Pacific Fleet headquarters, accompanied on the Trans-Siberian Railway by Zhdanov and other officials. They inspected various naval activities in the Far East until, on 15 April, they all were ordered back to Moscow. Shortly after arriving in Moscow, on 27 April, they were summoned to the Kremlin, where Kuznetsov and Zhdanov briefed Politburo members. The next day, Kuznetsov was named the People's Commissar of the Navy.

His appointment appears to have been still more evidence of Stalin's concern for the Far East situation and the potential role of the Soviet Navy in the Pacific theater.

Gorshkov, for his part, escaped the Stalinist purges for several reasons, among them his youth, non-membership in the Communist Party (he joined in August 1942), and the fact that his duty station was in the Far East. Service in the Pacific shielded Gorshkov and many others from charges of collaboration with the German "enemy," although no one was entirely safe from the NKVD. In 1938, having relinquished the *Burun* command but still assigned to the Pacific Fleet, Gorshkov briefly commanded a destroyer and next became chief of staff and then commander of a destroyer "brigade" (a large squadron). He was by that time a captain 2nd rank; his brigade consisted of 14 ships.

While in Vladivostok in 1933 Gorshkov met his future wife, Zinaida Vladimirovna Tarakanova. She was a neighbor of the girlfriend of a shipmate; she was also married and had a son. Her husband, quite a bit older, was a university professor. She initially refused Gorshkov's advances, but he pursued her for two years and, following her divorce, they were married in 1935.[15] His wife was well educated and had taken classes in English and Japanese. Gorshkov considered her son his own, and they would have two children together. Early in their marriage, to supplement his meager salary, she took in sewing and typing.

As the 1930s ended so did Gorshkov's service in the Far East. During those formative years he had been exposed to the privations of the Far East in comparison to the more comfortable and prestigious Baltic and Black Sea Fleets. At the same time, Gorshkov had experienced the state of quasi-war that existed between Japan and the Soviet Union in the Far East during the 1930s. He had been involved in naval support of the Red Army during some of the fighting between Japanese and Soviet forces of 1937–1939. In the Lake Khasan area in the summer of 1938, when open warfare erupted, he commanded naval units that delivered supplies and munitions to the ground forces and evacuated their wounded. For ten days in July–August 1938, a Soviet army—estimated at from 15,000 to as many as 30,000 troops, 100 to 200 aircraft, and a peak strength of 200 tanks—battled a maximum of 10,000 Japanese soldiers without tanks or air support. The Soviets defeated the smaller Japanese force, but their losses were considerable, an estimated 1,200 dead and 2,100 seriously wounded. The Japanese suffered more than 500 men killed and 900 wounded.[16]

The Soviet losses and delays in defeating the Japanese contributed to the 1938 recall, arrest, torture, and death of the commander, Marshal Vasiliy K. Blyukher, a Russian Civil War hero and one of the first five marshals of the Soviet Union. His replacement was Georgiy Zhukov. Gorshkov would have witnessed first the ineptitude of the Army's leadership and then the effectiveness of Zhukov, who would have several key roles in World War II and the immediate postwar period.

In November 1938 Gorshkov was involved in a disaster that could have ended his career—or worse. He was in charge of towing the new, incomplete destroyer *Reshitelnyy*. Built at the Komsomol'sk-on-Amur shipyard, the destroyer was being taken from Sovetskaya Gavan in the Tartar Strait to Vladivostok for completion and fitting out. Bad weather and the insufficient power of the tug caused the unfinished destroyer to run aground on the rocks off Cape Zolotov, near Vladivostok. The ship split in two and was lost.

At a meeting of the Defense Ministry Military Council in Moscow, with Stalin in attendance, Admiral Kuznetsov reported the loss of the new destroyer. Stalin asked whether everything possible had been done to save the ship, to which Kuznetsov answered in the affirmative. He also noted that Gorshkov, in charge of the tow, was an able commander and recommended that he not be blamed. Stalin remarked that should there be another such event things would not go as well, but in this case no one would be prosecuted.

In due course Gorshkov was relieved of command for the six months it took an investigative commission to complete its report. It placed blame on fleet commander Kuznetsov and then–Captain 3rd Rank Gorshkov, as well as on a number of other fleet staff officers. However, it also noted that because of Gorshkov's efforts all of the men on board the *Reshitelnyy* had been rescued. From this episode the young officer learned two lessons: first, because the sea could not be tamed, the Navy needed a dedicated search and rescue capability, as well as sea–going tugs—shortcomings he definitely fixed when he became head of the Navy; and second, attempts to carry out missions by force of will alone, without proper planning and assets, rarely result in success.[17]

This was actually the second time that Gorshkov's naval career could have been cut short by special commissions. The first was the hearing on his eligibility to take entrance examinations for the Frunze Higher Naval School; his parents could have been perceived as "enemies of the people." His survival in late 1938 may have been due to his not being a member of the Communist Party and, therefore, not subject to Party political proceedings into the loss of a new warship. Nonetheless, during his "suspension" ashore he was fearful of unpredictable consequences. His "punishment" was to read lectures in special classes organized by the fleet staff for rising officers.

Gorshkov was still contemplating his future when, in February 1939, Pacific Fleet commander Kuznetsov was chosen as a delegate to the 18th Party Congress and departed for Moscow. Word soon reached Vladivostok that Kuznetsov had been appointed the First Deputy Commander-in-Chief of the Navy and shortly afterward, in April, that he had become CinC Navy.

In late May, Gorshkov was called to the Pacific Fleet's personnel department. As he reported there he wondered if he would leave the building as a serving officer or as a former officer under arrest. Following pleasantries, he was informed that by order of the fleet commander dated 16 May he was to proceed to the Black Sea Fleet. War was clearly on the horizon. The action would be in the western fleets, and now he would have a chance to be a part of that action. In 1939 the Gorshkov family travelled by train across the Soviet Union, in what was likely the reverse of his previous solo, 25-day easterly journey, and in early June he reported to Black Sea Fleet headquarters in Sevastopol, on the Crimean Peninsula. Only when he had met with the fleet commander, Ivan S. Yumashev, did he learn of his assignment as the acting commander of a newly formed destroyer brigade, with particular responsibility to accept newly built warships.

Yumashev had been named Pacific Fleet commander in March 1939 but was still in Sevastopol in early June when Gorshkov reported. After the war Yumashev would be recalled from the Far East to become CinC of the Navy, still another manifestation of Stalin's interest in the Pacific area. Also, Stalin appeared to be pleased with the rearmament efforts of the Navy: he introduced Soviet Navy Day in July 1939 (the Day of the Russian Navy is still celebrated, on the last Sunday of each July).

In the winter of 1940–1941, finally successful after several previous attempts to arrange admission, Gorshkov attended the senior officers' course at the Voroshilov Naval Academy in Leningrad. This institution was at the level of the U.S. Naval War College; it and schools like it were the intellectual centers of the Soviet armed forces, and attendance was required for promotion to flag and general ranks. Gorshkov's classmates at the Voroshilov Naval Academy included Vladimir A. Kasatonov, who had been with him at Frunze a decade earlier, and Georgiy M. Yegorov; both would subsequently hold senior positions under Gorshkov.

The Naval Academy course was concluded after only four months in early April 1941; all officers were ordered to return to their ships and units. Yet another of Gorshkov's attempts to gain an academy education had been thwarted, albeit this time only partially. Later he would be quoted as having said, "The Academy does not make you smarter."[18] Still, he regretted not completing this level of formal education and continued to be a voracious reader of naval literature, actively pursuing self-education whenever possible.

Returning to the Black Sea Fleet, Gorshkov was a captain 1st rank after only ten years of commissioned service. The destroyer brigade he had commanded had been disbanded, and he was appointed to command instead the Black Sea cruiser brigade, comprising nine ships: the cruisers *Chervona Ukraina*, *Krasnyy Kavkaz*, *Krasnyy Krym*, *Voroshilov*, *Molotov*, and *Komintern* and the destroyer leaders *Moskva*, *Kharkov*, and *Tashkent*. War was coming, and Gorshkov was in an active theater with an important fleet command.

CHAPTER 4

Gorshkov at War, 1941

The conclusion which History will affirm [is] that the Russian resistance broke the power of the German armies and inflicted mortal injury upon the life-energies of the German nation.

—Winston S. Churchill, *The Grand Alliance* (1950)

Gorshkov's service in the Great Patriotic War—the Soviet term for the 1941–1945 conflict to expel the Nazi invader—would have profound influence on his later appointment as the commander-in-chief of the Soviet Navy and his ability to manage a revolution in naval warfare. His service in the Black Sea Fleet area during the war was to provide Gorshkov with combat experience of the need for innovation as well as personal contacts that would change his career and his life.

The Soviet Union was ill prepared for war in the summer of 1941. The nation's military services had not recovered from the massive loss of officers at all levels purged in the late 1930s; the rehabilitated shipbuilding industry had not yet produced the warships needed for war; and Stalin's efforts to postpone the conflict with Nazi Germany caused him to prevent certain military preparations from being carried out for fear of antagonizing Adolf Hitler. When the war began the Soviet Navy still operated many tsarist-era warships, but there were too few ships overall to achieve effective results in either the key Baltic or Black Sea theaters. In general, since the initiation of Stalin's drive for a major, ocean-going fleet, the Soviet Navy had been shifting toward battleships and large cruisers; construction of minesweepers, development of modern minesweeping gear, and the arming of ships with modern anti-aircraft guns, other weapons, and radar lagged behind.

War came to the Soviet Union early on the morning of Sunday, 22 June 1941, when German ground and air forces struck along a front extending some 2,000 miles, from Norway's North Cape to the Black Sea. More than three million German troops supported by approximately 1,300 aircraft delivered the devastating assault. The German *blitzkrieg* was totally successful along the entire front, driving the Soviets troops back with shattering losses. The signs of the onrushing Armageddon had been evident to Soviet military leaders in the weeks and days preceding the German attack: German troop movements near the borders, a slowdown in the deliveries of promised German war material to the Soviet Union, overflights of Soviet territory by reconnaissance aircraft, and, finally, the sudden sailings of German merchant ships out of Soviet ports.

In the Black Sea, indications of the coming conflict had become evident on 14 June—a week before the German assault. At that time the Black Sea Fleet was the second-largest of the four Soviet fleets, after the Baltic Fleet. The Black Sea force consisted of 1 of the Navy's 3 World War I–era battleships, the *Parizhskaya Kommuna* (formerly the *Sevastopol*), 6 cruisers, a dozen modern destroyers, 5 old destroyers, and approximately 45 submarines, plus light craft and torpedo boats (see table 4-1).

At the start of the conflict the Germans had no warships in the Black Sea, and their Rumanian allies had only 4 destroyers, 1 submarine, and some coastal craft. However, the German Air Force (Luftwaffe) could reach much of the western part of the Black Sea from airfields in Rumania. (During the war the Germans would transport to the Black Sea, via overland and river routes, 6 small,

Table 4-1. Soviet Naval Forces, June 1941

	Baltic Fleet	Black Sea Fleet	Northern Fleet	Pacific Fleet	Total
Battleships	2	1	—	—	3
Heavy cruisers★	2	3	—	—	5
Light cruisers★★	1	3	—	—	4
Destroyer leaders★★★	< 2	3	—	2	7
Modern destroyers#	12	8	5	10	35
Old destroyers	7	5	3	2	17
Guard ships / gunboats / large patrol ships	7	2	7	6	22
Submarines	65–69	44–47	15	85	209–216
Naval aircraft	656	625	116	(?)	

★   7.1-inch (180-mm) guns.
★★ 5.1-inch (130-mm) guns.
★★★ Also referred to as flotilla leaders.
Some ships were not completed until shortly after start of hostilities.
Sources: Jürgen Rohwer and Gerhard Hummelchen, *Chronology of the War at Sea* (London: Ian Allan, 1972); and Jürg Meister, *Soviet Warships of the Second World War* (London: Macdonald and Jane's, 1977). Sources vary on the submarine strengths.

Type IIB submarines of about 250 tons plus 23 minesweepers, 16 motor torpedo boats, 26 submarine chasers, 50 landing craft, and numerous cargo craft to provide afloat support for the German offensive.)[1]

Preparing for War

On 17 June 1941, Stalin received a report from Pavel M. Fitin, chief of the foreign intelligence section of his intelligence-security service—the NKVD—that "all preparations by Germany for an armed attack on the Soviet Union have been completed, and the blow can be expected at any time."[2] The source was an officer in the German Air Ministry. This warning, like others from the British intelligence services as well as his own, was curtly dismissed by Stalin as intentional *dezinformatsiya* (disinformation) intended to provoke him to start a conflict with Germany.

In mid-June the Black Sea Fleet was on maneuvers that were scheduled to conclude on 20 June with a debriefing of senior officers in Odessa. The vice commissar of naval affairs, Admiral Ivan S. Isakov, had been observing the threatening activity and at the last minute cancelled the debriefing, ordered all ships back to their homeports, and departed himself for Moscow on 21 June. Upon leaving he noted that on the previous day all German, Rumanian, and Turkish commercial vessels had departed Odessa, interrupting their loading and unloading.[3] Upon return to port all of Isakov's warships were ordered to top off fuel, ammunition, and stores and to assume Combat Readiness No. 2. At about five in the afternoon of 21 June—the day before the German attack—the decision was made by the Soviet High Command to bring all forces to No. 1 combat alert. Still, certain forward ground positions were to be left unmanned and no reconnaissance flights were to be flown over forward areas, for fear of provoking the Germans.

On 21 June, N. G. Kuznetsov, the naval commissar, sent the following message:

During 22 and 23 June a German surprise attack is possible. The attack may begin with provocative actions. Our mission is to not fall for any provocations which may complicate the situation. At the same time the fleets and flotillas are to be at full combat readiness to respond to surprise attacks by the Germans or their allies. I hereby order: Carefully conceal a transition to Combat Readiness No. 1. Conduct of reconnaissance in foreign territorial waters is categorically forbidden. No other activity without special orders is to be conducted. [signed] Kuznetsov.[4]

Not until 11 o'clock that night was Admiral Kuznetsov called to the office of the People's Commissar of Defense in Moscow and formally advised that an attack on the Soviet Union was probable in the very near future.[5] Kuznetsov immediately cabled and then telephoned the commanders of the Northern, Baltic, and Black Sea Fleets to direct them to be at full combat readiness. At 1 a.m. he reached the chief of staff of the Black Sea Fleet, and at 1:15 a.m. the fleet was ordered to Combat Readiness No. 1. (The war-warning telegram had not yet been received at fleet headquarters in Sevastopol.) At 3:07 a.m. the sound of aircraft approaching from seaward was heard in Sevastopol.

When the Germans began the invasion of the Soviet Union at 3:15 a.m. on 22 June it was already first light in Sevastopol and in Moscow. The commander of the Black Sea Fleet, Vice Admiral Oktyabrskiy, excitedly reported to Moscow, "An air raid has been carried out against Sevastopol. Anti-aircraft artillery is fighting off the attack. Several bombs have fallen on the city." The Soviet Navy had already blacked out its ships at night and taken other precautions as well. Gorshkov would later recall, "The war did not catch our fleets unawares, despite the fact that in the very first hours of it many naval bases were subjected to attack by the enemy air forces. The Soviet Navy did not lose a single warship or aircraft from the enemy's initial blow."[6] (In all, however, during the initial series of German air attacks almost one-fourth of the Soviet Union's 8,000 military and naval aircraft were destroyed, most caught on the ground.)

First Combat

The Soviet Black Sea Fleet's cruiser brigade, with nine ships— six cruisers and three destroyer leaders—was commanded by Captain 1st Rank Gorshkov. He flew his flag in the light cruiser *Chervona Ukraina*. Table 4-2 lists the six cruisers of Gorshkov's

Table 4-2. Black Sea Fleet Cruisers

	Completed	Standard Displacement	Main Gun Battery	Speed
Komintern	1905	6,338 tons	10 5.1-inch (130-mm)	23 knots
Krasnyy Krym	1925	6,934 tons	15 5.1-inch (130-mm)	29 knots
Chervona Ukraina	1927	6,934 tons	15 5.1-inch (130-mm)	25 knots
Krasnyy Kavkaz	1932	8,030 tons	4 7.1-inch (180-mm)	29 knots
Voroshilov	1940	8,800 tons	9 7.1-inch (180-mm)	35 knots
Molotov	1941	8,177 tons	9 7.1-inch (180-mm)	35 knots

command. The *Komintern* (formerly the *Pamyat Merkuriya*), essentially a training ship, would serve in the defense and evacuation of Odessa and Sevastopol before being bombed out of service early in 1942. The *Chervona Ukraina* was bombed by German aircraft at Sevastopol on 12 November 1941 and foundered. Thus, only four cruisers were available in the Black Sea for most of the conflict. These ships were small and under-gunned, and most were slow by Western standards.

In the evening of 21 June, Gorshkov had received permission to visit his family, and he and his wife had gone out for dinner and dancing. His relaxation was cut short near midnight by a messenger announcing an immediate recall of all military and naval personnel. Preparations for setting Combat Readiness No. 1 were already in progress on his flagship. When the sound of approaching aircraft was heard he immediately ordered all his ships to commence anti-aircraft fire. A surprised Admiral Oktyabrskiy called Gorshkov and asked who had ordered the firing. Gorshkov responded that he had. There was a pause on the line before Oktyabrskiy answered:

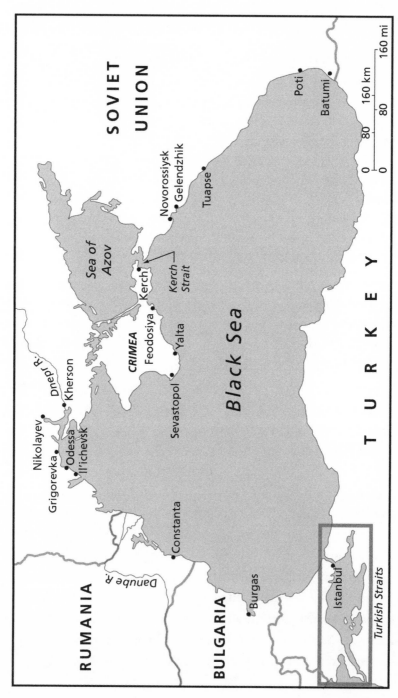

Map 4-1. Black Sea

"Molodets!" (Good man!) Tracer rounds arced into the sky, and Gorshkov's combat record began.[7]

At the start of the war the cruisers, including the *Chervona Ukraina*, destroyers, and purpose-built minelayers all laid defensive minefields off Soviet ports along the northern coast of the Black Sea. With the start of hostilities German aircraft too had begun planting mines near and in the harbors of Sevastopol and Nikolayev. These mines would inflict on both sides significant losses during the war.

The first major operation of Soviet warships in the Black Sea occurred on 26 June, when two destroyer leaders and naval aircraft attacked oil storage tanks, port infrastructure, and the railroad station and ammunition trains at the Rumanian port of Constanta, the main naval base available to the Germans on the Black Sea. The new cruiser *Voroshilov* and two destroyers provided cover to seaward. One of Gorshkov's destroyer leaders sank after striking a mine during the withdrawal; a second was heavily damaged by gunfire and air attack but managed to return to base. The *Voroshilov* suffered minor damage when a mine detonated close aboard.

By early July the Black Sea Fleet's major forces, including Gorshkov's cruiser brigade, had been forced to shift to a home port farther east—Novorossiysk. That port was farther from Luftwaffe airfields, but German aircraft did periodically strike it.

★ ★ ★

The 26 June attack and later hit-and-run raids were the only purely naval operations in the Black Sea performed by the Soviet Navy in this period. Gorshkov commanded some of the raids. All other naval operations in that theater were conducted in direct support of land operations, fulfilling the Navy's traditional role of supporting the Army.

Meanwhile, German-Rumanian forces were advancing rapidly into the Ukraine and approaching the port of Odessa, one of the largest cities on the Black Sea. The Axis forces threatened to cut off the city from the areas of the Ukraine still held by Soviet forces. Soviet cruisers and destroyers periodically provided gunfire support for the defending ground troops and struck Rumanian and German coastal installations behind the front lines. The Luftwaffe usually controlled the skies over combat areas; Soviet ships often were subjected to air attacks, mostly by Ju 87 Stuka dive-bombers.

In an effort to deny the Germans artillery positions from which they could bombard Odessa, a seaborne assault behind the lines, at Grigorevka, was planned for 22 September. Rear Admiral Lev A. Vladimirskiy, embarked in the destroyer *Frunze*, was to command the Soviet landing. However, the ship suffered heavy damage from German dive-bomber attacks while en route to Odessa and was run aground to prevent sinking. Vladimirskiy never reached the landing area. Direction of the landing fell to Gorshkov, who had to plan and command the assault operation "on the fly," making rapid decisions as the combat situation evolved.

Gorshkov was in command of a force of two cruisers—the *Krasnyy Kavkaz* and *Krasnyy Krym*—and two escorting destroyers, the *Boykiy* and *Bezuprechnyy*. The cruisers had on board a 1,700-man Naval Infantry (marine) landing force. Accompanying tugs, barges, and cutters were to take the troops ashore, early on the morning of 22 September. The amphibious landing was to be coordinated with 23 Soviet naval infantrymen parachuted behind the German lines to cause disruption. Air support was to be provided by land-based Soviet aircraft. Moments before the Naval Infantry paratroopers had jumped on their target and begun their attack, Gorshkov's cruisers and destroyers opened fire into the adjacent area, expending more than 3,500 rounds of ammunition. The cruisers had been ordered to retire before daybreak because of the threat of air attack, but the destroyers, including the *Besposhchadnyy*, which had joined the *Boykiy* and *Bezuprechnyy*, were to continue to support the assaulting troops.

Intense German air attacks were made throughout the day; Ju 87s damaged two of the destroyers and sank several lesser craft.

One Soviet report described the ferocity of the strikes by the infamous gull-winged Stuka dive-bombers:

> Ju 87 bombers in groups of 3 to 24 planes were diving on our ships all day. They dropped 16 aerial bombs on the *Bezuprechnyy*, but it emerged from the battle as the victor, repelling the raids with anti-aircraft fire, and maneuvering skillfully. Eighty-four aerial bombs were dropped on the *Besposhchadnyy*. The ship suffered severe damage: the raised forecastle was destroyed, and some of the compartments were flooded. But, thanks to the selflessness of the crew, the *Besposhchadnyy* reached Odessa under her own power, albeit in reverse.[8]

By sunset of the 22nd the Soviet assault forces had accomplished their objective. The Germans had been pushed back about five miles, having suffered a loss of 2,000 men killed and captured, according to Russian sources. The landing at Grigorevka was considered a major success amidst the uncountable Soviet reverses in the summer and fall of 1941. It was described as "one of the first naval landings in the Great Patriotic War and it led to significant operational results."[9] As a result of this landing and other Soviet efforts the German-Rumanian advance along the northern coast of the Black Sea was held up for two months, according to Soviet estimates. (During the 1941–1945 war almost 500,000 Soviet Navy officers and sailors would fight ashore as ground troops, forming 40 Naval Infantry brigades, 6 independent regiments, and several independent battalions. Some of these formations were called "naval-rifle units," and some were assigned to Army organizations, while the troops with the fleet were called Naval Infantry.)

Soon, however, German and Rumanian forces, having bypassed Odessa, were approaching the main Black Sea port of Sevastopol, in the Crimea. Two weeks after Gorshkov's amphibious landing it was decided to evacuate the port and major city of Odessa. Before its fall in October 1941, the ships and coastal craft of the Black Sea Fleet—in many cases escorted by Gorshkov's cruisers and destroyers—evacuated 350,000 civilians, 200,000 tons of industrial and military materiel, and, in the city's final moments, about 80,000 troops. The German-Rumanian advance continued. With the capture of Kerch on 16 November the whole of the Crimea was in Axis hands, with the exception of the besieged port city of Sevastopol.

During the horrific combat of the second half of 1941 Gorshkov gained experience in the direction of combined air-land-sea operations under fire. Interestingly, it was in the address of a fleet directive received on 22 September 1941, as the Grigorevka landing was under way, that he first realized that he had been promoted to rear admiral. The date of his promotion (16 September 1941) was less than five months before his 32nd birthday. He is often cited as being the youngest admiral in Soviet history.[10]

The following month, on 13 October, Gorshkov was assigned to command the Sea of Azov Flotilla. Two days later he was sitting amid sealed bags and boxes of documents in a Douglas C-47 Dakota aircraft taking off from Khersones airfield on the southern outskirts of Sevastopol and flying east into a new chapter of his life at war.

CHAPTER 5

The Sea of Azov, 1942

Before the operation Gorshkov visited the boats.
"You are faced with storming the Crimea to help
the Red Army liberate it more quickly from the fascist
invaders," he told the men of the Azov Flotilla. "Act
with initiative, decisively and boldly."

—Captain 1st Rank K. Vorobyev, "In the Rush of Combat,"
Morskoy Sbornik (no. 2, 1980)

The Sea of Azov is northeast of the Black Sea and washes the northern coasts of the Crimean–Kerch Peninsula and the Taman Peninsula. The narrow Kerch Strait between the peninsulas connects the Sea of Azov with the Black Sea. About 180 miles northeast of the Kerch Strait is the northern end of the Sea of Azov and the city of Rostov-on-Don, near the mouth of the Don River. Rostov is the transshipment point where cargo from the Volga and Don Rivers is loaded for the Black Sea and onward to the Mediterranean Sea and foreign ports.

The other principal ports of the Sea of Azov at the time were Mariupol and Taganrog, on the northern coast.[1] Mariupol ranked as one of the primary ports of the Soviet Union before World War II because of its accessibility to the Ukraine's industrial and agricultural regions and its convenience for the transshipment of coal from the Donets Basin and iron ore from the Kerch Peninsula. This city, also an industrial center in its own right, was the headquarters of Gorshkov's new command—the Azov Flotilla.

Most of the Sea of Azov is frozen from the end of November until mid-April, and all of its ports are icebound some of the winter. The sea is relatively shallow, with depths mostly some 25 feet and the deepest channel reaching only 50 feet. This enclosed sea—adjacent to the vital Ukraine and Black Sea regions—would be the scene of Gorshkov's combat activity for much of the war. Contrasting the Azov Flotilla with his previous command, a cruiser brigade, Gorshkov later wrote: "Now I had to command a flotilla basically comprised of mobilized civilian vessels, poorly armed and insufficiently adapted to execute the expected combat missions."[2]

A Fighting Retreat

After overrunning Odessa, the relentless German offensive rolled on, spilling into the Crimean Peninsula and besieging the large port city of Sevastopol, headquarters of the Black Sea Fleet. Other German troops advanced along the north coast of the Sea of Azov, taking Rostov-on-Don in November 1941. The Soviet High Command in late November ordered planning for a seaborne landing at several points around the Kerch–Feodosiya Peninsula to the east of Sevastopol to assist in the defense of that city and to delay further German advances.

Before the Kerch–Feodosiya landing, some of the Soviet combat troops allocated for the assault were instead sent directly into Sevastopol to assist in its immediate defense, thus weakening the planned seaborne operation. The landing plan called for troops of the 224th (Army) Rifle Division and 83rd Naval Rifle Brigade to be landed on the northern (i.e., Sea of Azov) shore of the Kerch Peninsula early on the morning of 26 December 1941, with simultaneous landings on the southern coast by the Black Sea Fleet.

However, for a number of reasons, including multiple regroupings, the landing force as finally assembled was to prove less than sufficiently trained and prepared for the mission.

For the seaborne landings the Black Sea Fleet and the Azov Flotilla, the latter under Gorshkov, would be subordinated to an Army *front* (roughly, an army group) commander. Assignment of naval and often air force units to a major Army command was both normal and expected under Soviet military doctrine. The Navy and Air Forces were considered specialized arms, whose primary purpose was to support the Red Army, which would conduct the main effort against the enemy. Gorshkov later would explain, "Joint operations between the Army and Navy have developed historically as a traditional feature of our military and naval art. Throughout all stages of history our military science has viewed the development and use of all branches of the Armed Forces as a single force for use in defending the state."[3]

Those problems facing the planned Kerch–Feodosiya landings were considerable. Some 40,000 Soviet troops were to be landed in the operation using fleet and flotilla forces, but not enough ships and small craft could be found to carry them. No specialized landing craft were available. Almost 300 barges, riverboats, cutters, and other small craft for the landings were commandeered from the local population. Obviously, such a vast variety of craft—with different speeds, capacities, and maneuvering characteristics—would be a nightmare to control and coordinate. Further, there was insufficient fuel (whether coal or wood) to employ even the polyglot flotilla that was assembled. Accordingly, a set of simultaneous surprise landings would be impossible to achieve.

Admiral Gorshkov persevered. The motley flotilla loaded troops, artillery, and vehicles during the day of 25 December, and that night his ships and small craft undertook to move 6,140 troops to the landing beaches along the Sea of Azov.[4] The next day there were storms of sleet and snow, the seas were rough, and the air temperature fell below the freezing point. Only three of his five landing groups were able to reach the shore on 26 December. The weather and some Luftwaffe interference delayed the others for several days. Additional troops were landed on the 28th, but the weather prevented further landings until the 30th. Only a few tanks and heavy guns were brought ashore, and the Soviet troops could only just survive German air and ground counterattacks; offensive action was impossible.

On the Black Sea side of the peninsula the landings were more successful, and the towns of Kerch and Feodosiya were retaken from the Germans. Gorshkov's key role in these landings—the largest Soviet amphibious operation of the war—was duly noted by senior Soviet ground and naval commanders. But the Soviet offensive soon came to a halt against stiffened resistance, and the subsequent Soviet efforts to penetrate the German defenses in the Crimea during February and April 1942 were failures.

Gorshkov later recalled: "During the war I participated in a number of amphibious assault operations . . . but the assault on the Kerch Peninsula in the winter of 1941 will remain in my memory as the most difficult and tragic."[5] Interestingly, although Moscow considered the landings a success, there was an investigation into Gorshkov's participation. An NKVD officer accused him of making statements not supporting the operation and of having insufficient confidence in its success. The investigative commission, however, did not find a basis for such an accusation; Gorshkov continued to hold his command and serve.[6]

The Soviet hold on the Kerch–Feodosiya Peninsula was short-lived. On 15 January 1942, German forces counterattacked and took Feodosiya. By early May Gorshkov's forces could no longer

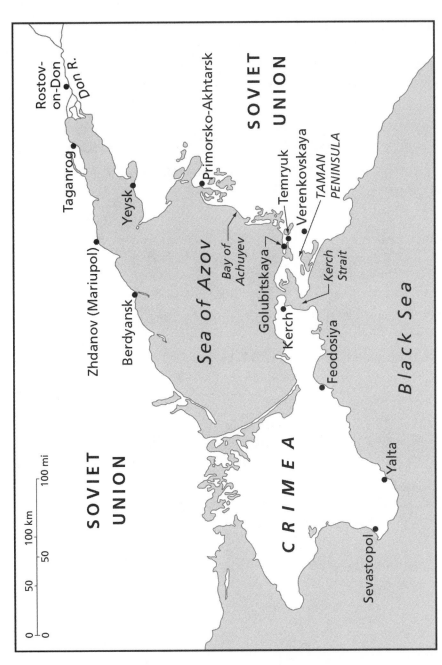

Map 5-1. Sea of Azov

delay the German advance. The Azov Flotilla was now employed in evacuating troops from the western end of the Kerch–Feodosiya Peninsula, across the five-mile-wide Kerch Strait. About 116,000 Soviet troops retreated from the eastern Crimea before German armored divisions cut off their escape routes; nevertheless, large numbers of Soviet troops and vast quantities of equipment were captured. Kerch was occupied by the Germans on 15 May, and as pockets of Soviet resistance were mopped up the surviving Soviet positions in the Crimea were sealed off except for the port of Sevastopol.

The Black Sea Fleet cruiser *Krasnyy Kavkaz* was damaged by German aircraft while engaged in shore bombardments during this period. She withdrew to Tuapse, on the eastern shore of the Black Sea, and remained there during this critical period.[7] The *Parizhkaya Kommuna*, the Black Sea Fleet's only battleship, suffered damage to her 12-inch (305-mm), main caliber gun barrels as a result of firing a fierce bombardment—more than 300 rounds—into German positions on the Kerch Peninsula. She withdrew to Poti, where she remained, unrepaired for the remainder of the war.[8]

The level of German air activity was almost overwhelming and would be until the decisive Battle of Stalingrad. As one Luftwaffe commander wrote during this period,

> In all we had assembled about 400 Stukas, bombers, and fighters on the airfields in the vicinity of Sevastopol. It meant that we had to keep 200 to 250 aircraft always ready for action every day.
>
> From the air Sevastopol looked like a painter's battle panorama. In the early morning the sky swarmed with aircraft hurrying to unload their bombs on the town. Thousands of bombs—more than 2,400 tons of high explosives and

23,000 incendiaries—were dropped on the town and fortress. A single sortie took no more than twenty minutes. By
the time you had gained the necessary altitude you were in
the target area. . . . Twelve, fourteen, and even up to eighteen
sorties were made daily by individual crews. A Ju 88 with
fuel tanks full made three or four sorties without the crew
stretching their legs.[9]

The Soviet forces in Sevastopol continued to hold out, supplied by
warships and cargo ships, which also took away the thousands of
wounded. From early May 1942, Soviet submarines too were pressed
into service carrying troops, munitions, and supplies to Sevastopol.
On 30 June, the Germans pushing relentlessly forward, the Soviet
High Command gave orders to evacuate Sevastopol by small craft
and submarines. Sevastopol—the last Soviet stronghold in the southern Ukraine and Crimea—fell to the Axis on 4 July. In total, during the defense of Sevastopol the Navy delivered 90,250 troops and
21,000 tons of military stores to the besieged city and brought out
29,845 wounded and some 15,000 civilians.

On 17 July the German armies, now in possession of all of
Crimea and the northern coast of the Sea of Azov, renewed their
push to the east-southeast. Their goal was the industrial river port
of Stalingrad and, ultimately, the oil fields of the Caspian Sea region.
On 28 July, Rostov-on-Don fell, even as Stalin issued his order:
"Not one step back!"

On the Sea of Azov, the task of Admiral Gorshkov's flotilla was
to help ground forces defend the naval base and city of Yeysk,
opposite Mariupol on the Taman Peninsula's northeast coast.
The German high command attached great importance to it as a
potential supply base to maintain the momentum of their eastward
advance. Gorshkov's ships and small craft joined two battalions
of Naval Infantry, three coastal defense batteries, and naval base
personnel in resisting the assault of a Rumanian mountain-rifle

division and a German SS regiment. The battle persisted for six days; the city fell only after the Germans assigned three more regiments to the task. Admiral Gorshkov's flotilla thus lost its bases at Yeysk and Primorsko-Akhtarsk, and the Soviet High Command directed the flotilla to move south, to Temryuk, near the mouth of the Kerch Strait.

On 11 August, with German forces on the coast north of Novorossiysk, the commander of the Soviet North Caucasus Front ordered the withdrawal of the effectively surrounded 47th Army and directed—via the Black Sea Fleet commander—Gorshkov's Azov Flotilla to assume the coastal defense of the Taman Peninsula and Novorossiysk. There was savage fighting as the Soviets attempted to slow the German columns advancing from the north and east. But the German advances could not be halted. There were no reserves for the Soviet defenders, and the flotilla's gunboats as well as the troops ashore soon expended virtually all of their ammunition. On the evening of 23 August the city of Temryuk and its naval base were abandoned, in effect giving the Germans control of the entire coastline of the Sea of Azov.

The Battle for the Caucasus

The German objective now was the Caucasus, the region between the Black Sea and Caspian Sea where lie major oil fields needed to power the German war machine. Also, further German advances eastward along the Black Sea coast would deny the Soviets their last major port—Novorossiysk—and the smaller ports of Tuapse and Poti. The defeats in the Crimea and the German threat to the Caucasus area to the northeast caused a major reorganization of the Soviet military commands in the region and the establishment of a new North Caucasus Front under Marshal Semyon M. Budennyy. The new front commander was given overall control of the remnants of the Black Sea Fleet.

Admiral Gorshkov's Azov Flotilla was pushed out of its home waters as the entire sea came under German control. His surviving ships and craft withdrew through the Kerch Strait. The main channel through the strait had been mined, and many of Gorshkov's smaller units were destroyed during the transit by German air strikes and mortar and artillery fire as well as by the mines. Still, during the period through 13 August more than 160 naval ships, small craft, cargo ships, and transports succeeded in breaking through into the Black Sea.

On 17 August 1942, the Soviet High Command created from part of Budennyy's force a Black Sea grouping that was to defend the coastal area between Novorossiysk (60 miles to the southeast of the Kerch Strait) and the smaller port of Sochi, farther southeast. This new command—the Novorossiysk Defense Region—was shortly placed under Major General Grigoriy P. Kotov; it consisted of the 47th Army, some of the ships and small craft of the Azov Flotilla, and a composite aviation group of 112 aircraft. The ground combat forces included several Naval Infantry battalions under the Novorossiysk naval base commander, Captain 1st Rank Georgiy N. Kholostyakov. The Germans had a more than two-fold advantage in troops.

Gorshkov would serve as the Novorossiysk Defense Region's deputy commander for naval operations and, significantly, became a member of the region's Military Council. "Military Council" was the generic Soviet term for a collective leadership entity consisting of the unit or area commander, his political deputy and chief of staff, and sometimes one or more other senior officers. All major decisions, both operational and administrative, by a unit or area commander had to be approved by his Military Council.

Gorshkov and his staff already had given considerable thought to the defense of Novorossiysk. On 17 August he submitted a proposal to the commander of the Black Sea Fleet, signed by Gorshkov's Military Council, arguing that, in part,

> the absence of a unified command in Novorossiysk does not ensure the most complete use of all capabilities for strengthening the defense and the terrain conditions. I consider it necessary to:
>
> 1. Immediately designate a unified commander for the sea and ground defense of Novorossiysk. . . .
> 2. Remove field units and move artillery from Taman Peninsula, evacuate Temryuk and bring them to defend Novorossiysk. This will provide up to two brigades of naval infantry and up to a regiment of field artillery.
> 3. Hold the Taman peninsula using coastal artillery until ammunition is exhausted.[10]

Also, in August 1942, Admiral Gorshkov had finally become a member of the Communist Party—a necessity for senior officers.

Initially, Gorshkov and the surviving ships and craft of his Azov Flotilla evacuated Army and Navy personnel and equipment from the southern coast of the Taman Peninsula to Novorossiysk. This operation, which lasted from 2 to 5 September, was subjected to nighttime attacks by motor torpedo boats. The Germans would claim to have sunk 19 ships and craft (aside from the German torpedo boat *S27*, sunk by her own torpedo). German forces began crossing the Kerch Strait on the night of 2 September and advanced along the coast toward Novorossiysk.

During the lengthy battle that ensued, 32-year-old Gorshkov commanded not only the local naval forces but also the direct defense of Novorossiysk, including its land approaches. He drew special notice for rapidly organizing naval troops to defend mountain passes through which German and Rumanian forces were threatening to advance into the city. According to one account, at one point, when there were no regular combat units from the 47th Army available, "Gorshkov ordered the Novorossiysk Naval Base commander to ... form detachments from staff personnel, the rear services establishments and afloat services, sending with them all who could bear arms regardless of their military rank, to form these detachments into artillery units (including anti-aircraft), and to send them to the [mountain] passes."[11]

The Germans made a determined assault, entering the outskirts of Novorossiysk on 5 September. On the eighth, 38-year-old Major General Andrey A. Grechko was appointed to command the 47th Army. This was Grechko's first major command, and in it he would meet and work with Gorshkov.[12] The center of the city and important harbor/naval base area were occupied by German forces on the ninth. Ships and small craft helped to evacuate the surviving Soviet troops—a frequent role of the Red Navy. On one sortie the destroyer *Nezamozhnyy* and the patrol ship *Shtorm* managed between them to evacuate 8,000 soldiers to Tuapse.

Still, the stubborn Soviet defenders prevented the Germans from seizing all of Novorossiysk or winning the use of its port, the most important harbor on the Black Sea east of Sevastopol. The front lines finally stabilized along the southern edge of the city on 10 September, in the area of the city's massive cement works. On 19 September, General Grechko was reassigned, and command of the 47th Army was added to Gorshkov's duties.

General Grechko was impressed by Gorshkov. From late September until late October 1942, when Gorshkov was acting commander of the 47th Army, Grechko led an adjacent army.[13] At the time the 47th Army is believed to have consisted of three rifle brigades, a mountain-rifle division, and two Naval Infantry brigades, plus smaller units. Grechko—who would become a postwar minister of defense—would certainly remember Gorshkov's decisiveness and effectiveness.

German troops were able to push around the Soviet positions at Novorossiysk and continue along the Black Sea coast, threatening the town of Tuapse, 95 miles southeast. Soviet 16th Army troops under General Grechko were able to halt the German drive, in part because the enemy forces were simply worn out and their lines of communications were over-extended. The all-important coastal road, which gave access to the south, remained in Soviet hands. Admiral Gorshkov would come to consider the defense of Novorossiysk as pivotal in the ultimate halting of the German advance in the Caucasus.[14]

Meanwhile, the issue of who would command the 47th Army, Admiral Gorshkov being only its acting commander, was being resolved. Gorshkov later wrote that one day he was at his headquarters when the telephone rang. Upon answering, he heard a characteristic Caucasus accent: "Hello, Comrade Gorshkov. Stalin speaking. There is an opinion here at the Stavka [Supreme Headquarters] to appoint you commander of the 47th Army. If you agree, you will have to say goodbye to the Navy—you will be given the rank of lieutenant general. What is your view of this?" After pausing a bit to consider such a fateful decision, Gorshkov said that he was grateful for the trust placed in him but asked Stalin to leave him in the Navy. Stalin replied, "Well, I understand you. I cannot blame you for your dedication to the Navy," and hung up.[15] (In April 1943 the 47th Army was to be transferred from the front organization to the Reserve of the Supreme High Command; this meant that it would be reconstituted and employed in important sectors to tilt the battle to the Soviets. According to Soviet writings, 23 armies were assigned this status at least once during the war; various corps and other units were similarly designated.)[16]

During the September–October 1942 time frame Admiral Gorshkov's wife and children, travelling independently from

Akhtarsk to Tbilisi, were briefly captured by a German–Rumanian group, but their identities were not discovered. When the local tide of battle changed they were able to get to the Soviet side and make themselves known. Gorshkov had learned that the Gestapo was extremely interested in his family and had sent a team to find them. All ended well: they reached Tbilisi, where Gorshkov briefly was reunited with them.[17]

During the fall of 1942 the Nazi empire reached the peak of its territorial expansion. Germans troops controlled Europe in the west to the French coast and the Pyrenees, to Norway in the north and North Africa to the south, and in the east to the Volga River, the major north–south waterway of the Soviet Union. Despite the massive size of Operation Barbarossa—the Germans had invaded the Soviet Union with 117 divisions—troops still were required to defend Norway and France against a possible Allied invasion, with increasing requirements for troops in North Africa.[18] This expansion was terminated in the battle for the industrial-port city of Stalingrad on the Volga River.

In these months the epic battle for Stalingrad, 400 miles north of the Black Sea coast, was being fought. From October 1942 until 1 February 1943, Soviet forces held the ruins of the city against massive German air and ground onslaughts. When the crucial battle ended the Germans and their allies had lost more than 730,000 men killed, wounded, or captured within the besieged city and in the attempts to break through the Soviet forces encircling the city.[19] Soviet losses in the battle were "substantial," but as Western invaders of Russia have always discovered, the country's supply of manpower is virtually inexhaustible. Most sources estimate Soviet losses in the lengthy battle at almost 480,000 killed or missing, another 650,000 wounded or sick.

But Stalingrad was in many respects the turning point of World War II in Europe.

★ ★ ★

As 1942 drew to a close Admiral Gorshkov was planning yet another assault landing—to liberate Novorossiysk. As he sat over his notes and maps he mused over the events of the waning year. They had been many and greatly varied, but the overall course of battle was changing: the German hordes had been stopped. But much fighting lay ahead before the invader would be completely expelled from "Mother Russia."

CHAPTER 6

On the Offensive, 1943–1945

By the end of 1942 the tide of war had unquestionably—and inalterably—turned in favor of the Allies in the Pacific, North Africa, and on the Eastern Front as Soviet and German armies were locked in mortal combat. Along the Black Sea coast the Soviet armies kept up pressure against German forces between Novorossiysk and the Kerch Strait. This area—the Taman Peninsula—soon became a pocket containing some 400,000 German troops who had been withdrawn from deeper penetrations into the Caucasus. The Soviets began an offensive on 27 January 1943, to retake the port city of Novorossiysk, a campaign that would last for nine months.

The initial Soviet amphibious landings near Novorossiysk established a beachhead that was maintained and expanded, but those forces were unable to liberate the city. For the next six months Soviet ships and craft ferried in reinforcements from nearby Gelendzhik and carried out the wounded. General Andrei Grechko, in his memoirs of the Caucasus battle, written when he was Minister of Defense (1967–1976), especially cited the Black Sea Fleet and the Azov Flotilla for their roles in preventing German seizure of this important region.[1]

Advancing Soviet forces reached the Sea of Azov in February 1943, and Admiral Gorshkov once more was assigned to command the reactivated Azov Flotilla, with headquarters at Yeysk. The flotilla again would consist of small craft and would have important roles in supporting Soviet ground operations in the battles to drive German forces from the Ukraine and Crimea, and destroying the German armies holding the Taman Peninsula. At the time the Germans also had forces on the Sea of Azov itself: in August 1943, they were believed to have consisted of 5 artillery cutters, up to 20 landing barges, 24 patrol boats, 3 torpedo boats, up to 11 patrol cutters, and 55 other naval craft.

During the spring and summer of 1943 the Soviet armies continued to drive the Germans from the Ukraine and prepare for the destruction of the German forces remaining on the Taman Peninsula. In late August, Admiral Gorshkov helped the 44th Army assault the important port city of Taganrog, on the northern side of the Sea of Azov, which had been held by the Germans since 1941. Gorshkov's flotilla shelled German positions along the coast and landed a small assault force. The city fell to Soviet troops on the last day of August 1943.

Mariupol, a short distance down the coast, was the next target of the Soviet steamroller. On one occasion in this phase a force that was put ashore was not joined by ground forces on schedule. In a most unusual move, the landing force was taken off. According to Gorshkov's chief of staff, Captain 1st Rank A. Sverdlov, "The progress of our [Army] troops on the sea flank was delayed too long. The counted on linkup of the landing force with the ground forces did not take place in the following twenty-four hours. Therefore, with the sanction of the army command, the landing force was withdrawn."[2]

The principal ground forces commanders in the area were Generals Rodion Ya. Malinovsky and Fedor I. Tolbukhin. Both men were highly thought of by Stalin, who prepared an order that covered the entire front page of every newspaper on 8 September citing the skill of the two generals in clearing the Donbas region. Gorshkov was working closely and continuously with these two officers. Stalin also cited the Azov Flotilla for its role in the Mariupol operation. The flotilla was transferred to the operational command of Tolbukhin's Southern Front on 2 September, and on the 8th the flotilla landed troops to the west of Mariupol. The city fell to the Soviets two days later. Mariupol then became the headquarters of Admiral Gorshkov.

Simultaneous with the Mariupol operation the Soviets undertook a massive assault into the German-held Black Sea port of Novorossiysk, beginning on the night of 10 September. The landing force, carried in 120 ships and small craft, consisted of 6,480 troops, including some 4,000 Naval Infantry. For nine months the Germans had fortified the area, and the jetties, piers, and breakwaters in the landing zone were heavily mined. The landing was supported by cruisers and destroyers of the Black Sea Fleet, as well as by army artillery. Soviet air forces and naval aircraft provided close air support, while small combat craft closed with the beach to add their firepower to the assault. Vice Admiral Lev A. Vladimirskiy was in command of the naval forces in the Novorossiysk assault.

The Novorossiysk landings later came to have major political significance, because of the presence in the landing force of 37-year-old, then-Colonel Leonid Brezhnev, a political officer. He apparently visited the beachhead several times. Over time his remembered role increased; Brezhnev himself later claimed to have planned the operation with the commander of the 18th Army. Rear Admiral Georgiy N. Kholostyakov, who was in charge of the actual landing operation, later recalled that Brezhnev had been an important participant in planning both the amphibious landings and the subsequent land offensive.[3] Gorshkov also was involved in the planning and may have worked with Brezhnev.

For the next half-century participation in the Great Patriotic War was to be looked on as tantamount in itself to heroism, and Brezhnev often would cite his role at Novorossiysk, where he was exposed to enemy fire. Even his ghost-written autobiography was titled *Malaya Zemlya* (Small Land), the local name for the landing area. Brezhnev was in fact involved with the Soviet offensive along the northern coast of the Black Sea following the landings, possibly having further interaction with Gorshkov.

Novorossiysk marked the easternmost major city of the German advance along the Black Sea coast. With Novorossiysk again in Soviet hands the Germans were displaced from the Caucasus region, except for some 400,000 troops left on the Taman Peninsula. The Soviets controlled most of the Black Sea, the peninsula's southern coast, and the Sea of Azov on the north. The Soviet front commander ordered the Black Sea Fleet and the Azov Flotilla to make a series of landings on the peninsula to constrict the German troops further. Gorshkov's Azov Flotilla prepared to land troops at the town of Temryuk, the main port on the northern coast of the peninsula.

At this point—on 19 September 1943—with most of the Sea of Azov liberated from the Germans, control of the Azov Flotilla was transferred to the North Caucasus Front, under Colonel-General Ivan Ye. Petrov. In a meeting with Admiral Kuznetsov, the naval commissar, and Marshal Aleksandr M. Vasilevskiy, who had been sent from Moscow to help coordinate the Soviet offensive, Admiral Gorshkov was told that his immediate mission was to help expel German forces from the Taman Peninsula and, after that, to prepare for an assault across the Kerch Strait and support the establishment of a lodgment there.[4]

For the assault on the Taman Peninsula, Gorshkov divided his relatively small force into two parts, sailing respectively from the port of Akhtarsk and the Bay of Achuyev. The main assault of 1,200 men in 33 landing craft went ashore near the village of Golubitskaya, west of Temryuk, while a smaller group of 200 Naval Infantry in seven craft landed near Chaykino, to the south of Temryuk. The landings were supported by gunfire from the flotilla and by 20 aircraft that strafed the German positions. Landing in the early morning of 5 September, the force met strong resistance but managed to get ashore and push inland to cut the vital east–west coastal highway. After three days of bitter fighting the Soviets captured Temryuk.

Gorshkov's flotilla then entered the Kuban River and followed it to Verenikovskaya, which his force also captured. The flotilla was again cited in an order published by Stalin.

In an effort to cut off retreat by German forces, the Soviets landed troops on the *western* bank of the Kerch Strait during late October and early November 1943, but superior German defenses entrapped the assault troops, eventually starving them out and destroying most of them. Tattered remnants made it back to the Taman Peninsula in early December.

In late December, while en route from Temryuk to one of the embarkation points, Admiral Gorshkov's vehicle struck a land mine. He suffered a concussion when his head hit the windshield, and he was thrown from the vehicle as it overturned; he sustained spinal damage that would nag him for the rest of his life. The fact that he had abandoned his customary automobile for an American-built Willys jeep and was thrown out rather than trapped and crushed likely saved his life. Gorshkov was forced to leave the war for a couple of months to convalesce.[5]

Meanwhile, the Germans began moving troops west across the strait and back into the Crimea. Despite their superiority at sea, the Soviets were unable to halt the withdrawal. The Germans crossed the four-mile strait safely with 256,000 men, 73,000 horses, 21,000 vehicles, 1,800 guns, and 100,000 tons of material.[6] Nor were there any serious casualties when the Germans used some 240 small ships and craft to withdraw from Kerch to Sevastopol. At the time in the Black Sea the Soviets still had 4 cruisers, 7 or 8 destroyers and destroyer leaders, 29 submarines, 67 motor torpedo boats, and a naval air arm of about 280 aircraft. The British liaison officer with the Black Sea Fleet described the failure as the result of "comparative inactivity ... [that] robbed Russia and her allies of the full fruits of the victory at Stalingrad. . . . In all of these operations there was no effective Russian naval intervention, although cruisers, destroyers and submarines were available at Poti."[7]

Further, the Soviet ships that did enter the combat area suffered grievous losses. On the night of 5–6 October two Soviet destroyers and a destroyer leader bombarded what were thought to be groupings of German ships in the harbors of Yalta and Feodosiya. The three destroyers instead encountered a German torpedo boat flotilla, but neither side suffered losses in the engagement. Then, on the morning of the sixth, while returning to base, Ju 87 Stuka dive-bombers attacked and sank all three of the Soviet warships; 780 crewmen were lost. After this setback a message was sent by Supreme Command to Admiral Kuznetsov and the North Caucasus Front commander: "The operation of the Black Sea Fleet of 6 October, ending in failure, unnecessary loss of personnel, and loss of three ships was conducted without the knowledge of the Front commander, notwithstanding that the fleet is subordinate to him. Conduct no operations without concurrence of the Front commander."[8] In contrast to the fleet's poor performance in the Black Sea, the flotilla under Admiral Gorshkov in the Sea of Azov had great success in supporting the Red Army's advance down to the Crimea. Of the Soviet flotilla's operations, the British liaison officer wrote, "We must give credit to the smaller Russian warships—the MTBs, the MGBs, gunboats, and all the miscellaneous craft used in the landings in the Crimea. Their tenacity and indifference to heavy losses were more conspicuous than the skill of the planners in coordinating the landing operations."[9]

The liberation of the Crimea—the diamond-shaped area between the Sea of Azov and the Black Sea—with its major port of Sevastopol and its airfields was the next Soviet objective in the southern region. In November 1943, Soviet land, air, and coastal naval forces gained another bridgehead on the Azov coast, near Kerch. For five and one-half months the sailors of the Azov Flotilla reliably supported the

Kerch crossing, supplying the Army with everything necessary for an offensive against the enemy despite fierce storms and rough winter seas. Ships large and small scurried across the strait around the clock, fighting winds, waves, and ice and braving the constant danger of mines that infested the waters. Also, the Germans launched heavy air strikes against the Soviet ships and small craft.[10]

The Germans held the Kerch beachhead through the winter of 1943–1944. Kerch was liberated on 11 April 1944, a victory the Azov Flotilla had facilitated by the delivery by sea of 240,000 troops with their artillery, tanks, and other vehicles to the Kerch Peninsula. The last remnants of German forces, pressed to the beach, laid down their arms on 18 May. Then, in a giant, two-prong attack, Soviet armies recaptured the Crimea. One prong thrust out from the Kerch beachhead, and the second swept down the western side of the Sea of Azov and across the top of the Crimea. The combination would liberate the port city of Odessa in April 1944. This maneuver isolated the Germans in the western Crimea; Soviet forces then turned eastward to clear the remainder of the Crimea. Admiral Gorshkov's flotilla had important roles in supporting the liberation of the Crimea.

Hitler delayed the evacuation of the Crimea until 9 May, by which time Soviet troops had reached Sevastopol, denying the use of its harbor to the Germans. The last remaining German troops in the city's outskirts surrendered on 12 May. Once again, however, the timidity of the Black Sea Fleet enabled the Germans to evacuate about 130,000 men from the beaches, including 6,000 wounded. There were losses among the German evacuation craft but primarily from Soviet air attacks; a senior German naval officer later wrote that "if the Russian Fleet had intervened, not one would have escaped from the Crimea."[11] The Black Sea Fleet was now commanded by Vice Admiral Fillip Sergeyevich Oktyabrskiy, who had relieved Vice Admiral Vladimirskiy in March 1944. Subsequently, Vladmiriskiy commanded not another fleet but a *squadron* in the

Black Sea until the end of the war. Oktyabrskiy had led the Black
Sea Fleet from 1939 to April 1943, and would again from March
1944 until 1948.

A New Flotilla . . . Briefly

On 13 April 1944, with naval operations in the Black Sea ending, the
Azov Flotilla was disbanded and reorganized into the newly established Danube Flotilla, named for the river that flows from the center of Europe into the western side of the Black Sea. Rear Admiral
Gorshkov was named flotilla commander, and on 3 May he and his
staff drove from Temryuk to Odessa.

Soviet armies continued moving west toward Moldavia and
Rumania. Gorshkov's flotilla landed troops that captured Akkerman
(now Belgorod-Dnestrovskiy), at the mouth of the Dniester River.
after only five days of battle, on 24 August Rumania ceased hostilities against the Soviet Union; the Red Army entered the capital,
Bucharest, on 31 August. Soviet troops then moved southwestward
into Hungary and Yugoslavia.

On 5 September the Soviet government declared war against neu-
tral while pro-fascist Bulgaria, to the south of Rumania. Soviet troops—
supported by Gorshkov's Danube Flotilla—prepared to invade that
country, but on 8 September the Bulgarians welcomed them with
bands and banners. As Soviet warships approached the Bulgarian ports
of Varna and Burgas, the surviving German ships and craft were scuttled, essentially ending the naval warfare on the Black Sea.

Gorshkov was promoted to the rank of vice admiral on 25 September
1944—at age 34. He thus had the same rank as Oktyabrskiy, the commander of the Black Sea Fleet.

To the west of Bulgaria lay Yugoslavia. After rolling through
Bulgaria, Soviet armies entered that country and linked up with
communist partisans led by Tito (Josip Broz). Gorshkov and his flotilla sailed up the Danube, through Rumania, Bulgaria, and into
Yugoslavia, supplying the Soviet ground forces, attacking the German

troops on the riverbanks, carrying out orders of the front commander, newly promoted Marshal of the Soviet Union Tolbukhin.
However, in early December 1944 an argument erupted between
Tolbukhin and Gorshkov. Tolbukhin had reportedly failed to support a landing of Naval Infantry by Gorshkov's river flotilla in the
Vukovar region on the Danube River in eastern Slavonia. Gorshkov
lost the argument and was dismissed as head of the Danube Flotilla
on 12 December.

Lessons Learned

Admiral Gorshkov's flotillas saw extensive combat service along the
Sea of Azov and the eastern coast of the Black Sea and then in
supporting Soviet armies as they moved westward. Gorshkov demonstrated his ability to support army commanders as well as his personal characteristics of flexibility and improvisation. For example,
he welded 76.2-mm gun turrets from disabled T-34 tanks onto the
decks of motor torpedo boats to increase their firepower.

The previous three and one-half years of war had given Admiral
Gorshkov sea-going and riverine experience in combat in large
ships (cruisers and destroyers) as well as in small combatants and supply craft. He had conducted joint amphibious operations, which the
Soviets considered "the most difficult and complex type of military
action"; he had the opportunity to command ground forces; also, he
had worked with key military and political personalities.[12]

Of particular interest was the appreciation that Gorshkov gained
for small craft operations, careful preparation of operations, and the
limitations of land-based aviation in supporting naval operations.
During the war the Soviet Navy landed approximately one-third of
a million troops in all theaters; more than one-third of those went
ashore in landings commanded by Gorshkov. It is important to note
that the amphibious practice of the Red Navy "developed along
its own paths, which differ considerably from the paths taken by
the naval art of foreign navies, primarily the U.S. Navy."[13] These

were largely riverine and coastal operations in support of ground combat operations, as opposed to the long-distance, often trans-oceanic amphibious assaults of the U.S. Navy. Soviet sources note that there were 114 amphibious landings in the war, 4 of them considered "operational" (*operativnyye*), or large-scale. One of those occurred in the Northern Fleet area, 3 in the Black Sea–Azov region—at Kerch–Feodosiya in 1941–1942, Novorossiysk in 1943, and Kerch–Eltigen in 1943.

With respect to air support, Gorshkov later would make repeated references, based on his war experience, to the limitations of land-based aviation: "Naval aviation was unable to successfully carry sufficient torpedoes against warships at sea which had been detected at long ranges from airfields. . . . Due to short operating range, weak armament, and short endurance, naval fighter aviation was not in condition to reliably cover forces at sea even at relatively short distances from shore. This considerably limited the employment of major fleet surface forces in zones accessible to hostile aircraft."[14]

Also confirmed by experience was Admiral Gorshkov's personal dedication to the assigned mission and his self-control when faced by superiors' decisions that were less than well thought out. Further, his few "failures" in the war did not draw down on him the severe and often tragic consequences that the Party could inflict on those who did not perform to the expectations of Stalin and the Party apparatchiks in Moscow.

CHAPTER 7

Rebuilding a Nation and a Navy, 1945–1953

And the fact that, despite all threats to destroy Communism, imperialism has not decided to unleash a new world war is explained primarily by the enormous growth of the might of the USSR.

—Admiral S. G. Gorshkov, *Morskoy Sbornik* (no. 12, 1972)

The war in Europe ended in May 1945. The Soviet Union's western fleets—inadequate as they had been when the war began—emerged from the conflict severely mauled. As during World War I, in the 1941–1945 conflict the Navy had fought in no major sea battles; the Pacific Fleet had been completely inactive until the last week of the war, when the Soviet Union entered the conflict against Japan. To the Western observer the Soviet Navy had not justified the pre-war investment in shipbuilding that Josef Stalin had made.

But the leadership of the Soviet Union viewed the matter quite differently: although the fleets had fought no significant sea battles, they had steadfastly had supported the Soviet Army—protecting its flanks, conducting amphibious landings, ferrying supplies and reinforcements, helping to defend ports under siege, and evacuating encircled ports and cities. The Navy had laid minefields to prevent German seaborne assaults and had interdicted enemy shipping. Hundreds of thousands of Naval Infantry and sailors from ships' crews had fought heroically on land in defense of their homeland, usually under local army commanders. Naval forces had defended the Kola Peninsula and had kept open the seaborne supply lines into Murmansk and Arkhangelsk. Major combatants, including even a battleship that had been sunk in shallow water, had served as artillery platforms in the defense of Leningrad. To the Soviet leadership with its land-oriented mind-set the Navy had done precisely what it should have done—serve as the loyal helper of the Red Army. Stalin often made it a point to heap praise upon the Navy. The Navy's leadership, in turn, was not slow to exaggerate the great contributions that it had made to the final victory.

The war devastated the Soviet Union. All industry in the western portion of the country had been heavily damaged, including the shipyards. Cities had been leveled. Counting the military and civilians, more than 20 million people had been killed, and millions more had been displaced. The survivors faced near-starvation diets for the near future. It would have been quite understandable if the Soviet leadership had reverted, with respect to the Navy, to some form of the Young School philosophy, that of building only small combatants and submarines, and those few in number. But this was not the case. Stalin again wanted a large, modern, ocean-going fleet.

As early as 28 July 1943, Stalin had declared that in the post-war period "the Soviet people [will] wish to see their fleet grow still stronger and more powerful." The war had made the Soviet Union a great power. Stalin had been welcomed in the highest Allied councils—he had sat at Tehran, Yalta, and Potsdam as an equal of Prime Minister Winston Churchill, President Franklin D. Roosevelt, and after the latter's death in April 1945, Harry S. Truman. A big navy befitted a great power.

On a more practical level, Stalin had not forgotten the limitations of the Soviet Union in the Spanish Civil War of 1936–1939, when Red merchant ships carrying aid to the Republican forces had been at the mercy of fascist warships and airplanes. Later, he had recognized the value of navies in several World War II campaigns. Should there be a future conflict between the capitalist and socialist worlds—a conflict that Stalin saw as "inevitable"—a powerful Soviet Navy could delay or halt American reinforcement across the Atlantic to the weakened Western European nations and prevent Allied assaults on Soviet territory. Stalin would be aided in developing a major navy by two factors: geography and German technology.

Red Army successes had expanded the territory of the Soviet Union to a size similar to its size at the peak of the tsarist empire and had mostly reversed what Lenin had ceded to make peace with Germany in 1917–1918. The Karelian Isthmus, taken from Finland, provided a protective land buffer for the city, port, and naval complexes of Leningrad. Reincorporation of the Baltic States of Estonia, Latvia, and Lithuania gave the Soviets year-around, ice-free ports on the Baltic Sea. Finally, the Red banner flew from the former German naval bases at Pillau (renamed Baltiysk) and Konigsberg (renamed Kaliningrad), with satellite naval bases at several other East German and Polish ports, as well as ports in Bulgaria and Romania on the Black Sea. Similarly, in the Far East, the northern half of the Korean Peninsula, the Kurile Islands, and Sakhalin were occupied by Soviet troops, improving the ability of the Soviet Navy to reach the open Pacific.

At the same time, the initial satellite status of Albania and Yugoslavia, the civil war raging in Greece, and Soviet demands on Turkey for joint control of the passage to the Black Sea gave promise of Soviet bases on and free entry to the Mediterranean—a desire of Russian naval leaders for two centuries. In addition, Soviet troops

had remained in northern Iran after the end of World War II, imply-
ing the potential for direct access to the Indian Ocean. An accom-
modation with the Iranian government might be reached for passage
through the southern half of that country, which had been occupied
by British troops during the war—or it might simply be "occupied."

The war-torn Soviet Union was reunited politically by Stalin,
often by draconian means, and a remarkable economic recovery
began. By 1947—only two years after the war ended—Soviet shipyards had begun construction of new classes of destroyers, cruisers,
and submarines, and plans were being drawn for aircraft carriers and
battle cruisers. The latter, a favorite of Stalin, would have 12-inch
(305-mm) guns, possibly capable of firing nuclear shells.

Although the outlook for the Soviet Navy was bright, the Black
Sea Fleet, in which Vice Admiral Gorshkov was again serving, was
second to the Baltic Fleet in priority and significance. The control of the straits connecting the Black Sea and Mediterranean by
Turkey—a NATO member—could inhibit Soviet access to the
Mediterranean in time of conflict, while British control of Gibraltar,
at the Mediterranean's exit to the Atlantic, and of the Suez Canal,
the route to the Indian Ocean, meant that the Black Sea Fleet would
have little chance of reaching beyond the Mediterranean should
Soviet naval forces even reach that sea and the Allies try to constrain
their operations.

Post-war U.S. military activity also made it clear that Soviet
advances into the eastern Mediterranean area would be countered. The U.S. government selected the battleship *Missouri* (BB 63),
escorted by a cruiser and destroyer, to return home the body of the
Turkish ambassador who had died in the United States in 1944.
The *Missouri* fulfilled both diplomatic and military roles by sailing through the Dardanelles and in to the Bosporus, arriving in
Istanbul in April 1946—a clear message of the range of U.S. naval
forces. She was followed into the Mediterranean later in 1946 by

an aircraft carrier task force that initiated the periodic and then continuous U.S. carrier deployments to the Mediterranean Sea for the remainder of the Cold War. From the 1950s those carriers embarked nuclear strike aircraft. These operations—coupled with U.S. military and economic assistance to Greece and Turkey—were a clear message to the Soviet regime of American political-military resolve to support allies in that region.

Stalin understood this situation. His oft-cited ultimatum to communist leaders during the Greek civil war bears this out: "What do you think, that Great Britain and the United States—the United States the most powerful state in the world—will permit you to break their line of communication in the Mediterranean Sea! Nonsense! And we have no navy. The uprising in Greece must be stopped, and as quickly as possible."[1]

The diminutive Black Sea Fleet could control its enclosed home waters, but in the Mediterranean it would be virtually defenseless against the aircraft from even a single U.S. carrier. Similarly, the Baltic Fleet was uncontested in that closed sea, but with Denmark in the Western camp this largest of Soviet fleets could easily be blocked from passing through the Danish Straits to enter the North Sea and Atlantic Ocean. The Soviet Northern (Arctic) and Pacific Fleets were too small and the former too distant from the Allied trans-Atlantic routes to threaten them seriously. To reach the Atlantic the Northern Fleet's surface ships and submarines would have to sail around Norway's North Cape, where they would be vulnerable to detection and air attack by yet another Allied nation. This overall situation was exacerbated in April 1949, with the formation of the anti-Soviet North Atlantic Treaty Organization (NATO), whose founding members included Britain, Denmark, Norway, and Turkey.

It was in this environment that Stalin again took up the construction of a major, ocean-going fleet. The first post-war, ten-year naval shipbuilding program envisioned the construction of almost 2,500 units:[2]

2 battleships	75 large amphibious ships
2 aircraft carriers	120 small landing ships
4 heavy cruisers	177 patrol ships
30 light cruisers	828 torpedo boats
188 destroyers	700 minesweepers
25 large (ocean-going) submarines	
204 medium submarines	
123 small (coastal) submarines	

This program also called for the completion of several unfinished pre-war ships. On the whole, it appears to have reflected a mixture of both the Old and Young School approaches to the composition of the fleet but basically continued the thrust of Stalin's pre-war "big Navy" program.

Admiral Kuznetsov Dismissed

Just as the post-war shipbuilding efforts were beginning, the Soviet Navy was shaken by criminal charges leveled at the Commander-in-Chief of the Navy. In early January 1947, Stalin dismissed Fleet Admiral N. G. Kuznetsov, who had commanded the Navy since 1939 and appeared to have had Stalin's confidence as he directed naval activities from Moscow during the war. Kuznetsov had been promoted to Fleet Admiral (*Admiral Flota*) at the end of the war. At that time Stalin had decided to divide the Baltic and Pacific Fleets each into two fleets.[3] Admiral Kuznetsov disagreed, and most of the naval staff supported his view. Stalin did not welcome opposing views. Also, the armed forces minister, Nikolay Bulganin, did not like Kuznetsov, apparently because of the Navy CinC's high principles and independence. Bulganin, close to Stalin, was known as a man to resent such attitudes in a colleague or, especially, in a subordinate.

Kuznetsov was demoted to rear admiral and sent to Leningrad as head of the higher naval schools—the equivalent of Western (undergraduate) naval academies. Then, in November 1947, Stalin ordered Kuznetsov and three other senior flag officers to Moscow. The others were Admiral L. M. Galler, head of the A. N. Krylov Naval Academy of Shipbuilding and Armament (i.e., technical war college); Admiral V. A. Alafuzov, head of the prestigious K. Ye. Voroshilov Naval Academy (i.e., command and staff war college);[4] and Vice Admiral G. A. Stepanov, Kuznetsov's deputy.[5] The four were good friends and over the years had often served together.

At naval headquarters the four admirals were told that they were under investigation to ascertain if they had overstepped authorized limits by passing information to foreign officials during the war, especially in regard to German T5 acoustic homing torpedoes, to the United States and Britain in 1944.[6] The torpedoes had been recovered from the German submarine *U-250*, sunk in the Gulf of Finland, which had been salvaged and towed to Kronshtadt for examination by Soviet engineers.

The four admirals were interrogated for two months. The torpedoes and other military equipment were cited in their interrogations as highly classified items. On 19 December 1947 Stalin signed a Council of Ministers decree bringing these former leaders of the Navy to trial. Court-martial proceedings began on 12 January 1948, the court's members appointed by Bulganin. When those proceedings concluded, the chairman of the court, Marshal Leonid A. Govorov, read the decree "acknowledging that the guilt . . . in this case has been fully proven and considering . . . that all of the defendants did great harm to the combat might of the Navy by their actions and thereby, in essence, committed a grave crime against our homeland."

The four admirals now would be tried by the Military Board of the Supreme Court of the Soviet Union. On 3 February all were pronounced guilty and sentenced, three of them to prison: Alafuzov and Stepanov to ten years, Galler to four years. These three were discharged from the armed forces. (Galler died in prison in 1950. Upon Stalin's death in March 1953, the judgment of the court was found to have been without basis, and in May all three were "rehabilitated," the survivors released from prison, and their ranks restored.[7])

Kuznetsov's sentence was quite different: reduction to rear admiral and effective exile as naval deputy to the commander of Far East Forces. Considering the fates of senior Soviet commanders charged with treason in the late 1930s, he was fortunate to have escaped imprisonment or worse; the leniency of the court was probably due to Stalin's deep-rooted favor—albeit limited—toward the man who had been his naval commander throughout the war. There also is the theory that Kuznetsov might have suffered more seriously but for his excellent relationship with Andrey Zhdanov, a member of the Politburo who was at times seen as the heir apparent to Stalin. Zhdanov's political base was Leningrad—the nation's shipbuilding center—and he had represented naval interests in the Politburo since 1935. (Zhdanov died in August 1948, apparently of a heart attack, although medical assassination later was charged by Stalin, in his announcement in January 1953 of a "doctors' plot" against Soviet leaders.)

Stalin appointed Admiral Ivan S. Yumashev to replace Kuznetsov as head of the Navy. Yumashev had been a sailor in the tsarist navy and had joined the Communist Party in 1918. He had advanced to flag rank, commanding the Black Sea Fleet in 1938–1939 and then the Pacific Fleet through World War II and until 17 January 1947, when he was appointed Commander-in-Chief and Minister of the Navy. Here again was evidence of Stalin's favoritism toward the Pacific Fleet. Yumashev would serve as CinC for four and one-half years, until 16 July 1951. During a Politburo meeting convened to consider shortfalls in the Navy's leadership, Stalin was to say, "He's weak, a very respected person, even my friend, but weak"—and remove him as CinC.[8] (Subsequently Yumashev served as head of the Voroshilov Naval Academy, until 1957, when he was retired from the Navy.)

Numerous other senior naval positions changed during 1947–1949 in the aftermath of the Kuznetsov dismissal. Admiral Fillip Oktyabrskiy ended his eight-year tenure as commander of the Black Sea Fleet and in 1949 became the First Deputy Commander-in-Chief of the Soviet Navy. In the ensuing shift of flag officers in the Black Sea, Vice Admiral Gorshkov, who had commanded the Black Sea surface squadron from December 1944, through November 1948, was assigned as chief of staff of the fleet on 9 November 1948. During Gorshkov's several years of service with Oktyabrskiy in the Black Sea the two officers apparently had worked well together. Thus, Gorshkov would have a friend in a senior position at naval headquarters in Moscow. (Vice Admiral Nikolay Efremovich Basisty succeeded Oktyabrskiy in command of the Black Sea Fleet.) The Soviet armed forces relied on staff planning and staff involvement in the direction of operations to a much higher degree than was the case in Western military services. This meant that Gorshkov again was exposed to higher levels of military and, inevitably, political activity.

Under Admiral Yumashev the Soviet Navy quietly but energetically went about its business: slowly the shipyards in the Baltic, Black Sea, Arctic, and Pacific areas began completing warships of post-war design, initially those at the lower levels of the shipbuilding plan. In 1950 the first *Skoryy* (Project 30*bis*)–class destroyers and Whiskey (Project 613)–class torpedo-armed submarines were completed, followed a year later by *Sverdlov* (Project 68*bis*), the lead ship of a class of large, impressive light cruisers.[9] The new cruisers, with a standard displacement of 13,600 tons and armed with 12 5.9-inch (152-mm) guns, soon became the "showboats" of the new Soviet Navy, often visiting foreign ports. More were on the building ways. Scores of destroyers and submarines were begun, and building schedules were prepared for 24 *Sverdlovs*, which were to be followed on the ways by the larger *Stalingrad* (Project 82)-class battle cruisers armed with 12-inch (305-mm) guns, as well as, eventually, by aircraft carriers.

Also, despite the political break between the Soviet Union and Yugoslavia in 1948 and the establishment of NATO in 1949 to counter its military ambitions, the Soviet Union was able to maintain a toehold in the Mediterranean in the satellite of Albania. However, the Vlore naval base there was used only between 1958 and 1961; for instance, four Whiskey-class submarines and the submarine tender *Viktor Kotelnikov* from the Black Sea were based in Vlore in 1960 for operations in the Mediterranean. (Two of these submarines were seized by the Albanians in May 1961, when that government broke with the Soviet regime.)

Within the overall Soviet defense picture, the Navy remained a favorite of Stalin. Nevertheless, the other services were being modernized with conventional weapons, and the Soviets were pursuing the development of nuclear weapons. The first Soviet atomic bomb was detonated on 29 August 1949—four years after the first U.S. nuclear weapons were tested and then used against Japan. But the development of nuclear weapons in the Soviet Union did not have the same impact on the armed forces that they did in the United States. In the United States these weapons led to considerable debate on service roles and missions and to the emergence of the U.S. Air Force as a separate and, to some political and military leaders, the predominant U.S. military service.

There was no analogous revision of Soviet military strategy, for several reasons. A key factor was that on the Eastern (Russo-German) Front during World War II, long-range/strategic bomber aircraft had not been perceived as a major factor in either Soviet or German combat operations. This was in sharp contrast to the American perception that strategic bombing had been a key factor—some would argue *the* factor—in the defeat of Germany, at least in the west, and then Japan. In the east, Soviet ground troops—supported by tactical aviation—had been the decisive factor. Against this backdrop, Stalin saw the Soviet ground forces as continuing to be the prime combat component; he envisioned the fleet as a supporting arm of the Army, including by coastal defense, and a part of some high-seas strategy against NATO navies (a strategy that never was spelled out).

The Return of Kuznetsov

As the first of the new warships were delivered to the Soviet Navy, Stalin also reorganized the service and then its leadership. First, in February 1950, the Ministry of the Armed Forces was reorganized into a separate Ministry of Defense (to direct the Army *and* the Air Forces) and a co-equal Ministry of the Navy. The Soviet Navy had existed as a separate commissariat from 1937 to 1946; before and after those years, until 1950, the Navy had been combined with the Red Army at the ministerial level.

In July 1951, Stalin recalled Admiral Kuznetsov from his exile in the Far East. There he had risen to command the Fifth Fleet and in January 1951, had been promoted to vice admiral—holding that rank for the second time in his career. Shortly thereafter he had been named to again command the Pacific Fleet and promoted to full admiral. He was reinstated on 20 July 1951 as the Commander-in-Chief of the Navy, Minister of the Navy, and a First Deputy Minister of Defense—again assuming the de facto positions that he had held from 1939 to 1947. At the same time, he was returned to full membership in the Central Committee of the Communist Party. He was awarded the rank of Admiral of the Fleet of the Soviet Union in March 1955.

At the 19th Party Congress in October 1952 the Central Committee had 127 full members, of whom 5 were active military officers: the Minister of Defense and 2 of his senior deputies; the chief of Army engineering and artillery services (involved in nuclear weapons development); and Kuznetsov.[10] The 19th Party Congress also was the first attended by Admiral Gorshkov as a candidate (non-voting) member of the Central Committee. He had become commander of the Black Sea Fleet on 2 August 1952, succeeding Admiral Basisty, who had been in the post since 1948. Among the other candidate members of the Central Committee were Basisty, now the Deputy Minister of the Navy (replacing Oktyabrskiy as Kuznetsov's principal deputy), and Admiral Semyon E. Zakharov, the head of the Political Directorate of the Navy. Thus, Gorshkov retained a close contact at naval headquarters in Moscow.

It is difficult for Westerners to comprehend the significance of membership in the Central Committee. Membership meant recognition of having reached the highest levels of the ruling Communist Party—a situation that would be analogous to U.S. military officers holding seats in Congress or being members of the president's cabinet while still on active duty. Beyond the prestige, members of the Central Committee had special access to the major government ministers, as well as to the "politicians" who were committee members.

In July 1951 Admiral Kuznetsov inspected the Baltic Fleet, taking a review of its warships. Afterward, at a conference of fleet officers, he described "the bright future of the Navy and the large shipbuilding program for the development of an ocean-going navy." He declared that "in the not-too-remote future, the Soviet Union would start the construction of aircraft carriers."[11] Admiral Kuznetsov was back; things were looking up for the Red Navy—and for Vice Admiral Gorshkov.

During this period *Skoryy*-class destroyers and Whiskey-class submarines began joining the fleets in large numbers, as well as the first *Sverdlov*-class cruisers; the new Soviet fleet was going to sea. But the progress made by the Soviet Navy during the early 1950s was tempered by the Korean War (1950–1953) and by the death of Stalin. The Korean conflict awakened the United States to the potential of Soviet and Soviet-supported military actions against Western interests. During the war, in which U.S. naval forces had several important roles, the active U.S. Fleet was considerably strengthened. Using relatively modern warships that had been mothballed in the reserve fleet after World War II, the fleet almost doubled its size during the three-year period. Also, and more significantly, the U.S. Navy was able to initiate a large construction program that initially included the start of one *Forrestal* (CVA 59)–class "super carrier" every year and a large number of nuclear-propelled submarines. At the same time, existing U.S. aircraft carriers were being modernized to operate attack aircraft that could deliver nuclear weapons, making the U.S. aircraft carriers collectively a primary strategic striking force. This last development, as well as the large size and global disposition of the U.S. Navy generally, would have considerable impact on the future of the Soviet Navy.

Stalin died on 5 March 1953, and with him were buried his plans for a large, conventional Soviet Navy. Almost immediately the naval shipbuilding programs were cut back. The *Skoryy* destroyer program was reduced; the *Sverdlov* light cruiser program was cut back to the six ships already finished and another eight then under construction; the planned *Stalingrad* battle cruisers and the aircraft carriers were cancelled altogether. Thus ended Soviet efforts of the Stalinist period to construct a large fleet to challenge Western sea power with conventional ships and strategy. The major ships of the Soviet fleet for the foreseeable future would be the *Sverdlov*-class cruisers, a collection of older cruisers, two outdated tsarist-era battleships, and the Italian-built war prize *Novorossiysk*, a modernized dreadnought armed with 12.5-inch (320-mm) guns.[12]

In the Black Sea Fleet, Admiral Gorshkov and his staff drew up plans to employ these ships should there be a future conflict against the Western naval powers.

CHAPTER 8

After Stalin

History shows that states which do not have naval forces at their disposal have not been able to hold the status of a great power for a long time.

—Admiral S. G. Gorshkov, *Morskoy Sbornik* (no. 12, 1972)

During Stalin's almost three decades of absolute power the Soviet Navy enjoyed a highly favorable position. The resulting allocation of resources to the Navy was not based on traditional considerations of geography, political circumstances, or military strategy. Rather, Stalin believed the Soviet Union needed naval forces to be a leading world power. He decided in the mid-1930s and again in the late 1940s that the "Soviet people" wished to see their fleet grow "still stronger and more powerful."

With Stalin gone, there was no longer support at the highest levels of government for a large, conventional ocean-going fleet, and without the late Andrey Zhdanov, who had been responsible for naval matters in the Politburo, there was no major advocate at the highest level of government for shipbuilding programs.[1] Almost within hours of Stalin's death changes were being made in the Soviet government, military hierarchy, and economic programs that would have profound impact on the Navy—and on Admiral Gorshkov.

Within a week the Ministry of Defense and the relatively short-lived Ministry of the Navy (1950–1953) were combined into a single ministry under Marshal Nikolay Bulganin, a political officer and obviously a compromise choice to direct the Soviet armed forces in a period of uncertainty. Admiral Kuznetsov remained as CinC of the Navy and was named one of the Deputy Ministers of Defense in the new organization.

The three other deputies were Army officers, including Marshal Georgiy K. Zhukov, who had been the most popular and possibly most able Soviet commander of World War II. (The other deputies, both marshals, were Aleksandr M. Vasilevskiy, who had been Stalin's Minister of Defense from 1949 to 1953, and Vasiliy D. Sokolovskiy, then newly appointed Chief of the General Staff.) Stalin, fearing Zhukov's popularity, had removed him from senior command positions in 1946 and relegated him to minor military assignments.[2] However, and for reasons not totally clear, Stalin had recalled Zhukov to Moscow late in 1952 to be Commander-in-Chief of Ground Forces (i.e., the Army) and a Deputy Minister of Defense.

Significantly, there were no Air Forces officers at this level of the political-military hierarchy of the armed forces or with full membership in the Central Committee. As discussed in the previous chapter, the Soviet Union had avoided developing an air power strategy after the war. Thus, Soviet military development could take a more logical—for the Soviet Union—land-power orientation in the post-Stalin period.

Following Stalin's death the new Soviet government ostensibly was led by Georgiy Malenkov, serving as prime minister and, initially, as first secretary of the Central Committee of the Communist Party. Malenkov was leading the effort to reshape Soviet policies to fit the post–Stalin environment. The large naval construction program initiated in the late 1940s was severely reduced, and overall defense expenditures declined in 1953 and 1954. These actions were part of Malenkov's two-phase approach: first, he believed that the all-devastating nuclear weapons made major-power warfare impossible, notwithstanding the Leninist dogma that war between communism and capitalism was inevitable; second, Malenkov called for an increase in consumer goods at the expense of the heavy industry that produced military weapons, including warships.

Both of Malenkov's contentions ran counter to the views of the Soviet military establishment. The military leadership could not accept Malenkov's declarations that a new world war "would mean the end of world civilization."[3] Instead, Marshal Zhukov himself declared that "one must bear in mind that one cannot win a war with atomic bombs alone" and called for the strengthening of Soviet conventional combat forces.[4] A contemporary Soviet Army manual on defense against atomic weapons stated, "Atomic weapons significantly exceed conventional weapons in their destructive force, but there are simple and effective means of defense. Troops which are well prepared for actions under the employment of atomic weapons can successfully accomplish their combat mission."[5] Also, of course, heavy industry would be required if the military weapons for conventional warfare, including naval forces, were to be built.

Although opposed to the views of Malenkov, the military leadership was able to survive because of the conflict among the factions of the Politburo. Marshal Zhukov himself had ordered the arrest of Lavrentiy P. Beria, head of the NKVD and deputy premier, in June 1953, in support of the Khrushchev faction.[6] In return for his services, a month later Zhukov was made a full member of the Central Committee. The concomitant downgrading of the secret police further enhanced the position of the Army.

Debates over the future of the nation's political, economic, and military policies continued during 1953 and 1954. Decisions were made about the future of the Soviet Navy as a part of the overall

efforts to cut back on heavy weapons procurement, to increase
international trade; also, they were in part a reflection of the belief
that large-scale conventional war was impossible in the nuclear
era. Coupled with the cutbacks and cancellations in warship programs, plans were made to replace the cruisers and some destroyers then on the building ways with submarines and small combat
craft and to shift other ways from warships to merchant ships and
fishing craft. The battleship ways at Molotovsk (Severodvinsk) in
the north and Komsomol'sk in the Far East would be allocated to
submarine construction as soon as the *Sverdlov*-class cruiser hulls
on their ways could be launched or scrapped; the Ordzhonikidze
(Leningrad) and Nikolayev (Black Sea) cruiser shipways were allocated to commercial shipbuilding.[7] Smaller shipways that had been
engaged in destroyer construction also were assigned to build submarines or merchant ships. At the same time, new shipyards were
established and older ones along the Baltic and Black Sea coasts
were enlarged specifically to build commercial ships. In addition,
large numbers of cargo and fish factory ships and fishing craft were
ordered from "socialist" (Eastern Bloc) and even from a few "cap-
italistic" countries. In 1964—shortly before his political demise—
Nikita Khrushchev declared that at the time 152 commercial ships
were being constructed in foreign yards to supplement Soviet
building efforts.[8]

As submarine construction was emphasized, so too were several technological developments, including ship-launched guided and ballistic
missiles, nuclear propulsion, and high-performance land-based naval
aircraft. With respect to submarines, beyond missile armament—
primarily for the land-attack role—Soviet industry was developing
nuclear-armed torpedoes, titanium hulls, and very highly automated
control systems. These advances would later be described by Admiral
Gorshkov as resulting from a "scientific-technical revolution." In

language that gave due credit to the political decision to build a non-conventional fleet, Gorshkov explained,

> In the mid-1950s, in connection with the revolution in military affairs, the Central Committee of our Party defined the path of fleet development, as well as the fleet's role and place in the system of Armed Forces in the country. The course taken was one which required the construction of an ocean-going fleet, capable of carrying out offensive strategic missions. Submarines and naval aviation, equipped with nuclear weapons, have a leading place in the program. Thus, there began a new stage in the development of the fleet and of its naval science.[9]

Admiral Kuznetsov, who during the late 1930s and again in the late 1940s had supported and directed Stalin's attempts to build a conventional (traditional) ocean-going fleet, was not the man to lead the revolution in naval development. There was a certain irony in the fact that on 3 March 1955 Kuznetsov, and the venerable I. S. Isakov were awarded the newly established rank of Fleet Admiral of the Soviet Union (*Admiral Flota Sovetskogo Soyuza*). That rank corresponded to Marshal of the Soviet Union—the highest military rank of the Soviet armed forces.

But even as Admiral Kuznetsov pinned on his "marshal's star," the ax was being sharpened. According to Khrushchev's memoirs, Kuznetsov continued to argue for major warships. Khrushchev recalled how, after a Kremlin meeting at which decisions on a Kuznetsov shipbuilding proposal were discussed and tabled:

> There was Kuznetsov waiting for me in the corridor. He started walking along beside me. I could tell he was extremely agitated. Suddenly he turned on me very rudely and belligerently.
>
> "How long do I have to tolerate such an attitude toward my navy?" he shouted.

"What attitude? What are you talking about? I think our attitude toward the Navy is perfectly good."[10]

I was upset by Kuznetsov's irritable, I'd even say dictatorial, mood. He had no right to expect the Party leadership just to rubberstamp his recommendations, and he certainly had no right to adopt a threatening tone of voice when talking to the head of the party.[11]

Kuznetsov continued to press for major warship construction with Khrushchev and other members of the Presidium (as the Politburo was known from 1952 to 1966). The admiral's days were numbered.

Gorshkov, the Black Sea Fleet commander since 1951, was promoted to full admiral on 3 August 1953, and a short time later began taking an active role in naval affairs in Moscow. Two years later, on 12 July 1955, he was named the First Deputy Commander-in-Chief of the Soviet Navy.

An event occurred shortly after Gorshkov moved to Moscow in 1955 that cast a shadow over the Black Sea Fleet and could even have endangered his position. On 28 October, following a short trial run at sea, the battleship *Novorossiysk*—pride of the Red Navy—dropped anchor in the Sevastopol roads. At midnight, after a critique of the exercise, the fleet commander, Vice Admiral Viktor A. Parkhomenko, departed the ship. As the admiral's barge neared the shore *Novorossiysk* shuddered from an underwater explosion. Admiral Parkhomenko immediately came back on board the stricken ship but failed—as did his deputy, the acting squadron commander, and the commanding officer of the ship—to take charge effectively. The command was given to get the ship towed aground to prevent her sinking. The under-powered tugs available could not move the ship, and less than three hours after the explosion *Novorossiysk* had flooded and capsized. Early estimates were that 200 or more of the 1,600 men on board were drowned or suffocated in the world's worst naval disaster since World War II.[12]

Soviet officials immediately suspected sabotage by "foreign agents." It soon became evident, however, that the loss had been caused by a mine—probably German—remaining unswept from the war. Several members of the Presidium were in the Crimea, and Nikita Khrushchev had them meet in Sevastopol to inspect the Black Sea Fleet and look into Navy problems. Khrushchev recalled a staff briefing of a recent exercise in which he and other leaders were told how the Soviet ships "devastated" the enemy forces, sailed through the Dardanelles, and prepared for an assault on the northwest coast of Africa. Khrushchev would write about the briefer, "And so forth and so on. He was terribly cocky. It made me sad to listen to him. Finally, I couldn't restrain myself any longer. I interrupted him and said: 'Stop! Wait! You keep talking with such certainty about how you've made short work of the enemy. . . . If this were a real war and not just a map exercise, your ships would all be lying on the bottom of the sea by now.'"[13]

Khrushchev had then berated the assembled naval officers for their lack of knowledge of the West's modern weapons. Although Khrushchev's memoirs lack accuracy in some respects, these impressions appear valid.

The immediate investigation into the loss of the *Novorossiysk* laid blame on fleet commander Parkhomenko, the fleet political officer, Nikolay M. Kulakov, and the squadron commander for failure to take immediate steps to run the ship aground by its own power and thereby prevent the capsizing.[14] Follow-on investigations, however, soon extended into other aspects of the Navy: shortcomings in training and discipline (a naval tanker had been lost in a collision in the Pacific) and extensive drunkenness. Marshal Zhukov is said to have cited the *Novorossiysk* sinking and general misbehavior by sailors—including fighting, stealing, drunkenness, and rape—in a secret letter to political officers. These revelations apparently further convinced Soviet Party officials that there was need for major change in the Navy's leadership.

Admiral Kuznetsov was gone. As the late professor Michael Parrish of Indiana University observed, "During his remarkable career Kuznetsov was twice Admiral of the Fleet of the Soviet Union, twice admiral, and three times Vice Admiral and Rear Admiral."[15]

CHAPTER 9

Gorshkov, Zhukov, and the Stalingrad Group

Khrushchev and Marshal Zhukov, defense minister
in the critical 1955–57 period of technological transition,
both managed to delude themselves that just as
long as [naval] forces were armed with nuclear
missiles they need only comprise relatively inexpensive
types, notably submarines, light surface craft, and
land-based naval aircraft.

—Commander Robert Waring Herrick, *Soviet Naval Strategy* (1968)

Admiral Gorshkov was appointed Commander-in-Chief of the Soviet Navy and a First Deputy Minister of Defense on 5 January 1956, At the time he was 45 years of age.[1] Gorshkov was advanced to the Navy's highest position because of his accomplishments and personal contacts—men with whom he had worked or who knew of his reputation. According to Khrushchev, "The question arose of whom we should appoint to replace Kuznetsov as Commander-in-Chief of the Navy. We asked Malinovskiy, and he recommended Gorshkov. I knew Gorshkov only slightly; I'd met him at the end of the war when he was in charge of our river defenses. Malinovskiy's recommendation was good enough for me."[2]

Marshal Rodion Ya. Malinovskiy was a Khrushchev confidant and at the time CinC of Soviet forces in the Far East; he, too, would become a First Deputy Minister of Defense in 1956 and a year later would replace Zhukov as Minister of Defense. The men who knew Gorshkov also included Khrushchev's protégé Leonid I. Brezhnev, who had served very briefly as head of the Political Administration of the Navy during 1953, and of course Kuznetsov and his Deputy CinC, Nikolay Ye. Basisty, under both of whom Gorshkov had served.

Admiral Gorshkov had a reputation for innovation; he was a tested combat leader who had commanded surface ships and been in action with cruisers as well as small craft; he had commanded troops ashore; and he had experience in staff work as chief of staff and deputy commander of the Black Sea Fleet. Khrushchev erroneously believed, or at least would write in his memoirs, that Gorshkov had been a submarine captain: "We counted it very much in his favor that he was a former submarine captain. He appreciated the role which German submarines had played in World War II by sinking so much English and American shipping, and he also appreciated the role which submarines could play for us in the event that we might have to go to war against Britain and the United States."[3]

After Kuznetsov's dismissal the two most senior Soviet flag officers were Admiral of the Fleet of the Soviet Union Ivan S. Isakov and Admiral Basisty. Isakov, the principal Soviet naval theoretician of the 1930s, had survived Stalin's purges to serve as Chief of the Main Navy Staff from 1941 to 1947, Deputy CinC Navy from 1947 to 1950, and Deputy Navy Minister from 1950 to 1956, under Kuznetsov.[4] But Isakov now was perhaps too old, his health questionable, and too conservative to direct major changes in naval policies. After the appointment of Gorshkov to the Navy's No.1 post, Isakov, at age 62, was named to the Inspector General Group of the Ministry of Defense.

Basisty had moved from command of the Black Sea Fleet to First Deputy CinC of the Navy in 1951. His credentials were impressive. Nevertheless, Basisty was superseded by Gorshkov as First Deputy in mid-1955 and he was reassigned in 1956 as Deputy

Commander-in-Chief "for military-scientific work." This latter position may have had great significance in view of the technological changes being made in the Navy, but it was in no way comparable in stature with that of the head of the Navy. (Subsequently, in June 1958, Basisty would follow Isakov to the Inspector General Group of the Ministry of Defense; he was to be retired in September 1960, at age 62.)

Younger candidates may also have been considered to head the Navy: possibly Andrey T. Chabanenko, head of the Northern Fleet; Yuriy A. Panteleyev, commander of the Pacific Fleet; and undoubtedly Arseniy G. Golovko, commander of the Baltic Fleet. Golovko was a leading flag officer, having become commander of the Northern Fleet in July 1940 at age 32. He, like Kuznetsov, had served in Madrid during the Spanish Civil War. A U.S. Navy intelligence evaluation in World War II noted, "He has a strong character, is keen, alert, aggressive, courteous." A more intimate view of Golovko came from an American naval officer who had met him in World War II. Kemp Tolley, later a rear admiral, would recall:

> Golovko met us at the door. The whole atmosphere of this place [his headquarters] and of the man Golovko himself were superior to anything we had so far encountered in the Red Navy....
>
> Golovko was frank and to the point. His answers were factual and precise. He spoke clearly and without hesitation, exhibiting a keen sense of humor. Undoubtedly, his time in Spain during the 1937 Revolution had been a broadening influence. He was short and stocky, stalking around rubbing his hands together, making no purposeless move, like a cat.[5]

Reportedly, Golovko was held in high esteem by his Soviet Navy colleagues. But he appears to have suffered by having commanded the Northern Fleet in the war, a secondary combat theater and away from Khrushchev (and Malinovskiy). Still, he had commanded the prestigious Baltic Fleet since August 1952; in late 1956—obviously with Gorshkov's approval if not by his selection—Golovko was named First Deputy CinC of the Soviet Navy. Golovko would serve in that role until his death in May 1962, at age 55, following a prolonged and serious heart ailment.

Admiral Gorshkov's appointment as Commander-in-Chief of the Soviet Navy was prompted by the desire to replace Kuznetsov and by changes in naval policies. His appointment soon became part of a widespread series of changes in the High Command of the Soviet armed forces. Because of the personalities involved and their impact on Soviet military politics and policies, these changes became significant to Gorshkov and the Soviet Navy.

The Military Ascendant

In February 1955, Georgiy Malenkov was ousted as premier, having been out-maneuvered by Nikita Khrushchev, who at the time enjoyed the support of the military leadership. Marshal Nikolay Bulganin—who had been the compromise Minister of Defense—succeeded to the premiership, and on 9 February Marshal Zhukov was appointed Minister of Defense. This marked the first time in Soviet history that a professional soldier rather than a commissar or political officer had been put in overall command of the Soviet armed forces.

Thus, the Red Army and Zhukov himself were elevated to greater power in the Soviet state and Khrushchev further enhanced his own position and his relationship with the armed forces. The month after Zhukov's appointment, six officers received promotions to Marshal of the Soviet Union, the highest rank in the Soviet military structure—except for *Generalissimus*, a rank assumed by Stalin in 1945 and previously held only by Count Suvorov, hero of the war with Napoleon in the early 1800s. Four other officers were made marshal of a branch of the armed forces, and soon afterward six generals were promoted to General of the Army, the equivalent of marshal of a branch. At least 13 of these 16 men were members of what was known as the "Stalingrad Group," men who had fought in the decisive winter battles of 1942–1943 around Stalingrad and had been associated with Khrushchev during that period.[6] Significantly, all six of the officers promoted to Marshal of the Soviet Union had been among the closest wartime military associates of Khrushchev— *not* of Zhukov. Among the six was Andrey A. Grechko. At the time of this promotion Grechko held the important command of the Soviet forces in East Germany, which included 20 of the best-trained and best-equipped divisions in the Red Army. Grechko had long been a close associate of Khrushchev.

The Army's professional officers prospered under Zhukov, but political officers did not. From 1946 the political activities within the Soviet armed forces had been directed by the Main Political Administration (MPA) of the Army and Navy, under which each service had its own political directorate, staffed mainly with specially trained political officers. The MPA was an organ of both the Ministry of Defense and of the Central Committee of the Communist Party. This made MPA officers responsible to the Party leadership outside the military chain of command.

At the 20th Communist Party Congress in 1956 the head of the Army's Political Directorate was downgraded from candidate member of the Central Committee to a member of the Audit Commission of the Army and Navy. The representation on the Central Committee of the state security (secret police) agencies were reduced from the ten full and candidate members at the 19th Party Congress in 1953 to only two full members and one candidate at the 20th. Simultaneously, the number of professional military officers in the Central Committee was increased. At the 20th Congress Admiral Gorshkov, recently appointed Commander-in-Chief of the Navy, was named a candidate member. But no other naval officers sat in the Central Committee, as a result of the changes taking place in the naval leadership and the general downgrading of the Navy discussed below.

The downgrading of the role of political officers in the armed forces under Marshal Zhukov reached down into the tactical units of the Army. From the outset of Bolshevik rule loyal party members, often with no military knowledge or experience, shared command with military officers; all orders requiring the signature of both the military commander and political commissar. By 1928 most commanders were considered sufficiently loyal to exercise "one-man control." Stalin's purges of military officers from 1937 to 1939 led to reintroduction of political commissars and the concept of "dual control," which was imposed again from 1941—after the German invasion—until late 1942, when, with Red armies taking the offensive, the military commanders were again given control, but with political deputies. In mid-1955 the position of political officer *(zampolit)* was abolished at the company, squadron, and battery levels. The commanders of these line units—professional military officers— now became responsible for the political education of their men. At intermediate levels the role of political officers also was downgraded. Similar changes were made in the Navy. Zhukov also sought to limit political officers to the rank of colonel or (naval) captain 1st rank.

At the Party conferences in the Army's military districts in late 1956 strong criticism of military political organizations was voiced. Continued efforts were made to lessen further the influence of the Party within the armed forces and to raise the status of professional officers. Reversing a policy that had stood since the Russian Revolution, Marshal Zhukov declared that "criticism of the orders and decisions of commanders will not be permitted at Party meetings."[7]

In 1955, under the leadership of Khrushchev and Zhukov, military appropriations were increased 123 percent over the previous year, most of the additional funds going to new weapons. In the Ground

Forces the rifle divisions were increasingly upgraded to motorized rifle (i.e., armored infantry) divisions, and new tanks and other weapons were introduced. Trained manpower shortages, however, forced a reduction in the overall size of the armed forces; the decision was made in August 1955 to demobilize some 640,000 men and in 1956 to drop another 1,200,000 from the active-duty forces.

Marshal Zhukov himself was performing in political and diplomatic roles in addition to his military activities. During July 1956, he accompanied Khrushchev and Premier Bulganin to the summit conference at Geneva, and he directed the military operations that countered the revolts of that year in Poland and Hungary. He travelled still farther afield in January–February 1957, visiting India without other high-level Soviet leaders. That visit, to inspect the Indian armed forces—which would increasingly use Soviet weapons—received extensive coverage in the Soviet press. Gorshkov himself would sponsor massive Soviet assistance to the Indian Navy, including surface ships and diesel-electric submarines.[8]

Marshal Zhukov reached the apex of his career in June 1957, when opposition to Khrushchev increased within the Presidium. Dissatisfaction with Khrushchev's policies had brought about a crisis in the 11 full members of that body. In addition to the full members, there were in the Presidium 7 candidate members without voting rights, Zhukov among them. When challenged for leadership, Khrushchev declared that he could be ousted from the Presidium only by the Central Committee that had elected him. At Zhukov's direction the Air Forces rapidly transported Khrushchev supporters from throughout the Soviet Union to Moscow, making possible his political survival. Zhukov also addressed troops in the Moscow area during the crisis, probably in an effort to deny their support to the anti-Khrushchev group.

Following Khrushchev's political triumph, Zhukov was elected to full membership in the Presidium. This was the first time in Soviet history that a professional soldier was accorded full membership in that supreme body. Thus, Zhukov achieved the highest political position then existing to complement his military post as Minister of Defense. He now had Party, government, and military power that could make him to a direct threat to Khrushchev.

Some four months later Marshal Zhukov was dismissed from his unprecedented military and political positions. In the first week of October 1957, Zhukov embarked in the Black Sea Fleet cruiser *Kuybyshev* for a goodwill visit to Yugoslavia. The commanding officer of the ship, Captain 1st Rank Vladimir V. Mikhailin, assembled his crew, to whom his distinguished passenger declared, "On the day of our voyage's beginning, the fourth of October, Soviet scientists accomplished the world's first launching of an artificial earth satellite, which is a great attainment of our Soviet science and technology."

The euphoria that Zhukov undoubtedly felt as the *Kuybyshev* steamed through the Dardanelles, into the Mediterranean, and then up to the Adriatic coast of Yugoslavia soon was dispelled. His reception from Josip Broz Tito was neither warm nor enthusiastic, and Soviet press coverage of the trip ebbed. At Khrushchev's request, Zhukov delayed his return to Moscow for a brief diplomatic mission to Albania. Arriving in Moscow on 26 October, Zhukov was met at the airport by a delegation of senior military officers, who took him straight to a meeting of the Presidium. There a debate began, of the results of which the next morning the newspaper *Pravda* published a brief announcement:

> The Presidium of the Supreme Soviet of the USSR appointed Marshal of the Soviet Union Rodion Yakovlevich Malinovskiy Defense Minister of the USSR.
>
> The Presidium of the Supreme Soviet of the USSR relieved Marshal of the Soviet Union Georgiy Konstantinovich Zhukov from the post of Defense Minister of the USSR.[9]

Post-Zhukov Reorganizations

In the wake of the fall of Marshal Zhukov, most of the Soviet High Command was reorganized.[10] Significantly, his dismissal was not interpreted as an attack against the military establishment. Although Zhukov had had great popularity in the Soviet Union, he had not been politician enough to make use of this popularity; the High Command was fractionated, most of the important positions going to members of the Stalingrad, or "southern," group loyal to Khrushchev and—of course—to the Party itself. The most prominent of these was Marshal Malinovskiy, who became Minister of Defense. He was not, however, given the seat on the Presidium that had been accorded to Zhukov. Malinovskiy also had served with Republican forces in the Spanish Civil War during 1936–1937 and thus was one the few Soviet officers with military experience outside of the Soviet Union to have served in senior positions during World War II. Except for a temporary demotion after the defeat at Rostov (at the northern end of the Sea of Azov), Malinovskiy had a distinguished wartime record, had commanded one of the Soviet armies at Stalingrad, and was now in close contact with Khrushchev.

In another such shift, Marshal Andrei Grechko returned to Moscow from his command in East Germany to become Commander-in-Chief of Ground Forces (i.e., the Army) and a Deputy Minister of Defense. The only non-Khrushchev marshals to retain senior positions were the two other first deputies: the Chief of the General Staff, V. D. Sokolovskiy, and the commander of the Warsaw Pact forces, Ivan S. Konev. Konev had been a spokesman for the Stalingrad Group, but he and Sokolovskiy were the only two marshals on the active list who had not served with Khrushchev at either Stalingrad or on the Ukrainian front. In 1960 those last two holdovers from the Zhukov administration were retired, and that May Grechko moved up to command the Warsaw Pact forces and became a First Deputy Minister of Defense. Of future significance to the Soviet Navy was that Grechko favored large-scale battle exercises—and, of course, the fact that Admiral Gorshkov had served with both Malinovskiy and Grechko during the war.

Also significant in the post-Zhukov changes was the assignment in 1958 of Colonel General Filipp I. Golikov, a professional Army intelligence officer, as head of the Main Political Administration. This appointment placated potential political opposition to the naming of a hard-line political officer to the important MPA post and installed another officer of the Stalingrad group loyal to Khrushchev in an important position. At the same time, Admiral Vasiliy M. Grishanov was named head of the Navy's Political Directorate (and thus a deputy to Golikov). Grishanov had served in the Baltic, Northern, and Pacific Fleets. Although he had not served with Gorshkov, he had performed well, as evidenced by his subsequent longevity as the head of the Navy's political activities—more than two decades, from 1958 until 1981.

With the replacement of the last Zhukov incumbents in the Soviet High Command, Khrushchev was able to accelerate his changes to the armed forces. These changes related to Khrushchev's belief that intercontinental missiles would be the primary weapons of future wars and to his desire to reduce conventional military forces accordingly. In 1960, Khrushchev announced the reduction of the armed forces by another 1,200,000 men, including 250,000 officers, over the next 18 months. (The Berlin crisis in mid-1961 halted some of these reductions. Then, on Victory Day celebrating the end of World War II—9 May 1961—Khrushchev promoted 372 marshals and generals to their next highest ranks, and awarded more than 300 colonels general stars. These promotions went largely to technical officers, especially men with experience in missiles and other modern weapon systems. These officers formed a new elite, more privileged than either career officers steeped in conventional warfare or the political officers. Of major significance, these technical officers generally were reluctant to become involved in political activities. Minister of Defense Malinovskiy explained the change in the structure of the Soviet officer corps: "Without high levels of technical training, without knowing the basics of physics and mathematics, it is impossible to conduct modern military operations expertly."[11]

These dismissals and promotions caused demoralization among the traditional elements of the armed forces. General Staff colonel-turned-Western spy Oleg Penkovskiy wrote:

> The entire Army is in a state of turmoil; everyone in the Army recalls Stalin and says that under Stalin things were better: that is, Stalin never insulted the Army, but this scoundrel [Khrushchev] has dismissed good officers from the Army. And now this same scoundrel lifts his goblet high and drinks a toast, saying, "I love the Army." The officers say to themselves, "You scoundrel, right now you are drinking a toast to my health, and tomorrow I must die for you. If I do stay alive, then two years from now you will throw me out again."[12]

Penkovskiy was over-reacting with regard to method—military officers were being *dismissed* by Khrushchev; they had been *purged, disposed of,* by Stalin. Still, he appears to have reflected the feelings of a major segment of the Soviet officer corps.

Khrushchev's advancement of technicians and his Stalingrad "clique" included an increase in the number of military men in the Central Committee, a move that gave the military more influence in Soviet political affairs (as did, of course, his initial appointment of Zhukov to the Presidium). From the 20th Party Congress in 1956 to the 22nd in 1961 the number of officers who were full (voting) members more than doubled, from 6 to 14, and the candidates (nonvoting) also increased, from 12 to 17. More than two-thirds of these 31 officers could be identified clearly as members of the Stalingrad group. At the 22nd Congress, Admiral Gorshkov and Admiral Vitaliy A. Fokin, commander of the Pacific Fleet, were elected full members of the Central Committee, and Admiral Andrey T. Chabanenko, commander of the Northern Fleet, was elected a candidate member.

In fact, the military establishment as a whole—including the Navy—was enjoying an increasing role in Soviet political and national activities.

The New Armed Services

One other aspect of Khrushchev's redirection of the Soviet military establishment was the reorganization of the armed services. The principal service was the Ground Forces (i.e., Army), the Navy and Air Forces supporting. At the end of World War II the Air Forces had finally become a separate arm, albeit not equal in status to the Army and Navy.

The Soviet leadership had long emphasized defense against air attack, and this concern manifested itself in May 1954 in the form of a separate service—Protivovozdushnoy Oborony Strany (Air Defense of the Country). Referred to as PVO-*Strany*, the new service consisted of the Soviet fighter-interceptor aircraft, anti-aircraft guns (and later surface-to-air missiles), and the related air-defense warning and control activities. Soviet Naval Aviation (Morskaya Aviatsiya) was forced to turn over all of its fighter aircraft to PVO-*Strany* (albeit with the Navy retaining bombers, reconnaissance, and anti-submarine aircraft).

In 1954–1955 the Soviet Air Forces, in turn, was forced to transfer their Tu-16 Badger turbojet bomber aircraft armed with air-to-surface missiles to the Navy for the anti-ship role. This loss of Badgers to the Navy further weakened the position of the Air Forces, as did the shift of the operational command of Dalnaya Aviatsiya (Long-Range Aviation) and troop-carrying transport aircraft to the direct operational control of the Soviet High Command. Naval Aviation—with bombers, reconnaissance, and anti-submarine aircraft—remained completely under Navy control.[13]

Peter the Great (1672–1725) was reputed to have declared: "Any ruler that has but ground troops has one hand, but one that has also a navy has both." He established St. Petersburg as Russia's capital, established the Russian Navy, and established the nation's shipbuilding industry. *U.S. Naval Institute photo archive*

Gorshkov and other naval officers were caught up by the "Old School" versus "Young School" debates of the 1920s and 1930s. The former advocated a big-ship navy for the Soviet Union, but the economy could not support such a program. Hence, many tsarist-era warships, like the battleship *Marat* (formerly *Petropavlovsk*), shown here in 1937, were retained in service. *Imperial War Museum*

Josef Stalin in the 1930s and again after World War II planned to construct a large, ocean-going fleet as advocated by the "Old School" naval strategists. Beyond conceiving grandiose shipbuilding programs, at times he became involved in the details, such as the anti-aircraft armament of warships. Here at the "Big Three" meeting at Yalta in February 1945, he wore a marshal's uniform. *U.S. Naval Institute photo archive*

Flagman 2nd Grade Nikolay G. Kuznetsov (*left*) as the Pacific Fleet commander. The Soviet regime long rejected the rank of "admiral." The various grades of general and admiral were belatedly introduced in the Soviet armed forces on 7 May 1940, when seven Soviet naval officers were given admiral ranks. *Authors' collection*

Gorshkov experienced considerable combat during World War II in the Black Sea, Sea of Azov, and Danube River areas. He held significant commands ashore and afloat and—of particular importance—worked closely with several Army commanders and political leaders. This 1944 photo (*right*) was taken when he led the Danube Flotilla. *U.S. Naval Institute photo archive*

Admiral Kuznetsov twice served as commander-in-chief of the Soviet Navy, being the prime architect of Josef Stalin's plans to build a major, ocean-going fleet in the 1930s and, again, immediately after World War II. Both plans were aborted. *U.S. Army*

Stalin's massive pre–World War II shipbuilding program was terminated with the German attack on the Soviet Union in June 1941. This aerial photo shows the unfinished super-battleship *Sovetskiy Soyuz* on the building ways at the Ordzhonikidze (Baltic) shipyard in Leningrad in June 1942; she was scrapped on the ways after the war. *Authors' collection*

Fleet Admiral Kuznetsov twice commanded the Soviet Navy as Stalin charged him with building an ocean-going fleet. He was unable to do so for reasons beyond his control. Kuznetsov was fired by Nikita Khrushchev when he again tried to build such a fleet. Here he stands with Fleet Admiral E. J. King, head of the U.S. Navy, at Yalta in February 1945. *U.S. Naval Institute photo archive*

The only major surface ship class of the Stalin-Kuznetsov shipbuilding plan of the late 1940s to reach fruition was the *Sverdlov* light cruisers. Fourteen of these ships were completed as all-gun cruisers; one was converted to a guided missile ship and two became fleet flagships. This is the *Aleksandr Suvorov* in the Philippine Sea during the *Okean*-70 multi-ocean exercises. *U.S. Navy*

Nikita Khrushchev succeeded Stalin as head of the Soviet government. With his leadership colleagues, Khrushchev tore up the plans for a large, ocean-going fleet and selected Admiral Gorshkov to head the Navy—to consist primarily of submarines and land-based strike aircraft. He greatly underestimated the admiral. *Authors' collection*

Nuclear-propelled submarines were initiated during the Stalin-Kuznetsov regime. However, under Admiral Gorshkov—who built modern surface warships—the submarine force became the hallmark of the Red fleet. This is the torpedo-attack submarine *K-4* (November class). Unlike the U.S. Navy, which built several prototype submarines before entering series production, Soviet shipyards began the nuclear submarine era with the series production of attack, cruise missile, and ballistic missile submarines. *Malachite Design Bureau*

Soviet submariners "watch the watchers," looking up at a British aircraft that sighted this submarine on the surface. Under Admiral Gorshkov the strategic missile submarines became a key component of the Soviet Union's nuclear striking forces—some analysts would say *the* most significant component because of its expected survivability against a Western pre-emptive attack. *Royal Navy*

After more than three decades of efforts by some Soviet naval officials to initiate an aircraft carrier program, Admiral Gorshkov accomplished that goal, beginning with the two-ship *Moskva* class. The *Moskva* and her sister ship *Leningrad*—seen here—were hermaphrodite helicopter carrier-missile cruisers, the progenitors of true aircraft carriers for the Soviet Navy. *Authors' collection*

Admiral Gorshkov was elevated to full, voting membership in the Central Committee of the Communist Party in 1961. Thus, as Navy Minister he held a significant political position as well as having a military role. Here, at the 24th Party Congress in 1971, he met with a delegation of the Lebanese Communist Party. *Novosti*

Soviet Naval Infantry—in chemical-biological protective gear—ride a tank ashore during an amphibious exercise in the Baltic area. The tank landing ship visible behind them is similar to the one that had just unloaded this tank into the surf. The "marines" also came ashore in amphibious landing vehicles. Admiral Gorshkov, who had worked closely with Naval Infantry during World War II, had reestablished the force. *Authors' collection*

Admiral Gorshkov sent his warships far and wide: This Kresta I-class missile cruiser and Foxtrot diesel–electric submarine were part of a task force that sailed through Hawaiian waters in the fall of 1971. More often these ships operated in the Western Pacific, Indian, and Atlantic Oceans, the last providing support of Soviet political–economic interests in the Caribbean area and in Africa. *U.S. Navy*

While building a major surface fleet, under Admiral Gorshkov the principal combat elements of the Soviet Navy were submarines and land-based strike aircraft. Here two Typhoon-class submarines—the world's largest undersea craft—are seen at their Nerpichya base in Litsa Fjord in the Arctic region. These SSBNs had a unique design, with their 20 strategic missiles *forward* of the massive sail structure.
Rubin Design Bureau

The Soviet "spy ship," *Gidrofon* was typical of the Soviet AGIs that tracked U.S. and NATO forces, both to observe and learn from Western operations and in part to provide targeting data should the Cold War turn "hot." Here the *Gidrofon* monitors the aircraft carrier *Coral Sea* (CVA 43) during flight operations in the Gulf of Tonkin during the Vietnam War. *U.S. Navy*

Admiral Gorshkov also employed warships in the "tattletale" role, such as this Kashin–class destroyer keeping close watch on a U.S. aircraft carrier in the Mediterranean. Beyond observing and providing targeting data on U.S. and NATO forces, this Kashin could add additional anti-ship missiles on the target. The A-4 Skyhawks in the foreground at the time could be employed in nuclear strikes against Soviet targets. *U.S. Navy*

Soviet warships ranged far and wide under Admiral Gorshkov. These sailors from a Kashin-class missile destroyer are going ashore on liberty. Foreign port visits throughout the Third World helped Admiral Gorshkov explain the political value of his fleet and their long-range operations to the Soviet leadership. These operations also had significant military value for the Navy. *Authors' collection*

Admiral Gorshkov joined Minister of Defense Dimitri F. Ustinov (*right*) in meeting Indian Defense Minister Ramaswamy Venkataraman in New Delhi in March 1984. Some 30 marshals, generals, and admirals were in the Soviet delegation to further enhance military and industrial relations with India. The Soviet Navy under Gorshkov enjoyed a close relationship with India. *World Wide Photos*

The largest warships constructed by any nation after World War II—except for aircraft carriers—were the four nuclear-propelled battle cruisers of the *Kirov* class, completed from 1980 to 1998. The *Frunze*, renamed *Admiral Lazarev* in the post-Soviet era, is seen here in 1987; two of these ships survived in post–Cold War service. They were impressive ships with potent anti-air, anti-surface, and anti-submarine weapons. *U.S. Navy*

After almost a half-century of Soviet discussions about aircraft carriers, Admiral Gorshkov was able to bring that type of warship into the Soviet fleet. In view of the cost of these ships and opposition from political and military leaders, Gorshkov's success was remarkable. But in the post-Soviet era only one of these ships has survived the demise of the Soviet Navy—the *Admiral Kuznetsov. Authors' collection*

Admiral Sergey G. Gorshkov. He subsequently was raised two additional ranks: to Fleet Admiral and to Fleet Admiral of the Soviet Union. The other officers to hold that ultimate naval rank were Nikolai G. Kuznetsov and Ivan S. Isakov. *Authors' collection*

Khrushchev's interest in the development of long-range missiles as the prime striking force of the Soviet Union led to the formal establishment on 14 December 1959, of the Strategic Missile Troops (Raketnyye Voyska Strategicheskogo Naznacheniya—usually known as the Strategic Rocket Forces, or SRF) as a separate service. SRF was given responsibility for the development and operation of all Soviet intermediate-range and intercontinental ballistic missiles (IRBMs/ICBMs). This was unlike the contemporary U.S. Strategic Air Command, the specified command that controlled all land-based ICBM and strategic bombers. However, establishment of the SRF did lead to the Soviet decision to delay further Navy development of strategic (ballistic) missile submarines.

With the establishment of the Air Defense and Strategic Rocket Forces, the Soviet Union had three combat services and two branches:

Ground Forces (Army)
Navy
Air Forces
Strategic Rocket Forces
National Air Defense Forces

With this reorganization there were now in the Ministry of Defense three "first deputies." The five service chiefs became simply deputy ministers, as did the heads of five specialized support services (Rear Services, Military Construction, Inspector General, Weapons Development, and Civil Defense).

The Soviet military policies that evolved between the death of Stalin in 1953 and the restructuring of the Soviet armed forces through the early 1960s set the stage for a "revolution" in the Soviet Navy.

CHAPTER 10

Building a Revolutionary Fleet

It is difficult to review the evidence of Soviet maritime expansion, especially over the past 15 years, without being struck by the persistence and purposefulness with which the Soviets have pursued their maritime programs.

—*Soviet Maritime Expansion,* U.S. Defense Intelligence Agency (1971)

Stalin's successors made rapid decisions about the future of the Soviet Navy as a part of their efforts to cut back the expenditures on heavy weapons and procurement and to increase international trade. These decisions were in part a reflection of the belief that conventional war—including naval campaigns—was impossible in the nuclear era. Coupled with the cutbacks and cancellations in warship construction programs, plans were made, as noted in chapter 8, to replace the cruisers and some destroyers on building ways with submarines or smaller combat craft and to shift other building ways from warships to merchant ships and fishing craft.

As also noted earlier, the large warship building ways at Severodvinsk (Molotovsk) in the north and Komsomol'sk in the Far East would be allocated to submarine construction as soon as the *Sverdlov*-class cruiser hulls on them could be launched or scrapped; the Baltic (Ordzhonikidze) and Black Sea (Marti-Nikolayev) cruiser shipways would be redirected to commercial shipbuilding. At the same time, new shipyards were established, and older ones along the Baltic and Black Sea coasts were enlarged specifically to build commercial ships. The amount of shipyard capacity allocated to naval construction soon fell to about one-half of what it had been at the time of Stalin's death. The Soviet Union was reverting to the Young School philosophy with respect to naval forces, although that term was no longer in vogue.

The emphasis with respect to ocean-going warships would now be on submarines. Large submarine fleets were a Russian tradition, and while Stalin had seen them as only adjuncts to his large, conventional surface fleet, Khrushchev and most Soviet political leaders now saw them as the principal arm of the Navy. Under both tsars and commissars Russia had demonstrated a special interest in submarines, and reportedly Stalin had sought no fewer than 1,200 submarines in one iteration of his post-war 20-year shipbuilding program, although according to available records smaller numbers were more realistic. The medium-range Whiskey (Project 613)–class diesel boats—incorporating features of the German Type XXI U-boat, the most advanced undersea craft of World War II—were mass-produced at four shipyards, and when the last unit was completed in 1957 a total of 236 had been built. In one year alone 90 of these units were launched, as well as several undersea craft of other designs—an ominous indication of Soviet industrial capacity just one decade after World War II had devastated it.[1]

The "Revolution"

The Soviet Navy already had several naval missile programs under way—both strategic and tactical—initiated under the Stalin-Kuznetsov regime. Admiral Gorshkov accelerated these efforts. His target was specific: the U.S. Navy's aircraft carriers that operated nuclear strike aircraft that could reach targets in the Soviet Union from launching sites in the Norwegian Sea, eastern Mediterranean, and Sea of Japan. To obtain missile-firing ships rapidly, Gorshkov directed that unfinished destroyers be fitted with a modified Army missile, designated SS-N-1 by NATO intelligence.[2] This effort produced the Kildin and Krupnyy destroyer classes (NATO code names). These ships—and submarines carrying cruise missiles—would be supplemented by land-based Tu-16 Badger bombers armed with anti-ship missiles. Soon the Navy was also being provided with the large Tu-20/Tu-95 Bear-D long-range reconnaissance aircraft, that could seek out targets for the Soviet ships and submarines. They could also provide guidance for over-the-horizon strikes against Western aircraft carriers to submarines armed with the later SS-N-3 Shaddock–series anti-ship missile.

These missile developments were part of what Soviet officials described as a scientific-technical "revolution" in military affairs. Admiral Gorshkov explained:

> In the mid-1950s, in connection with the revolution in military affairs, the Central Committee of our Party defined the path of fleet development, as well as the fleet's role and place in the system of Armed Forces in the country. The course taken required the construction of an ocean-going fleet, capable of carrying out offensive strategic missions. Submarines and shore-based naval aircraft, equipped with nuclear weapons, have a leading place in the program. Thus, there began a new stage in the development of the fleet and of its naval science.[3]

In addition to developing a fleet for the anti-carrier role, Admiral Gorshkov was able to accelerate the development of both cruise missiles and ballistic missiles for the land-attack role—for strikes against strategic targets in Western Europe *and* in the United States. This latter development had a parallel in the U.S. Navy's Regulus strategic cruise missile, which could be launched from submarines on the surface as well as from surface warships.

In the realm of strategic missiles, the Soviet programs initially outpaced those of the U.S. Navy. The latter's uniformed leaders in the post–World War II era were mostly "carrier admirals," men who "pushed" aircraft carrier programs, in part to provide the nuclear strike capability that was seen by many as the key to the Navy's "survival" in the nuclear era.[4] These admirals had fought the political carrier-versus–B-36 strategic bomber battle in the late 1940s, a debate that had led to cancellation of the first planned U.S. "super carrier," the *United States* (CVA 58). They were not about to fight another political battle with the Air Force to obtain a submarine-launched ballistic missile that would compete with the massive (1,000-missile) Intercontinental Ballistic Missile (ICBM) program.

The Regulus cruise missile being developed by the U.S. Navy was not considered a "political" threat to manned, carrier-based aircraft; indeed, the naval aviation community was largely responsible for the development of Regulus—essentially an unmanned airplane with a nuclear warhead.[5] Sea-based ballistic missiles were another issue, for the U.S. Navy—but not so in the Soviet Navy. The Soviets chose both cruise missiles and ballistic missiles from the start, building on advances made by German missile programs during the war. As early as 16 September 1955, an adapted Red Army ballistic missile was launched from a surfaced submarine. This launch, from a modified Zulu (Project 611)–class diesel-electric submarine, came 4½ years *before* the first launch of a U.S. Polaris Submarine-Launched Ballistic Missile (SLBM). Development already was under way in the Soviet Union on liquid-propellant missiles that could be launched from submarines on the surface (NATO SS-N-4 Sark) and, subsequently, while submerged (NATO SS-N-5 Serb). Soviet submarine design bureaus could modify quickly: Zulu-class submarines already on the building ways with vertical tubes for two SS-N-4 missiles. Construction soon was initiated of the more advanced diesel-electric Golf (Project 629) and nuclear-propelled Hotel (Project 658) classes, both carrying three SLBMs.

Submarines armed with the SS-N-4 and SS-N-5 nuclear-tipped ballistic missiles could be forward deployed to help compensate for the limited range and reliability of these early Soviet land-based strategic missiles. Also, planning was under way for large, 16-missile nuclear submarines generally comparable to the U.S. Polaris craft—the Yankee (Project 667) design. At the same time, the initial submarine-launched cruise missiles—with nuclear warheads—were intended for the strategic land-attack role, in particular the widely distributed P-5 (NATO SS-N-3c Shaddock). These missiles initially were fitted in Whiskey-class conversions, then in purpose-built nuclear Echo I (Project 659), Echo II (Project 675), and diesel-electric Juliett (Project 651) submarines. However, the land-attack variant of the Shaddock was replaced in the early 1960s, following the establishment of Strategic Rocket Forces. These submarines were refitted with surface-launched, anti-ship Shaddock missiles and were soon considered to represent a major threat to U.S. aircraft carriers.

The Soviet decision to develop anti-ship cruise missiles was in essence another indication of the return to the Young School philosophy: the Soviets would counter Western aircraft carriers with missiles launched from aircraft, surface ships, and, eventually, from submarines, just as earlier navies had sought to counter costly battleships with far less expensive torpedo boats and submarines. As Khrushchev would relate in his memoirs, "The Americans had a mighty carrier fleet—no one could deny that. I'll admit I felt a nagging desire to have some in our own navy, but we couldn't afford to build them. They were simply beyond our means. Besides, with a strong submarine force, we felt able to sink the American carriers if it came to war. In other words, submarines represented an effective defensive capability as well as reliable means of launching a missile counterattack."[6]

An Emphasis on Submarines

The second post-war, ten-year naval shipbuilding program (1956–1965) was focused on submarines and sea-launched cruise and ballistic missiles. It also gave emphasis to developing nuclear propulsion, primarily for submarines.

While the Whiskey medium-range submarine program was still under way, the larger Zulu diesel torpedo-attack boat and the Quebec

(Project 633) coastal submarine were being built also, albeit in smaller numbers. The Quebec's closed-cycle diesel plant was not successful; and several accidents occurred. Counting older boats of wartime design, the Soviet submarine fleet peaked at some 475 submarines in 1958, after which there was a decline as the older craft were retired at a faster rate than new boats were constructed.

The first Soviet nuclear submarine, the November (Project 627)–class submarine *K-3*, began her sea trials on 4 July 1958—2½ years after the USS *Nautilus* (SSN 571) got under way.[7] Almost simultaneously, construction began in Soviet shipyards of the nuclear-propelled Echo cruise missile and Hotel ballistic missile submarines. (This was in sharp contrast to the intervals between the first U.S. nuclear torpedo-attack, cruise missile, and ballistic missile submarines.)

As the problems with the early Soviet nuclear submarines were solved (see below), these submarines went farther and remained at sea longer. By the late 1960s the second generation of nuclear submarines was going to sea:

- Charlie/Project 670: cruise missile submarine armed with the world's first underwater-launch anti-ship missiles (eight P-70 Ametist/NATO SS-N-7).
- Victor/Project 671: torpedo-attack submarine introducing new acoustic quieting levels, especially in the Victor III/Project 671RTM variant, earlier than expected by Western intelligence.
- Yankee/Project 667: ballistic missile submarine, analogous to the U.S. Polaris submarines but with several advances (e.g., ability to launch missiles while moving, whereas U.S. submarines had to hover in the water column). Significantly, the Yankee was capable of launching 16 strategic SLBMs and also the R-27K (NATO SS-NX-13) anti-ship ballistic missile.[8]

While these submarines appeared to be "logical" successors to the "HEN" (Hotel-Echo-November) series of nuclear submarines,

Soviet designers were in fact pushing the technological envelope during this period, initially producing three highly advanced designs:

- Alfa/Project 705 Lira: A high-speed (41–42 knot) torpedo-attack submarine with a titanium hull, a liquid-metal reactor, escape chamber for the entire crew, and a remarkable degree of automation that reduced the crew to only 30 men.[9] The basic project was proposed in 1957, design work was started in 1960, and the first of seven units was completed in 1971.
- Papa/Project 661 Anchar: A cruise missile submarine, also with a titanium hull and liquid-metal reactor plant, the world's fastest manned undersea craft, achieving 44.7 knots in trials. Development began in late 1959; the only unit appeared in 1969. The program ended then, although series production had been envisioned, owing to a combination of the high cost of the submarine and alternative, more advanced submarine designs.
- Mike/Project 685: A torpedo-attack submarine and the world's deepest diving combat submarine of its time (3,300+ feet). The *Komsomolets* was intended to evaluate a dozen advanced submarine technologies. Design work began in 1966 with completion of the *Komsomolets* in 1983. (She was lost in the Norwegian Sea to fire on 7 April 1989.)

All three of these submarines were fabricated of titanium, a metal lighter and significantly stronger than steel, corrosion resistant, and also non-magnetic, hence not detectable by magnetic anomaly detection systems. The Soviet Union was—and Russia remains—the only nation capable of large-scale production, welding, and assembly of titanium structures.

The Papa and Mike did not enter serial production in large part because of their high costs but also because of the development of more advanced submarine designs. The prototype Alfa, completed in December 1971 with her radical nuclear plant, suffered major technical problems. She never became operational and suffered a major accident in 1974. Six operational units followed, being completed to a modified design. These were the most highly automated undersea craft ever produced. The Malachite Bureau was awarded the Order of October Revolution in 1981 "for creating the first fast, automated Design Project 705 submarine."

Again, the Alfa SSNs were overtaken by more advanced submarine designs, while their liquid-metal nuclear plants continued to experience problems. "She was many years ahead of her time and so turned out to be too difficult to master and operate," according to Radiy Shmakov, a senior Soviet submarine designer.[10]

Admiral Gorshkov pressed radical surface ship as well as submarine designs while continuing the production of relatively conservative classes. The latter permitted Gorshkov to attain numbers that would not be affordable if he strove for an "all-high-tech" fleet. Also, a major effort was undertaken to provide smaller craft with anti-ship missiles. The Soviet Navy, with a requirement to defend long coastlines in conjunction with the state security services often adjacent to hostile states, has always emphasized small combat craft. Those craft, armed with torpedoes to defend against hostile amphibious attack, would be supplemented from 1958 onward by missile craft armed with the ubiquitous SS-N-2 Styx anti-ship missile. Soon these craft were being transferred to allied and to Third World navies. (Western naval leaders were shocked on when on 21 October 1967, from the shelter of Alexandria harbor, Egyptian missile boats launched four Soviet Styx missiles to sink the Israeli destroyer *Eilat*, steaming just beyond the 12-mile territorial sea. This was the first enemy ship to be sunk by surface-to-surface missiles.)

But it was the massive submarine effort of the immediate postwar period that would provide, even in the Gorshkov years, the basis for continued construction of large numbers of advanced-technology submarines, far outpacing the West in this vital area (see table 10-1).

Table 10-1. Cold War Submarine Production (Completed 1946–1991)

Type	United States	Soviet Union
Diesel-electric	21	399
Closed-cycle	—*	21
Nuclear-propelled	170	231
Totals	*191*	*651*

*The U.S. Navy built one closed-cycle propelled submarine, the midget *X-1* (SSX 1), completed in 1955.

Building Surface Ships

While Admiral Gorshkov was able to adapt smaller ships rapidly to carry out coastal defense missions, the development of larger warships was a more difficult political issue. Khrushchev opposed large warships; they were, in his opinion, expensive, vulnerable to modern weapons, required large crews, and made too heavy demands on Soviet industry: "Gone were the days when a heavy cruiser and the battleship were the backbone of a navy. It still made a beautiful picture when the crew lined up smartly at attention on the deck of a cruiser to receive an admiral or call on a friendly foreign port. But such ceremonies were now just an elegant luxury."[11]

Khrushchev specifically directed Admiral Gorshkov to dispose of the large warships. The Soviet leader's private directions to Gorshkov were soon amplified in public: In April 1956, Khrushchev visited England in the new *Sverdlov*-class cruiser *Ordzhonikidze* and was quoted as declaring that such ships were good for firing salutes and little more.[12] That summer, when General Nathan Twining, the U.S. Air Force Chief of Staff, visited Moscow he was told by Khrushchev that "admirals are always looking backward and living in the past." Visiting the United States in 1959, Khrushchev revealed his views to another

U.S. officer: "We were starting to build a big fleet of ships, including many cruisers. But today they are outmoded. Cruisers have a very short range. They are enormously expensive. We are scrapping 90–95 percent of them, including some that were just on the verge of being commissioned. From now on we will rely mainly on submarines."[13]

While Khrushchev's statements as remembered may vary somewhat from what he actually said, they certainly reflected his perceptions. In response, Admiral Gorshkov rapidly disposed of the three surviving tsarist-era battleships; the ex-Italian *Novorossiysk* had already sunk and would be raised and cut up for scrap. But Gorshkov did retain most of the older cruisers, as well as 14 of the new *Sverdlov*-class ships, completed between 1952 and 1956. Three additional *Sverdlovs* were launched but not completed, and three unfinished hulls were scrapped on the building ways.

Thus, Admiral Gorshkov was able to maintain a large (and costly) cruiser force; he would actually increase their numbers during the Khrushchev era with the larger and more modern ships of the *Sverdlov* class. Gorshkov argued that new surface warships were needed to support the undersea fleet. Drawing on historical precedent, as was the Soviet style, he later explained, "A modern fleet, designed to conduct combat against a strong enemy, cannot be only an undersea fleet. The underestimation of the need to support submarine operations with aircraft and surface ships cost the German High Command dearly in the last two wars."[14]

In particular, it was pointed out that one of the reasons for failure of the German "unrestricted submarine war" was the absence of such support, which forced submarines to operate alone. "Therefore, in giving priority to the development of submarine forces, we believe we have a need not only for submarines but also for various types of surface ships. The latter, in addition to giving combat stability to the submarines, are intended to accomplish a wide range of missions both in peacetime and in war."

Table 10-2. Soviet Major Surface Warship Strength

	Completed	1950	1953	1956	1959-1960	1985
Battleships						
Ex-tsarist	1904–1915	3	3	3	—	—
Novorossiysk★	1914	1	1	—	—	—
Cruisers						
Svetlana★★	1928	1	1	1	—	—
Krasnyy Kavkaz	1932	1	1	—	—	—
Admiral						
Makarov★★★	1935	1	1	1	—	—
Kirov class	1940–1944	6	6	5	4	—
Chapayev class	1949–1950	5	5	5	5	—
Sverdlov class	1952–1956	—	6	14	14	8
Missile-Armed Cruisers						
Kynda class	1962–1965	—	—	—	—	4
Kresta I class	1967–1969	—	—	—	—	4
Kresta II class	1969–1978	—	—	—	—	10
Kara class	1973–1980	—	—	—	—	7
Slava class	1982–1992	—	—	—	—	1
Kirov class#	1980–1988	—	—	—	—	2
Aviation-Missile Ships						
Moskva class	1967–1968	—	—	—	—	2
Kiev class##	1975–1982	—	—	—	—	3

★ Former Italian battleship *Julio Caesare.*
★★ Formerly named *Krasnyy Krym.*
★★★ Former German light cruiser *Nurnberg.*
Nuclear-propelled; two additional ships subsequently were completed in 1988 and 1998.
A fourth ship of this class was completed in 1987.

Indeed, there are indications of confrontations between Khrushchev and Admiral Gorshkov. For example, in January 1960, Khrushchev told the Supreme Soviet that "the submarine forces assume great importance while surface ships can no longer play the part they once did."[15] Gorshkov responded in agreement—but with an important qualification: "Surface ships can no longer play as important a role as they played in the past."[16]

Still, at one point Khrushchev was interested in having a "surface strike force." In the early 1960s a widespread and increasingly radical pro-independence movement achieved independence for the Congo, which became the Republic of Congo–Léopoldville. Virulent disagreements between factions within the Congo, the continued involvement of the Belgium government in Congolese affairs, and intervention by major parties of the Cold War led to five years of conflict and political instability, from 1960 to 1965. The United States sent ships to the African coast to demonstrate support for one faction, and the Soviet regime believed that the United States might send in troops.

"We had no way to interfere or to help our friends," wrote Sergey Khrushchev, son of the Soviet leader.[17] "Admiral Gorshkov proposed sending a cruiser and a pair of destroyers, but it became clear that they would run out of fuel and that it was doubtful that we could supply them at such a distance from Soviet bases. The idea smacked of adventurism and was quickly rejected." But the Soviet leader feared that "victory" by the parties supported by the United States would be viewed as a defeat for the Soviet Union:

> He summoned Admiral Gorshkov—I was present at the meeting—and Boris Yevstafyevich Butoma, chairman of the Committee on Shipbuilding, and asked: "How much would it cost and how long would it take to build a rapid response squadron? One that would show the power and flag of the Soviet Union in support of our friends anywhere in the world?"

It took about a week to obtain a preliminary estimate. The report the specialists prepared for Father calculated that it would take about five years to build the fighting ships and auxiliary vessels, and that the squadron would cost about five billion rubles.

In reply, Father simply mumbled, "Rather a lot. We'll find better uses for all that money."

He never raised the question again.[18]

The First Missile Ships

The first major surface combatant ships initiated under Admiral Gorshkov were the Kynda-class missile cruisers, with a full load displacement of some 5,500 tons with the large SS-N-3 Shaddock cruise missile—initially developed for surface ships and submarines as a land-attack weapon (Soviet P-5) and then for the anti-ship role(P-6). The lead ship of the class, the *Groznyy*, was laid down in June 1959, indicating that a construction decision had undoubtedly been taken shortly after Gorshkov became came to Moscow. Khrushchev, as critical of these cruisers as he was of virtually all large surface ships, wrote:

> As I recall, we decided to build four cruisers—one for the Baltic, one for the Black Sea, one for the Far East, and the fourth I forget for where. They were good solely as showpieces, and very expensive showpieces at that. After the first one was finished—and the second one almost finished—we had second thoughts about whether to build the other two at all. We exchanged opinions in the leadership and decided to go ahead as a concession to the military, which was in favor of these ships. Our naval commanders thought they looked beautiful and liked to show them off to foreigners. An officer likes to hear all the young sailors greet his command with a loud cheer. That always makes a big impression.[19]

Admiral Gorshkov was able to obtain Presidium backing for the four Kynda-class missile cruisers, and plans were drawn up for a larger cruiser for the anti-carrier role. Construction also was begun on a series of anti-aircraft missile destroyers with gas-turbine engines; the first of these ships, designated the Kashin class by NATO, was launched in the winter of 1962–1963, shortly after the first of the Kynda class. These were the world's first warships with all-gas-turbine propulsion, another Soviet naval innovation, providing a maximum speed of 38 knots. The impact of these new Soviet ships on the more-perceptive Western naval leaders was significant. One of the first public commentaries, albeit not by leaders but by two junior U.S. Navy officers, observed: "If both Soviet and Western strategists are currently having to reassess their evaluation of Soviet sea strength, one of the principal reasons is the construction of the Kynda-class guided-missile frigates."[20]

A New Command Team

Upon his arrival in Moscow in 1955, first as deputy and then as commander-in-chief of the Navy, Admiral Gorshkov was met by an existing headquarters staff. Nikolay Ye. Basisty, his predecessor as first deputy CinC, was reassigned as a deputy CinC "for military scientific work" and then, two years later, to the Ministry of Defense General Inspectorate; he was retired in 1960 at age 62. Gorshkov was, in turn, replaced as first deputy CinC of the Navy by Admiral Arseniy G. Golovko, age 50, who had been Northern Fleet commander during the war and commander of the Baltic Fleet from 1952 to 1956. He had been an obvious competitor to Gorshkov for the post of head of the Navy.

Admiral A. V. Komarov, who had become head of the Political Administration of the Navy after the battleship *Novorossiysk* disaster in 1955, was replaced in 1958 by Admiral Vasiliy M. Grishanov, who thereby suffered a slight demotion after earlier assignments as political officer of the Pacific Fleet and of the then-premier Baltic Fleet. Grishanov as head of the Navy's political administration was thus a deputy to Filipp I. Golikov. Apparently Grishanov had not previously worked with Admiral Gorshkov. However, he was said to have been a close friend of Leonid Brezhnev, head of the government from 1964, and obviously performed well, as evidenced by his subsequent longevity as the head of the Navy's political staff—from 1958 until 1981.

Another significant Navy shift in the period was the appointment of aviation general Ivan Ivanovich Borzov as first deputy CinC for Naval Aviation late in 1957. The 42-year-old Borzov had been highly decorated for leading air strikes against German shipping in the Baltic and Black Sea during World War II. He also was considered highly reliable from a political viewpoint, having been one of the officers who publicly declared themselves in favor of Zhukov's dismissal in late 1957. Before his appointment to the Moscow post Borzov had commanded naval aviation in the Northern Fleet and then in the Baltic Fleet.[21]

Thus, Admiral Gorshkov was able to develop rapidly his own command team to help him direct the Soviet Navy during this period of revolutionary change. Further, as the only naval officer then holding membership in the Central Committee and so the political as well as the military head of the Soviet Navy, he was without competition. Gorshkov's genius in initiating change in the Navy has perhaps best been described by Professor John Erickson, the dean of analysts regarding the Soviet defense establishment during much of the Cold War:

Caught between the traditionalism of the Soviet military establishment in general and the eccentric exuberance of Nikita Khrushchev in particular, Admiral Gorshkov picked his way with great care. Supported by a whole *eskadra* [squadron] of Soviet admirals safely in retirement, he deftly turned

Khrushchev's main argument against him, repeating in all political dutifulness that submarines may be the "main striking force," but adding the rider that they require "comprehensive combat support." Much turned on that term "comprehensive."

Against heavy political odds, Gorshkov mustered substantial support for a better balanced naval force, which included large surface ships.[22]

CHAPTER 11

New Directions

The Navy . . . is capable of not only defending our
maritime borders but also of destroying enemy forces
on the seas and oceans, as well as of delivering powerful
blows against targets located on other continents.

—Marshal Rodion Ya. Malinovskiy, *Sovetskiy Flot* (25 February 1959)

Admiral Gorshkov was brought to Moscow to change the direction of the Soviet Navy—to manage the "revolution in naval affairs." He initiated or accelerated several programs, the Kynda-class missile cruiser being among the earliest and most visible evidence of the new directions of the Red Navy. But the Kynda program was short-lived. The fourth Kynda was laid down in 1962, and no more followed. Planning for a larger cruiser armed with Shaddock anti-ship missiles was stopped. In 1960 the Soviet Navy was stripped of its fighter aircraft—needed to provide air cover for the Shaddock-armed cruisers. The Navy's estimated 1,500 to 2,000 fighters were transferred to PVO-*Strany*, reducing Naval Aviation from as many as 4,000 aircraft and perhaps 90,000 men in the late 1950s to about 850 aircraft and one-half the personnel.

Almost simultaneous with these changes in the air and surface programs, the Soviet Navy's Submarine-Launched Ballistic Missile (SLBM) program was truncated. Only 23 of the diesel-electric Golf and 8 of the nuclear-propelled Hotel submarines were completed, and planning for more advanced SLBM programs—similar to the

U.S. Polaris project—essentially was halted. Termination of the SLBM programs was related to Khrushchev's establishment of the Strategic Rocket Forces in 1959 as a separate military service. Thus a key part of Admiral Gorshkov's efforts to build a revolutionary fleet were thwarted—at least for the moment.

Reacting to New Threats

Khrushchev's plan was to reduce the size of the Soviet Union's conventional armed forces in favor of a nuclear strike force—operated by the Strategic Rocket Forces—and to fight the West instead with trade and support of "wars of national liberation" in the Third World. This plan fell apart when John F. Kennedy became president of the United States in January 1961. Kennedy, elected in a campaign that had publicized a "missile gap" sparked by impressive Soviet satellite launches and ICBM tests, began a buildup of U.S. strategic and conventional military forces. He accelerated the development of the Polaris SLBM and Minuteman ICBM programs, increased the number of naval ships in commission, and built up "special forces," most notably the U.S. Army's Green Berets and the Navy's SEALs (SEa Air Land teams) to fight Soviet-sponsored insurgents in the Third World.

This major buildup in U.S. strategic offensive and conventional forces created confusion in the Kremlin and led to major reconsiderations in defense planning. The recently decided Soviet defense policies emphasizing ICBMs were found wanting, as was Soviet missile development in general, with major technical problems being encountered. Several revisions in defense planning were initiated, and in a move to overcome shortfalls in the ICBM program, Khrushchev ordered medium-range ballistic missiles and nuclear-capable strike aircraft to be based secretly in Cuba. The ensuing Cuban missile crisis of October–November 1962, demonstrated that, first, the United States was willing to use conventional military force against the Soviet Union, at least in the Western Hemisphere but possibly elsewhere as well; second, the U.S. strategic offensive weapons could overwhelm those of the Soviet Union; and third, the Soviet Navy was unable to support an overseas adventure. The last factor was significant for Admiral Gorshkov: Early plans during the buildup of strategic weapons in Cuba included the dispatch of surface warships to escort the arms-carrying merchant ships, In the event, these plans were quickly dropped, as were proposals to carry the nuclear missile warheads to Cuba in submarines. Indeed, the Soviet Navy would prove unable even to support the movement of arms to Cuba by sending nuclear-propelled submarines to the western Atlantic—only a few diesel-electric submarines were dispatched. The early Soviet nuclear submarines—the HEN series— had suffered major engineering problems. The rapid development of nuclear propulsion and poor quality control in Soviet industry had led to a number of nuclear incidents and accidents. Several of these submarines suffered propulsion breakdowns at sea and had to be towed back to port, sometimes with significant damage and casualties. Admiral Igor Kasatonov later wrote that Admiral Gorshkov and the Northern Fleet commander agreed that it was impossible to send the unreliable nuclear submarines to Cuba: "Relatively long voyages of the Soviet nuclear submarines were only begun in 1962. [There] was no assurance in the reliability of their nuclear plants."[1]

In the early planning for the Cuban undertaking—given the Soviet code name Operation Anadyr—Admiral Gorshkov and his key advisors had planned to base surface ships and submarines in Cuban ports. The submarines were to operate off the U.S. Atlantic coast, while both the warships and submarines were to be prepared to prevent American ships from approaching Cuba to carry out amphibious landings or to impose a sea blockade of the U.S. base at Guantanamo Bay. The submarines would include four nuclear-propelled ballistic missile submarines of the Hotel type, each armed with three short-range ballistic missiles with nuclear warheads. There also would be seven diesel-electric submarines armed with torpedoes, some of which would have nuclear warheads. The surface force would consist of two *Sverdlov*-class gun cruisers, two guided missile destroyers, and two gun destroyers, complemented by a dozen of the new missile-armed small combatant craft (NATO Komar). These craft each had two anti-ship missiles, weapons against which U.S. warships had no effective defense at that time.[2]

Ashore, in addition to support personnel, the Navy would establish an aviation mine-torpedo regiment with 33 Il-28 Beagle light bombers, and there would be a regiment of S-2 Sopka (NATO SSC-2b Samlet) coastal defense cruise missiles. Also, the Navy planned to send four nuclear mines to Cuba, to stop American submarines from attacking the Soviet ships in their anchorages. (Significantly, the Soviet Union was the only nation to develop nuclear mines during the Cold War.[3]) To support the submarine and surface forces in Cuba, the Soviet Navy would send two submarine tenders, two tankers, two cargo ships, and a repair ship. The main fleet base would be in the Havana area, secondary bases in the ports west of Havana—that is, Mariel, Cabañas, and Bahia Honda.[4]

The total naval personnel needed to man those ships, submarines, aircraft, and missile units would be almost 6,000 men. Preparations proceeded at a rapid pace, but in midst of them the decision was made not to send the naval forces to Cuba, because of the fear that they would be too provocative to the American leadership. Instead, only five Foxtrot diesel-electric torpedo submarines and the Komar missile craft were dispatched to Cuba, the latter as deck cargo on merchant ships.

In the aftermath of the missile crisis, even while the Soviet missiles and bombers were being withdrawn from Cuba, Deputy Foreign Minister V.V. Kuznetsov told an American official, "We will live up to this agreement, but we will never be caught like that again." Soviet military programs were accelerated, and long-range plans were revised.

Several changes to the suspended naval programs were put in hand, and, most significant, in March 1963 there was a top-level realignment of the country's economic management—just three months after a long-planned reorganization had occurred. A new Supreme Economic Council was established, headed by Dmitriy Ustinov, the longtime chief of armament production. This appointment gave military planning clear priority in the national economy after Khrushchev's earlier attempts at a more balanced approach. In the aftermath of Cuba there also were several changes within the defense establishment's senior leadership; some pundits saw indications that Khrushchev might soon be forced to give up his own positions.

The events of 1961–1963 had considerable impact on the Soviet Navy. They enhanced the stature of the Navy within the Soviet armed forces, for naval forces could help to counter the U.S. Navy's Polaris submarines, and Soviet SLBM-armed nuclear submarines could help to redress the "missile gap," which actually existed in the early 1960s but in favor of the United States. Also, naval forces could potentially support future Soviet political-military forays into the Third World.

Anti-Polaris Efforts

For the Soviet Navy the U.S. acceleration of the Polaris program brought to the fore the mission of strategic anti-submarine warfare in defense of the Soviet homeland—the No. 1 military priority. The Kyndas were soon replaced on the building ways at the Zhdanov (Northern) shipyard in Leningrad by the interim Kresta I class of cruisers. The new class mounted only one-half of the Kynda's Shaddock missile battery (four launcher tubes with no reloads versus eight tubes plus eight reloads in the Kynda). However, the Kresta I had improved anti-aircraft and helicopter capabilities, the former to defend against Western carrier-based aircraft in the absence of Soviet naval fighters, the latter for target detection and anti-ship missile guidance.

Only four of these ships were built before the mature Kresta II design appeared: a large anti-submarine ship—*Bolshoy Protivolodochnyy Korabl* (BPK)—with eight long-range SS-N-14 anti-submarine warfare (ASW) missiles replacing the earlier ship's four Shaddock anti-ship weapons.[5] At the same time, the Nikolayev South yard, in the Black Sea area, began building the *Moskva*-class hermaphrodite missile cruisers–ASW helicopter carriers. These ships, the first aviation ships to be constructed in the Soviet Union, were intended to counter the U.S. Polaris submarines in seas adjacent to the Soviet Union.

With a full load displacement of almost 18,000 tons, the *Moskva*, completed in 1967, and her sister ship the *Leningrad*, finished the following year, were the largest warships yet built in the Soviet Union. Their design was unique, leading some Western analysts to believe that the *Moskva*s were built with a hull design intended for larger Shaddock missile cruisers that were never laid down.

Despite carrying 18 ASW helicopters and being fitted with the most advanced Soviet anti-aircraft and anti-submarine weapons, the *Moskva*s were incapable of coping with the Polaris threat. By 1967 the U.S. Navy had 41 Polaris SLBM submarines in service, at least one-half of which were always at sea, each armed with 16 nuclear missiles. Also, the improved Polaris A-3 missile, which had become operational in 1964, had a range of 2,500 nautical miles, reducing the potential effectiveness of the *Moskva*s, which, without air cover, could not operate that far from land. No more *Moskva*s were built; instead, Soviet designers began planning significantly larger and more capable ASW aircraft carriers. The Kresta II series continued in production, ten of these ASW cruisers being built through 1978; almost simultaneously, the Nikolayev North shipyard produced the larger (9,700-ton) Kara class of ASW cruisers, of which seven were built through 1979. A Kresta II or Kara could effectively serve as a command ship for ASW forces seeking to protect Soviet submarines (including strategic missile submarines) from Western submarine and anti-submarine forces.

This pro-submarine mission appears to have been the ratio-
nale for several major Soviet programs of the period, all justified
by Admiral Gorshkov's pointed observations that it had been the
failure of the German Navy to support U-boats adequately in the
two world wars that had prevented those submarines from prevail-
ing. Most noteworthy of these programs would be the *Kiev*-class
aircraft carrier. Although again hermaphrodite ships, mounting both
long-range anti-ship missiles, as well as advanced anti-aircraft and
anti-submarine weapons, the *Kievs* operated Vertical/Short Takeoff
and Landing (VSTOL) aircraft and thereby represented a major step
in Soviet aircraft carrier development. The *Kiev*, completed in 1975,
had a full-load displacement of some 43,000 tons, the new record
for the largest warship to be constructed in the Soviet Union. Three
sister ships would follow. Significantly, in addition to embarking
VSTOL fighter aircraft and helicopters and having a heavy anti-
aircraft and ASW armament, the four *Kiev*-class ships each had eight
SS-N-12 Sandbox anti-ship missiles. (These missiles were the much-
improved successor to the SS-N-3 Shaddock.)

There was, of course, another consideration: even as these cruisers
were being built Admiral Gorshkov would note, "We must be prepared . . . on the whole territory of the world ocean."[6] These cruisers
and aviation ships were modern, multi-purpose ships. As the Soviet
Navy began to operate farther afield on the world's oceans, these
large, graceful-looking warships would personify Oliver Cromwell's
adage, "A man-of-war is the best ambassador."

The large ASW cruiser program—almost two new ships per
year—soon was supplemented by specialized anti-submarine destroyers, as well as land-based ASW aircraft and ASW submarines. The
latter consisted primarily of the Victor (Project 671) class of nuclear-
propelled attack submarines, faster and deeper-diving than their
American contemporaries. Finally, this emphasis on strategic ASW
to counter U.S. strategic missile submarines did not preclude either
the continued construction of large numbers of submarines for the

anti-ship/anti-carrier role or, at the same time, a new program of strategic missile submarines.

Nevertheless, even as these larger, more capable surface warships were being produced, Admiral Gorshkov was careful not to argue from simplistic comparisons numbers of ships of specific types in the American and Soviet fleets—as did American naval leaders calling for more shipbuilding funds from Congress. Rather, wrote Gorshkov, "We have had to cease comparing the number of warships of one type or another and their total displacement (or number of guns in a salvo or the weight of this salvo), and turn to a more complex, but also more correct, appraisal of the striking and defensive power of ships, based on a mathematical analysis of their capabilities and qualitative characteristics."[7]

Strategic Strike

Soviet SLBM development was slowed with the 1959 establishment of the Strategic Rocket Forces. However, the on-going U.S. strategic forces buildup and technical problems with Soviet ICBM development gave the Soviet strategic missile submarine program new life, accelerated by the Cuban missile fiasco; the directive creating the new SLBM/SSBN system was adopted on 24 April 1962. The new SLBM submarine design externally resembled the U.S. Polaris submarines, a submarine class to which NATO gave the confusing and ironic code name Yankee. Armed with 16 ballistic missiles, the Yankee (Project 667A) design showed evidence of having been ordered into construction with the highest priority. Production was undertaken at two shipyards, Severodvinsk in the north and Komsomol'sk in the Far East.

The first Yankee SLBM submarine was completed in 1967, the year that the 41st and last U.S. Polaris submarine first went to sea. The Yankee initially carried the liquid-propellant R-27 (NATO SS-N-6) missile with a range of some 1,200 nautical miles, significantly short of the range of contemporary U.S. submarine missiles but sufficient to allow Soviet submarines to remain a thousand miles off the American coasts and target most of the nation's population and industry and almost all its major ports and naval facilities.[8]

The U.S. Department of Defense announced in April 1970, that Yankee-class missile submarines were being maintained on station in the western Atlantic on a regular basis, with some 1,200 to 1,500 miles of the East Coast.[9] Regular Yankee SSBNs off the U.S. West Coast would follow.

Yankee submarine production reached a peak of eight units commissioned and another eight launched in 1970—about the time that the Soviet Navy equaled the United States in total number of nuclear submarines of all types in service. Afterward, Yankee production slowed as yards prepared for the follow-on Delta SLBM submarines (Project 667B); 34 Yankee submarines were built. The Delta I submarines, which began to enter service in 1972, were the world's largest submarines built up to that time. More significant than their size was the fact that the Delta I initially carried the liquid-propellant R-29 (NATO SS-N-8), with a range of more than 4,000 nautical miles. This meant that Delta I submarines could remain in Soviet waters in the Barents Sea or off Kamchatka or in the Sea of Okhotsk in the Pacific while targeting virtually the entire United States. This capability would invalidate the existing Western anti-submarine strategy, which called for intercepting Soviet ballistic missile submarines (as well as torpedo-attack and cruise missile submarines) as they transited from their bases or holding areas to missile launching positions off the American East and West Coasts.[10]

Thus, under Admiral Gorshkov's direction—a surface warfare specialist by his early fleet experience—the Russian-Soviet emphasis on submarines continued with new fervor. Indeed, commenting on this situation, then–Vice Admiral H. G. Rickover, head of the U.S. nuclear-propulsion program, wrote: "The Soviets are embarked on a program which reveals a singular awareness of the importance of seapower, and an unmistakable resolve to become the most powerful maritime force in the world."[11]

By this time the massive Soviet investment in large, specialized ASW cruisers, helicopter carriers, and destroyers had begun to make sense to Western observers. For many it had been difficult to conceptualize how these ships would be employed outside the range of land-based air support to "provide combat stability" to the Soviet submarine force. Now, with Soviet strategic, nuclear-powered ballistic missile submarines (SSBNs) operating in the Barents Sea, Arctic Ocean, and northern Pacific *within* range of land-based or carrier-based air support, the deployment concept became obvious: these ships would protect the Soviet SSBN operating and transit areas from prowling Western SSNs and ASW aircraft.

Additional torpedo-attack and cruise missile submarine classes were begun during the 1960s, continuing the Soviet pattern of not only large numbers of submarines but also simultaneous development of multiple classes. While the emphasis was on nuclear-propelled submarines, the Soviet design bureaus and shipyards continued to produce diesel-electric attack boats. The Soviets apparently believed (and the Russians still do) that modern diesel submarines can undertake certain missions as effectively or more so than nuclear submarines, especially in regional waters, at far less cost in resources and manpower. Further, non-nuclear submarines could be provided to Third World countries, in some cases earning hard currency and in others improving relationships (and possibly dependency) and perhaps gaining political-military influence.

The Rebirth of Naval Infantry

A final development in this period demonstrated another dimension of the future course and emphasis of the Soviet Navy under Admiral

Gorshkov—the rebirth of Morskaya Pekhota, the Naval Infantry, or marines. The Naval Infantry, which fought ashore with the Red Army in World War II, had been disbanded in 1956.

That situation did not last even half a decade. By the early 1960s, moves were under way to reconstitute the Naval Infantry. For example, responding to a then-recently published official volume *Voyennaya Strategiya* (Military Strategy), a senior naval officer wrote, "The ground forces would be in a terrible quandary, to say the least, in attempting the invasion of enemy territory across the sea."[12] Then, on 24 June 1964, a front-page pictorial in the newspaper *Krasnaya Zvezda* (Red Star) showed marines coming ashore in amphibious personnel carriers. It was announced that these newly formed units had conducted amphibious landings during joint operations with other Warsaw Pact forces.

The reconstitution proceeded slowly. Units were established in the Baltic and Pacific Fleets in 1963, followed by the Northern and Black Sea Fleets in 1966. The Caspian Sea Flotilla would have to wait until 1994. Naval Infantry—about 500 marines from the Baltic Fleet—participated in the Moscow parade on 7 November 1967, commemorating the October Revolution, the first time the service had been seen on parade in Red Square since World War II.

There was a rapid growth of Naval Infantry during the next few years as each of the four fleets was provided with specialized amphibious assault ships to transport marines and amphibious personnel carriers to send them ashore. Beginning in the early 1970s, the Soviet Navy also began to deploy air-cushion landing craft that could carry marines long distances at high speeds in coastal waters. Also, in the early 1970s Naval Infantry troops were reported afloat with the Soviet squadron deployed to the Mediterranean.

During the 1970s the size of the Naval Infantry had stabilized at about 12,000 men, with a regiment each in the Northern, Baltic, and Black Sea Fleets and apparently a two-regiment brigade in the Pacific Fleet. While some Western strategists suggested that such a small marine force was merely a showpiece without meaningful combat capability, the potential role of a trained amphibious assault cadre had been spelled out by Soviet spokesmen:

> Landed as tactical amphibious forces, Naval Infantry units are capable of seizing islands, naval bases, ports, coastal air-fields, and also sectors of the sea coast on their own and, where necessary, with attached specialized fleet subunits. In amphibious landings of larger scale involving units and combined units of ground forces, the Naval Infantry may operate as part of forward detachments, as the first wave of an amphibious landing . . . or assault detachments . . . seizing a beachhead . . . and holding it to support the landing and supply of the amphibious force main body.[13]

Of course, in peacetime or crisis a few hundred marines at the right place at the right time in the Third World could shift a coup or local conflict in favor of the Soviet-supported side, as American and European marines have demonstrated on numerous occasions.

Admiral Gorshkov's interest in the re-establishment of the Morskaya Pekhota was obviously personal and direct, in view of his own experience with wartime amphibious operations in the Black Sea and Sea of Azov and of the practical value of marines for the envisioned expanded role of the Soviet Navy in the potential Third World "adventures."

Assignments and Awards

During 1962–1964, as these new naval programs were being put in hand, Admiral Gorshkov changed his senior deputies, bringing in men who would direct the next phase of Soviet naval development. First, Admiral Vladimir A. Kasatonov, Gorshkov's classmate and successor as Black Sea Fleet commander, in 1962 was appointed to command the Northern Fleet, which had become the Navy's most important force. That summer Admiral Nikolay N. Amelko took command of the Pacific Fleet and Admiral Serafim Ye. Chursin of the Black Sea Fleet. Only the Baltic Fleet commander, Vice Admiral Aleksandr Ye. Orel, appointed in May 1959, remained of the previous fleet commanders.

Admiral Golovko, the First Deputy CinC of the Navy, died in May 1962, opening up that key position to a Gorshkov appointee. Admiral Vitaliy A. Fokin, the Pacific Fleet commander from 1958 to 1962, became the first deputy CinC. He may have been a placeholder until Admiral Kasatonov could have commanded the Northern Fleet for a respectable period. In the event, Fokin would die of a massive heart attack in January 1964; Admiral Kasatonov became the First Deputy CinC, and Admiral Nikolay D. Sergeyev became the Chief of the Main Navy Staff, the No. 2 position at naval headquarters. Both men would serve in those important posts for more than a decade.

Three other flag officers should be mentioned as having key roles in this phase of Gorshkov's rebuilding of the Soviet fleet. First, Colonel General of (naval) Aviation Ivan I. Borzov was moved from first deputy to the commander of Morskaya Aviatsiya in May 1962; he too would serve more than a decade in that post. Engineer-Admiral Nikolay V. Isachenkov, the Deputy CinC of the Navy for Shipbuilding and Armaments, had technological direction of the Navy from 1952 until February 1966, when he was taken ill and replaced by his deputy, Engineer-Admiral Pavel G. Kotov.

Although none of the changes in the naval high command were directly attributable to the Cuban missile crisis; that situation had led to dissention between Khrushchev and the High Command. The Chief of the General Staff, Marshal Matvey V. Zakharov, and two of his deputies were transferred to less responsible posts. Marshal Sergey S. Biryuzov, a key figure in the development of the Air Defense

Forces, briefly was given command of the Strategic Rocket Forces in a belated effort to overcome the shortcomings in ICBM programs that had contributed to the need to place ballistic missiles in Cuba. However, in April 1963, Biryuzov was named Chief of the General Staff, essentially the No. 2 position in the Ministry of Defense. He was killed in an air crash late in 1964, and Zakharov then succeeded his own successor.

★ ★ ★

As the Soviet Navy gained more capabilities, especially with the deployment of Yankee-class ballistic missile submarines, there was need for more coordination of these weapons within the Soviet General Staff. In 1958, Admiral Nikolay I. Vinogradov, former Deputy Chief of the Main Naval Staff, was named one of several deputy chiefs of the General Staff. He was succeeded in his Navy position in 1962 by Admiral Chabanenko, former commander of the Northern Fleet (and a 1931 classmate of Gorshkov). The assignment of Chabanenko from the Northern Fleet, where most Soviet nuclear-propelled submarines were based, and his subsequent ten years on the General Staff gave Gorshkov increased influence with that important body. This thesis was reinforced by the appointment in 1972 of Fleet Admiral Semyon M. Lobov as Assistant Chief of the General Staff. Lobov had been the first Soviet officer to reach the rank of fleet admiral while serving in an operational command—the Northern Fleet from 1964 to 1972, the period of introduction of the Yankee and Delta submarines. Upon his appointment in 1972 he had the same rank level as the Chief of the General Staff, General of the Army Viktor G. Kulikov.

The large programs of the 1960s for surface ships, submarines, naval aircraft, and missiles gave the Soviet Navy a new level of prestige within the Soviet hierarchy and a higher stature to Gorshkov himself. Indeed, in late 1966, Gorshkov could write: "For the first time in its history our Navy was converted, in the full sense of the word, into an offensive type of long-range armed force. Along with the Strategic Missile Troops the Navy had become the most important weapon the Supreme Command had, one which could exert a decisive influence on the course of an armed struggle on theaters of military operations of vast extent."[14]

Admiral Gorshkov's coupling of the Navy with the Strategic Rocket Forces was particularly significant, for there now could be no question among the national leadership of the importance of strategic nuclear weapons. Although Gorshkov's next paragraph noted, "this potential must be brought to bear in full measure in the struggle with a strong naval enemy," this is usually interpreted in the West to mean the employment of SLBMs against *naval* targets, such as ports and shipyards. This was a circumlocution similarly employed by American naval planners in the late 1940s and 1950s to justify the development of sea-based strategic weapons that would compete with U.S. land-based strategic forces (i.e., U.S. Air Force manned bombers and, later, land-based ICBMs).

In October 1961, at the 22nd Party Congress, Gorshkov was elevated to full (voting) membership in the Central Committee. Not since Kuznetsov's dismissal five years earlier had a naval officer held full membership. Also elected to full membership was Admiral Fokin, then still commander of the Pacific Fleet, marking the first time in Party history that two naval officers had held full membership. In addition, Admiral Chabanenko, commander of the Northern Fleet, was named to candidate membership.

Six months later, on 28 April 1962, the rank of Fleet Admiral (*Admiral Flota*) was reestablished in the Soviet Union, having been abolished in 1955 when the rank of Fleet Admiral of the Soviet Union was introduced, and still remained as the ultimate naval rank. Gorshkov was awarded the fleet admiral rank in 1962, an indication of the Navy's increasing prestige. Three years later, on 7 May 1965, after Leonid Brezhnev had succeeded Khrushchev, Gorshkov was belatedly decorated for his performance in the Great Patriotic War with the Hero of the Soviet Union, the highest award that the Soviet government could bestow.

In 1967, as the helicopter carrier-missile cruiser *Moskva*, the Yankee-class ballistic missile submarines, and the large ASW cruisers were going to sea, Admiral Gorshkov was awarded the rarified rank of Fleet Admiral of the Soviet Union. This promotion, on 20 October, made Gorshkov the third (and final) Fleet Admiral of the Soviet Union, his predecessors being Kuznetsov and Isakov.

In 1969 and 1970, after Gorshkov's promotion, the importance of the Navy was made further manifest in the promotion to fleet admiral of Admirals Kasatonov, Lobov, and Sergeyev. Admirals Nikolay I. Smirnov, at the time commander of the Pacific Fleet (having succeeded Amelko in 1969), and Georgiy M. Yegorov, commander of the Northern Fleet (succeeding Kasatonov in 1971), were promoted to that grade in 1973.

However, despite the shipbuilding programs, promotions, and awards, Admiral Gorshkov still faced a difficult course ahead.

CHAPTER 12

Selling a Balanced Navy

Every time ruling circles in Russia failed to properly emphasize development of the Fleet and its maintenance . . . at a level necessitated by modern-day demands, the country either lost battles in wars or its peacetime policy failed to achieve designated objectives.

—Admiral S. G. Gorshkov, *Morskoy Sbornik* (no. 4, 1972)

Admiral Gorshkov's campaign to develop a modern and effective fleet was long and tortuous. Beyond overcoming Khrushchev's dictum that large surface ships should be scrapped in favor of missile-armed submarines and aircraft, Gorshkov had a continuous battle against senior civilian and military leaders— and even some naval officers—who saw the shipyards at Leningrad, Nikolayev, and Severodvinsk consuming vast quantities of steel, electrical, and then electronic components, as well as other resources scarce in a country in all-out competition with the West. Once built, the warships required highly trained crews—large numbers of skilled men who also were in great demand for industry and the other military services.

According to Gorshkov,

We had among us, unfortunately, some extremely influential "authorities" who felt that with the appearance of atomic weapons the Navy had completely lost its importance as a branch of the Armed Forces. In their opinion, all of the primary missions in a future war could, supposedly, be carried out quite without the participation of the fleet, even in those cases when to do so would require deployment for combat operations on the broad sea and ocean expanses. A frequent assertion of the time was that single missiles, placed on land launchers, would be sufficient for destroying strike dispositions of surface warships, and even submarines.[1]

A New Soviet Strategy

Marshal Rodion Ya. Malinovskiy, the Minister of Defense from 1957 to 1967, certainly was a supporter of Gorshkov. But the revolution in military affairs of the middle and late 1950s addressed issues far greater than naval matters, for the advent of ballistic missiles and nuclear weapons was demanding new military strategies. Particular efforts were begun in May 1957, to bring "scientific method" to the development of new strategies, the Soviet General Staff beginning formal discussions the following year. Beginning in 1960 a series of top secret writings on the problems of future war began to be published as the "Special Collection" in the classified Defense Ministry journal *Voyennaya Mysl* (Military Thought).[2]

In 1962, however, Marshal Malinovskiy declared, "The task of propagandizing [in the sense of disseminating and inculcating] the progressive views and conclusions of Soviet military doctrine is highly important because some units of military personnel still live with old, outmoded notions about the nature of modern warfare."[3] By that year the views of the Soviet military leadership were sufficiently developed for publication in an open forum—the volume *Voyennaya Strategiya* (Military Strategy) under the overall editorship of Marshal Vasiliy D. Sokolovskiy.[4] This was the first major Soviet work on military strategy since the mid-1920s. While most of the book addressed overall strategic and defense issues, there was significant discussion of the Soviet Navy. After briefly discussing the

operations of the Navy in World War II—"mainly in inland seas"—
Marshal Sokolovskiy and his all-Army contributors declared, "In a
future world war the fleet may have more responsibilities. The world
oceans will be the theaters of military operations for the Navy":

> The main aim of military operations for naval forces and in
> naval theaters is the defeat of the enemy fleet and disruption
> of his naval and sea communications lines. In addition, there
> may be the task of delivering nuclear missile strikes against
> coastal targets, support of the ground troops, the carrying
> out of maritime shipping, and protection of our own sea
> lines of communications. The presence of a fleet of missile-
> carrying nuclear submarines and naval missile-carrying
> aircraft will make it possible to conduct naval operations
> decisively against a strong naval enemy.[5]

This was—from a traditionalist's viewpoint—a major concession to
the aspirations of the Navy. But even this was not enough. Admiral
Vladimir A. Alafuzov, the Deputy Chief of the Main Naval Staff in
1944–1945 and head of the Naval Academy (i.e., Naval War College)
from 1945 to 1953, took the lead in calling for still more concessions
to the Navy in argumentative reviews of *Military Strategy*. For example, Marshal Sokolovskiy and his colleagues had claimed that even
submarines were vulnerable, asserting that "submarines can be successfully combatted by anti-submarine submarines with missiles and
torpedoes, by planes, by anti-submarine surface vessels with hydro-
foils and armed with nuclear weapons, and also by destroyers, fast
torpedo boats, and helicopters."[6]

This catalog of anti-submarine forces was a criticism of the Navy's
considerable investment in submarines, especially nuclear-propelled
undersea craft, as well as an attempt to reduce the perceived threat
from U.S. Polaris missile submarines. Admiral Alafuzov's most bit-
ing critique of *Military Strategy* was that its Army contributors had

declared "without any basis whatever . . . that the missile-carrying nuclear submarine is in reality vulnerable and that an effective means against it 'is the homing missile launched from a submarine or surface ship.' Such an unproven conclusion seems brash and unconvincing. Apparently, the indisputable fact that nuclear submarines will operate only when submerged was not taken into consideration."[7]

The Navy's opposition to even the comparatively favorable first edition of *Military Strategy* led to specific changes in a revised second edition that appeared in 1963. Some of these changes only compounded the misstatements of the previous editions, but there were significant changes, such as:

> Combat with missile-carrying submarines has now been shifted to great distances from the coast—to the open seas and oceans. The former coastal system of anti-submarine defense will now be ineffective against missile-carrying submarines. For successfully combating them, a reliable system of reconnaissance is necessary which will ensure the timely detection of enemy submarines, particularly those carrying missiles, the exact determination of the coordinates of their location, and the guidance of active weapons against them.[8]

This second edition of *Military Strategy* also contained several significant, albeit small, additions that pointed to the increased recognition of the Soviet Navy. The phrase "on the oceans" was added in a lengthy statement about future Navy missions, and to the list of targets assigned to the Strategic Rocket Forces were added missile strikes on enemy naval bases, ports, and centers of the shipbuilding industry by "missile-carrying nuclear submarines."

Admiral Gorshkov's efforts were having success: The Navy—obviously backed by the Party leadership and at least some Army officers—was achieving new status in Soviet defense policy. The Party backing was, of course, essential, because of the centralized control of both industry and the military by the Party leadership— that is, the Presidium (after April 1966, renamed the Politburo).

With Khrushchev's fall from power in October 1964, the Navy gained increased support at the highest level of national leadership. Khrushchev was replaced as Party chief by Leonid Brezhnev, his protégé, who had been a member of the Presidium since 1957. Brezhnev had been under enemy fire in the landings at Novorossiysk in September 1943, and had served as the chief political officer of the Navy in 1953. The No. 2 man in the post-Khrushchev government was Andrey N. Kosygin, a native of Leningrad, the country's shipbuilding center and a close associate of the late Andrey Zhdanov.

Minister of Defense R.Ya. Malinovskiy, credited by Khrushchev with proposing Gorshkov to head the Navy, was a supporter of Gorshkov until his own death in 1967. Malinovskiy's successor was Marshal Andrey A. Grechko, who had been closely associated with Gorshkov in the Black Sea–Caucasus operations. Grechko, like Malinovskiy, was made a candidate member of the Presidium upon his appointment as Minister of Defense. During the reshuffling of the Politburo in April 1973, Grechko became a full member of the ruling body, the first professional soldier to serve in the highest government body since Marshal Zhukov's abortive tenure in 1957.

One other appointment to the Politburo (as now known) should be considered in regard to Navy issues. In the 1973 reorganization Georgiy V. Romanov, the First Secretary of the Leningrad region's Communist Party, became a candidate member of the Politburo. The 50-year-old Romanov became the youngest member of the Soviet ruling group. He was a 1953 graduate of the Leningrad Shipbuilding Institute and had worked as a researcher in, and then section chief of, the ship design bureau at the Zhdanov shipyard before becoming engaged full-time in Party work in Leningrad.[9] In March 1976, he would become a full member of the Politburo. Thus, he represented additional support for the Admiral Gorshkov and Navy at the highest level of the government.

Within the Navy

There were debates on naval strategy within the Navy as well at this time. Such principles as concentration of and cooperation among naval forces and maneuver were the subjects of these intramural debates, which were touched off by Rear Admiral Kazimir A. Stalbo in 1961 in *Morskoy Sbornik* and other publications.[10] Promoted to vice admiral, Stalbo continued to write frequently, generally as a spokesman for Admiral Gorshkov's views. The issues included whether the concentration of firepower was to be achieved through the maneuver of ships, aircraft, and submarines, or by weapon trajectories, or by the number of missiles fired or the yield of their nuclear warheads.

Admiral Gorshkov himself became a major participant, with his byline articles appearing frequently in *Morskoy Sbornik* and other Soviet journals. They often were controversial and called attention to differences within the Soviet military hierarchy and the Navy. In contrast to the platitudes that usually appeared under the bylines of Soviet military commanders, Gorshkov's articles were well-developed expositions of the background, problems, and often of proposed solutions.

To some observers Admiral Gorshkov's most significant single article was "The Development of Soviet Naval Science," published in *Morskoy Sbornik* in 1967. It outlined the impact on the Navy of the 1950s revolution in military strategy. Arguably, however, much more impressive—and significant—was his "Navies in War and in Peace" in the February 1972 issue of *Morskoy Sbornik*.

Captain 1st Rank Mikhail S. Monakov's superbly written and sourced biography of Gorshkov, titled simply *GLAVKOM*, the Russian equivalent of "CinC"—points out that by the late 1960s the admiral had grown tired of answering inquiries from the General Staff. Those inquiries reflected misunderstanding of the capabilities and missions of the Navy. He decided to break his prolonged public silence and to embark on a series of articles that would eventually be the foundation for his seminal work *Seapower of the State*. Monakov quotes Admiral Gorshkov as recalling, "Leading the Navy, speaking with our academic scholars and naval research scientists, organizing the operational training of the fleets and central organs, I ever more thought of the necessity of my personal participation in bringing to light many issues facing the country and navy in the course of the missile and nuclear stage of its development."[11]

The Gorshkov Series

The February 1972 article mentioned above was the first in a series of 11 in which Admiral Gorshkov declared that he was writing to "define the trends and principles of the change in the role and position of navies in war and also in their employment in peacetime as an instrument of state policy."[12] The *Morskoy Sbornik* series—running to almost 55,000 words—appears to have been intended for internal education and clarification among the senior policy officials, as well as domestic, navy audiences. Unlike in the United States, where military leaders periodically take their causes to the Congress and the open press in search of political support, in the Soviet system such support must be developed within the confines of the Politburo and lesser government institutions.

A condensation of the Gorshkov's series appeared in the General Staff journal *Voyennaya Mysl*, demonstrating that he had sufficient confidence in his views to further "educate" the general leadership of the defense establishment. Subsequently, the series was published in the Soviet Union and in the West in book form, as *The Seapower of the State*.[13]

Numerous appraisals of the series and subsequent book appeared in the Western professional press (see the selected bibliography).

Indeed, the U.S. Naval Institute, the Navy's professional (but private) society, collected the initial articles in a book, *Red Star Rising at Sea*.[14] Admiral Elmo R. Zumwalt Jr., the Chief of Naval Operations when the *Morskoy Sbornik* series began, provided an overall introduction; each of the collection's 11 chapters was accompanied by a commentary by a senior U.S. naval officer. These commentaries were apparently required by the Naval Institute's Board of Control to "qualify" or "explain" the series to American readers. All of these flag-level contributors were retired, except for Vice Admiral Stansfield Turner, at the time President of the Naval War College (and later Director of Central Intelligence in the Jimmy Carter administration).

Admiral Zumwalt, in his introduction, identified what he considered three important aspects of the series:

> What we are seeing in Gorshkov's series is [first,] the rationale for decisions already taken by the Soviet hierarchy. Gorshkov is not advocating new departures in Soviet policy. He is recapitulating the arguments which have already proven persuasive in launching the Soviets on a campaign to acquire a naval force—in Gorshkov's words—"second to none." . . .
>
> The second point is Gorshkov's emphasis on technology, and the crucial influence it exerts on naval weapons and tactics. Gorshkov has shown himself adept at introducing advanced technology into the Soviet Navy, and in focusing his efforts on those areas where technology promises the highest battle pay-off—electronic warfare, missiles, and advanced propulsion techniques. . . .
>
> Finally, Gorshkov gives us a clear indication of Soviet mission priorities. In this area he is careful to distinguish between peacetime and wartime missions. As the title of his series suggests, he believes navies can be as important in advancing the state's political objectives in peacetime as they are in defending vital national interests in war.[15]

Some Western analysts argued over whether the Admiral Gorshkov series and book represented views already accepted by the Soviet leadership or if the admiral still was having to agitate for an expanded fleet and naval role in Soviet military strategy. In either case, the Gorshkov work was definitely a guide to the probable future development of the Soviet Navy, at least under the stewardship of Gorshkov. James McConnell, a leading U.S. analyst of Soviet defense policy, wrote that Gorshkov was in his articles "performing a well-known function of military theoreticians—formulating a 'concrete expression of doctrine,' i.e., a military-scientific work which takes doctrine as its point of departure, rationalizes it and draws out its detailed implications, so that it can be implemented."[16]

The breadth of subjects addressed by Gorshkov in his series was considerable—national policy affecting navies, the economic relationship of the state to the navy, tactics, surface ships, submarines, naval aviation, amphibious warfare, inter-service cooperation, naval forces in the political presence role, the need for emphasis on education and training in the navy, the need for innovation in the fleet, and others. Many American and Western European reviewers of Gorshkov's writings compared him with Alfred T. Mahan, the U.S. naval officer whose classic work *The Influence of Sea Power upon History, 1660–1783*, published in 1890, became a primer for the German kaiser and President Theodore Roosevelt in the building of their navies.[17] In a commentary accompanying the first Gorshkov article in *Red Star Rising at Sea,* Rear Admiral George H. Miller, a leading U.S. naval strategist, concluded,

Admiral Gorshkov is without doubt one of the foremost authorities on naval strategy of modern times. His writings should be studied as assiduously as European statesmen studied Alfred Thayer Mahan's works during the years preceding World War I. They are of considerable importance in determining the nature and scope of the big-power competition to be expected in the years to come.

One can find very little if any material in this first installment which is not important. All of it is deadly serious.[18]

Admiral Miller was correct. The value, however, of Admiral Gorshkov's writings to the West lay not in the guidance it implied as to how its leaders should use navies, as with Mahan's. Rather, they were a guide to the planned Soviet use of navies—and commercial and research ships—on the world's oceans. Of particular significance was Gorshkov's definition of supremacy at sea and control of the sea: "The Mahan theory of 'supremacy at sea,' according to which only a general engagement of major line forces could lead to a victory, which was considered indisputable, had a considerable effect on the one-sided trend in the development of navies. This theory did not at all take into account not only the near future, but even the notable trends in the development of [contemporary] naval technology."[19]

Admiral Gorshkov preferred to Mahan the Russian naval strategist and historian Rear Admiral Vladimir A. Belli, who wrote, "To achieve superiority of forces over the enemy in the main sector and to pin him down in the secondary sectors at the time of the operations means to achieve control of the sea in a theater or a sector of a theater, i.e., to create such a situation that the enemy will be paralyzed or constrained in his operations, or weakened and thereby hampered from interfering with our execution of a given operation or in our execution of our own operational mission."[20] Thus, while the United States and its key allies sought to operate warships and merchant ships in numerous sea areas in support of far-ranging maritime interests, the Soviet Union would seek superiority of naval forces in only the "main sector" of a conflict and "pin down" U.S. forces elsewhere to prevent them from reinforcing the main sector. The Soviet Navy's *Okean* exercises, discussed in the following chapter, provide support for this thesis.

CHAPTER 13

To the World's Oceans

In time of peace a superior warship on the spot can
achieve results not obtainable in other ways and without
regard to the purpose for which the ship was built.
What counts is the existence of the Soviet Navy, not
the original motives of its builders.

—Sir James Cable, "Political Applications of Limited Naval Force" (1970)

Warships have been used to carry out national interests both in
war and in peace since man first used ships in coastal waters
for fishing and trade. Periodically tsarist Russian warships were useful in carrying out the nation's political goals, on occasion exerting
influence on seas and oceans far from Russia's borders. The most significant examples of such distant operations were the Russian fleets
in the Mediterranean during the Napoleonic era. These warships
fought several victorious battles and carried out successful amphibious assaults against Corfu and other islands.

But too often Russian naval forces were impotent because of the
indifference of Russian governments to the navy, inefficiencies and
corruption within the Russian Admiralty, the devastation wrought
on the nation by revolutions and civil war, and the losses in World
War II. From the end of World War II into the 1960s, Soviet naval
forces played no role on the international scene—the existing fleet
was of no significant help to Soviet foreign policy. This especially

was evident during the Cuban missile crisis of 1962. After Stalin's death in 1953, as Khrushchev and his colleagues sought to extend relations with the West as well as the Third World, Soviet warships began to make foreign port visits. The newly completed cruiser *Sverdlov* represented the Soviet Union at Britain's Coronation Review at Spithead in June 1953. A year later the *Ordzhonikidze* of that class visited Helsinki, and the similar *Admiral Ushakov* visited Stockholm. In October 1955, the *Sverdlov* and her sister ship the *Aleksandr Suvorov*, with Admiral A. G. Golovko (then commanding the Fourth Fleet in the Baltic) embarked, called at Portsmouth, England. The following April the *Ordzhonikidze* carried Party Secretary Khrushchev and Marshal Nikolai Bulganin on a state visit to England. More ship visits to Western and Third World nations followed, and the practice was accelerated with Admiral Gorshkov's selection as head of the Navy.

After decimating Stalin's naval construction program, Khrushchev approved a modest naval program for defense of the homeland—submarines and aircraft armed with anti-ship missiles—in part by destroying U.S. aircraft carriers that could threaten the homeland with nuclear strike aircraft. Then, as noted in the preceding chapter, after the Kennedy-McNamara decisions to accelerate the buildup of U.S. strategic weapons, the Soviet Navy again acquired a major strategic role, initially marked by the large-scale construction of the "modern" Yankee ballistic missile submarines.

Navies in Peace

By the mid-1950s Admiral Gorshkov and other Soviet naval leaders had begun to think of the future Navy as an ocean-going fleet that could effectively support Soviet state interests on distant seas in peace as well as in war. It has become convenient to point to the Soviet setback in the Cuban missile crisis of October 1962 as the beginning of the Soviet naval buildup. But by that time the first generation of nuclear submarines already was at sea; the *Moskva*, Kashin, and Kynda classes of missile-armed warships were on the building ways; and Soviet ship design bureaus were hard at work on other, larger, and more capable surface warships, as well as advanced submarines.

The development of aircraft carriers had been proposed in the late 1930s in connection with Stalin's plans for an ocean-going fleet, and again immediately after World War II. Finally, in the early 1960s, detailed design work actually began on a "true"—full flight deck—aircraft carrier. The technical requirements were approved in 1968, and the keel was laid at Nikolayev on the Black Sea for the first *Kiev*-class carrier in 1970. Allowing for the ordering and manufacture of long-lead-time components, the decision to go ahead with the program would have had to have been made in time for its inclusion in the 1966–1970 Five-Year Plan and the third (1969–1979) post–World War II Shipbuilding Plan.

There are indications that the Suez crisis of 1956 and the subsequent Israeli invasion of Sinai and Anglo-French assault on Egypt may have marked the start of the Soviet buildup, and the carrier decision. In a speech at the U.S. Naval War College, Rear Admiral George H. Miller, a leading U.S. strategist, postulated that "the year 1956, the year of the Suez crisis, can be marked as the beginning of what I regard as the Soviet break-out from historical confines of their landmass competition for world power and influence."[1] According to Miller, the American failure to support the Anglo-French assault at Suez was "the signal . . . that Suez, long regarded as a critically important strategic crossroads of the western maritime powers, was no longer considered of vital importance to U.S. interests, and that the U.S. itself had backed away from massive retaliation as its main military option, and had indeed itself been deterred by its own nuclear retaliation threat from taking appropriate action in its own interest." The Suez assault occurred in 1956—the year that Gorshkov became CinC of the Soviet Navy.

The Soviets were helpless to interfere with the Anglo-French-Israeli assault on Egypt, which, under President Abdel Nasser, had recently nationalized the Suez Canal. The Soviet regime was seeking to make Egypt a client—a key foothold in the critical Middle East area. Only after the administration of President Dwight D. Eisenhower had announced its absolute opposition to the Anglo-French assault could Moscow "take action," threatening missile attacks against Britain and France if the invasion were not halted. Moscow also warned Israel—which had initiated the assault—that its very existence was at stake.

Following the cease-fire, the Soviet government threatened to send military "volunteers" to help Nasser. The Soviets did not have the conventional military forces to intervene beyond the lands that bordered on the Soviet states, nor could they confront the West at sea. In recalling the events of 1956, Khrushchev was to write that "before that time, the Soviet Union—and Imperial Russia before it—had always treated the Near East as belonging to England and France . . . [B]y 1956, we were able to step in and assist President Nasser and the Arab peoples."[2]

Soviet appreciation of the value of military use of the sea has been reinforced several times in the years since the Suez crisis by the use of U.S. naval forces to support American national interests: in Lebanon (1958), Cuba (1962), the Dominican Republic (1965), Vietnam (1964–1973), again in Lebanon (1983–1984), and Grenada (1983). The initial 2001 "assault" into Afghanistan—a land-locked country—by U.S. forces was launched from aircraft carriers and from surface warships firing Tomahawk land-attack missiles; the strikes were followed by special operations forces, carried by helicopters from the carrier *Kitty Hawk* (CV 63), operating in the Arabian Sea. Great Britain too had used aircraft carriers to carry out "peacetime" operations, from West Africa to the Middle East and Indonesia.

The use of U.S. naval forces was almost always successful. Admiral Gorshkov's series "Navies in War and Peace"—by its content as well as its title—showed his awareness of this situation. In particular, his penultimate article in the 1972–1973 series notes, "Owing to the high mobility and endurance of its combatants, the Navy possesses the capability to vividly demonstrate the economic and military power of a country beyond its borders *during peacetime*. This quality is normally used by the political leadership of the imperialist states to show their readiness for decisive actions, to deter or suppress the intentions of potential enemies, as well as to support 'friendly states.'" (emphasis added).[3] This view of the peacetime role of the Soviet Navy was echoed in a U.S. intelligence report of the mid-1970s: "Naval activity and port visits, particularly in the Third World, probably have improved the Soviet Union's position with some foreign political leaders, but it has irritated others. . . . [I]n many countries, especially developed countries with a maritime tradition, naval activity is perceived as an important element in the international political balance. As long as this view continues to be prominent, the Soviet Navy's peacetime operations will have significant political impact."[4]

After briefly discussing the technological advancements in the warships employed for gunboat diplomacy, Admiral Gorshkov continued his assessment of naval peacetime roles with a fundamental observation:

> Consequently, the role of the navy is not limited to the execution of important missions in armed combat. While representing a formidable force in war, it has always been a political weapon of the imperialist states and an important support for diplomacy in peacetime owing to its inherent qualities which permit it to a greater degree than other branches of the armed forces to exert pressure on potential enemies without the direct employment of weaponry.

And today the imperialists are striving to use the quality of navies, such as the capability of making a visible demonstration of force, to put political pressure on other states and to support the diplomatic moves of one's own country to deter potential enemies.[5]

Turning from his discussion of the political uses of naval forces by the West, both historical and current, Admiral Gorshkov advised his readers, "There is still another side to the question[:] . . . [w]ith the emergence of the Soviet Navy onto the ocean expanses, our warships are calling with continually greater frequency at foreign ports, fulfilling the role of 'plenipotentiaries' of the Socialist countries. In the last three years alone, some 1,000 Soviet combatants and auxiliaries have visited the ports of 60 countries in Europe, Asia, Africa, and Latin America. More than 200,000 of our officers and rated and non-rated men have visited the shores of foreign states."[6]

Soon after in his text, Admiral Gorshkov offered a forecast of the future: "Further growth in the power of our navy will be characterized by an intensification of its international mission. While appearing within our armed forces as an imposing factor in regard to restraining imperialist aggression and ventures, at the same time the Soviet Navy is a consolidator of international relations, strengthening friendship and cooperation among peace-loving nations."[7]

Into the Mediterranean

In mid-1954 Gorshkov, then a vice admiral and commander of the Soviet Black Sea Fleet, led a cruiser and two destroyers on a visit to communist Albania, the first Soviet naval visit to the Mediterranean since the 1930s. There were a few more ship visits to Albania and Yugoslavia during the next few years.

A continuous Soviet naval presence in the Mediterranean began in mid-1964, when a cruiser and two destroyers passed through the Turkish Straits and entered the "central sea." The move came shortly after President Lyndon Johnson had advised the Turkish prime minister that if Turkish troops landed on trouble-plagued Cyprus and the Soviet Union responded with military action, Turkey could not be assured that the United States would come to its defense. This was a watershed point in Turkish-American relations—both members of NATO. Subsequently, the Turkish foreign minister visited the Soviet Union for a week of discussions. Unquestionably, the passage of the Soviet ships through the Turkish-controlled straits was on the agenda. Strengthened Soviet-Turkish economic relations followed those talks.

During 1964 the Soviet Navy maintained an average of five ships in the Mediterranean. Thereafter, the number gradually increased, with numerous port visits, especially to Algeria, Egypt, and Syria. (The U.S. Sixth Fleet in the Mediterranean at the time generally consisted of some 35 ships, including 2 large aircraft carriers with some 150 aircraft on board, as well as an amphibious squadron with about 2,000 Marines embarked. The carrier-based aircraft included several squadrons of nuclear-capable strike aircraft.)

With the start of sustained out-of-area—that is, out of "home area"—deployments in 1964 the emphasis initially was on the Mediterranean, for the decade 1964–1973. In the five from years 1965 to 1969, more than one-half of those deployments were to the Mediterranean. Only beginning in 1970, the year of the multi-ocean *Okean* exercises, were there more ships deployed in the Atlantic and other areas, albeit with the Mediterranean still having about 40 percent of the out-of-area "ship days."

Of the Soviet Navy's out-of-area deployments in the decade 1964 through 1973:[8]

25%   submarines (nuclear and conventional, strategic and general purpose)

23%   surface combatants and amphibious ships

53%   auxiliaries (including intelligence collection ships [AGIs] and merchant ships operating under naval supervision).

When the next Arab-Israeli conflict erupted, in June 1967, a steady stream of Soviet naval ships began passing through the Turkish Straits until there were about 70 in the Mediterranean. After that war the Soviets maintained an average of 35 to 40 ships in the Mediterranean, including 10 to 15 surface combatants (cruisers, destroyers, frigates). At times these included one of the *Moskva*-class missile-helicopter carriers, two or three amphibious ships, six or seven diesel-electric submarines, and an occasional nuclear submarine, plus 10 to 15 auxiliary ships. Airfields in Egypt were used from 1967 to 1972, to enable Soviet land-based reconnaissance and anti-submarine aircraft to operate over the Mediterranean without overflying Greece or Turkey, both NATO members.[9] Those aircraft, with Soviet Navy crews, usually wore Egyptian markings. At times Soviet aircraft were sighted at bases in other Arab countries, including the former U.S. Wheelus Air Force Base in Libya. In addition to being in a position to confront the U.S. Sixth Fleet during the Arab-Israeli conflict, the Fifth Eskadra—as the Soviet naval force in the Mediterranean was known—placed ships in major Egyptian harbors to deter Israeli attacks against those ports. Reflecting on this period, Rear Admiral Petr N. Navoytsev would declare, "The presence of the Soviet Navy in the Mediterranean is a most important factor for stabilization in that troubled area of the globe."[10]

Soviet capabilities for rapid reinforcement of the Fifth Eskadra were demonstrated in October–November 1973, when within a few days of a new outbreak of hostilities between Israel and Egypt and Syria, Soviet ships again began steaming south through the Dardanelles. A second group of submarines from the Northern Fleet began passing through the Strait of Gibraltar, doubling the Soviet submarine force in the Mediterranean.[11]

By early November, when the 1973 crisis in the Middle East reached its peak with the threat of unilateral Soviet intervention unless Israeli troops withdrew from certain territory, there were 96 Soviet naval units in the Mediterranean: 27 cruisers, destroyers, and frigates; 2 Nanuchka–class missile corvettes; 8 amphibious ships; 36 support ships; and 23 submarines, several of which were nuclear propelled. The surface ships and submarines were armed with a total of 88 anti-ship missiles. The U.S. Sixth Fleet reached a strength of 60 ships during the crisis. The U.S. force, however, contained 3 large aircraft carriers with some 200 aircraft embarked, while the only Soviet combat aircraft in the immediate Mediterranean area were an estimated 12 Tu–22 Blinder turbojet bombers based in Iraq.

Battle for the First Salvo

The proximity of two battle fleets in the eastern Mediterranean during the 1973 crisis brought to the fore Admiral Gorshkov's concept of the "Battle for the First Salvo" (sometimes translated as "The Battle *of* the First Salvo"). The concept called for the concentration of Soviet forces and the targeting of U.S. formations to deliver an overwhelming, pre-emptive strike at the commencement of hostilities, ideally destroying, or at least crippling, the enemy's ability to fight. The concept recognized that despite the advantage of surprise, the attacking Soviet units might themselves not survive the encounter. According to Gorshkov, "The battle for the first salvo is taking on a special meaning in naval battle under present day conditions (conditions including the possible employment of combat means of colossal power [nuclear weapons]). Delay in the employment of weapons in a naval battle or operation inevitably will be fraught with the most serious or even fatal consequences, regardless of where the fleet is located, at sea or in port."[12]

The concept of achieving naval superiority for at least a limited time or location by a concentrated pre-emptive attack was not new in Russian or Soviet naval thought; it goes back to the tsarist era. It was further developed by naval strategists in the early days of the Soviet Union as a solution to the problem of how a weaker navy might deal with a more powerful enemy. U.S. Navy analyst Robert Herrick pointed out that this concept remained a constant throughout the changes and permutations of Soviet naval doctrine over the years.[13]

A particularly dramatic illustration of this first-salvo tactic *almost* took place during the Arab-Israeli war of 1973, when the Soviet Fifth Eskadra was arrayed for a pre-emptive strike on the three U.S. aircraft carriers and two helicopter carriers of the U.S. Sixth Fleet. The U.S. attack carriers were operating aircraft armed with nuclear weapons and were within striking distance of the Soviet Union. In the face of the increased tension of the U.S.-Soviet confrontation, the Soviet Navy was prepared, as its doctrine dictated, for a pre-emptive strike on the carriers. The confrontation is detailed in an exhaustive study of the incident published in the U.S. *Naval War College Review*:

> Largely due to unrivalled U.S. air superiority in the region, first-strike was given special importance in the 1973 exercises, reflecting Soviet "battle of the first salvo" doctrine. In his 8 January 1973 journal entry, Semenov [Captain 1st Rank Yevgeniy Semenov, Chief of Staff of the Soviet Fifth Eskadra at the time] writes of an officers' briefing on anti-carrier warfare: "Ship attack groups need to use all weaponry for assaults on aerial attack groups: missiles, artillery, torpedoes, jet-propelled rockets—the whole lot—since it is unlikely that anything will remain afloat after an air strike. We are all kamikazes."[14]

An important aspect of the first-salvo concept, of course, was precise targeting of key Western warships (as well as submarines) during a crisis and at the very start of hostilities. The "tattletales" entrusted with that task were omnipresent in U.S. and NATO naval exercises and "observing" forward-deployed U.S. aircraft carriers. Beyond noting how the ships and forces operated, the tattletales could provide real-time targeting for over-the-horizon weapons. Indeed, it became a standard joke that some tattletales had the NATO signal book and that task force commanders could signal them when changes in course were planned.

Some of these tattletales were dedicated intelligence collectors (AGIs), some were warships—destroyers or frigates. In time many Soviet destroyers were fitted with—in addition to their standard anti-aircraft/anti-ship weapons—*aft-firing* Styx-type missiles, to add their "voices" to the incoming long-range missiles as they sped away.[15] Of course, U.S. and NATO forces also were dogged by Soviet torpedo-attack and cruise missile submarines.

Significantly, neither of the two *Moskva*-class missile-helicopter carriers was in the Mediterranean during the fall 1973 crisis, nor the *Nikolayev*, lead ship of the latest Soviet ASW cruisers of the Kara class, which had made her Mediterranean debut a few months earlier. The absence of these ships may have indicated that the reinforcement of the Mediterranean *eskadra* was less than an all-out effort. Indeed, the initial posture of the Soviet force was not threatening—rather meant to demonstrate the potential of Soviet naval power and practice for the "next time." However, during the later phases of the crisis, in late October, Admiral Zumwalt, the U.S. Chief of Naval Operations at the time, would recall, "I doubt that major units of the U.S. Navy were ever in a tenser situation since World War II ended than the Sixth Fleet in the Mediterranean was for the week after the alert was declared."[16] The Commander, Sixth Fleet agreed: "The U.S. Sixth Fleet and the Soviet Mediterranean Fleet were, in effect, sitting in a pond in close proximity and the stage set for the hitherto unlikely 'war at sea' scenario was set. This situation prevailed for several days. Both fleets were obviously in a high readiness posture for whatever might come next, although it appeared that neither fleet knew exactly what to expect."[17]

The Soviets derived considerable benefit from the 1973 war and the confrontation with the Sixth Fleet. These benefits were political and diplomatic, including the Arab oil embargo of the West and the reopening of the Suez Canal under Egyptian control. There also was a sharp division within NATO as the European members—except for Portugal—refused to help in the U.S. shipment of needed war supplies to Israel.[18] The Soviet Navy thus had played a key role in the crisis and confrontation of October 1973.

And Nuclear Strike?

Closely related to the concept of the Battle for the First Salvo was Soviet nuclear doctrine. The initial Soviet nuclear doctrine postulated that any war with the West would inevitably and rapidly escalate to a strategic nuclear exchange. This concept was in line with the defense policies of Nikita Khrushchev, who sought to reduce large (and expensive) conventional military forces in favor of a minimal strategic force—primarily intercontinental ballistic missiles—and "unconventional" efforts against the West, such as wars of national liberation in the Third World.

For the first decade of Soviet nuclear strategy, the Soviet leadership believed that "in the very first minutes of the war the belligerents may use up their missiles and aircraft . . . along with their stockpiles of nuclear weapons, in order to destroy and devastate the enemy's most important targets throughout his entire territory." This statement by the Chief of the Soviet General Staff, Marshal of the Soviet Union V. D. Sokolovskiy, in his *Military Strategy* (1962), reflected the model of *immediate* escalation.

This outlook—coupled with the Soviet "embarrassment" in the Cuban missile crisis—led to the Soviet Navy fully regaining its role in strategic strike, with acceleration of the Project 667/Yankee ballistic missile submarines. Also, Soviet surface ships and submarines were rapidly being armed with nuclear anti-ship and anti-submarine weapons; with all submarines carrying nuclear torpedoes.

Also, unlike the U.S. Navy, the Soviet Navy was building nuclear defense features into its ships. Major warships and specific small missile craft all had a "citadel," where the crew could operate the ships protected from nuclear weapon effects. Also provided were decontamination stations for crewmen passing from the outside— where they wore protective suits—into the protected areas.

By a decade later, in the post-Khrushchev period, this attitude toward nuclear conflict had been modified significantly. Writing in 1976 in *Krasnaya Zvezda*, the daily newspaper of the Ministry of Defense, a general officer warned that a conventional conflict in Europe "carries with it constant danger of being escalated into a nuclear war." This meant that a nuclear exchange was no longer automatic at the start of a conflict; rather, there was a distinct danger of its occurring during the course of a conventional conflict. But the same article also implied that even a Soviet–NATO conflict reaching a nuclear phase would not necessarily become an all-out, intercontinental nuclear exchange between the Soviet Union and the United States.

By the 1980s, Soviet writers on strategic doctrine were addressing the possibility that a conventional conflict with the West could last for several months. While Soviet combat forces—including the Navy—still were being configured to fight extended conventional conflicts, it remained important for the combat forces to be able to conduct *all* types of military operations.

To Distant Seas

The increased Soviet naval activity in the Mediterranean was followed by an increase in operations in other areas, as new ships joined the Soviet Fleet and Admiral Gorshkov's officers and sailors gained at-sea experience. In the post-Stalin period there was great political interest in the Indian Ocean, which washes the shores of the Asian subcontinent and eastern Africa, both areas in which former European colonies were becoming independent. Also, the continued strife between Pakistan and India was of considerable attraction to the leadership in Moscow. Here was rich ground for Soviet political and economic activity—supported by merchant shipping and possibly by naval forces.

The first Soviet naval visit to the Indian Ocean area occurred in February 1965, when Rear Admiral Georgiy F. Stepanov in the destroyer *Naporistyy* visited the Red Sea port of Massawa, Ethiopia. This was the start of a regular schedule of Soviet warship visits to Massawa; Admiral Gorshkov himself made a visit there with the destroyer *Gnevnyy* in January 1967. Massawa was soon joined by other ports on the Soviet calling list: Admiral Nikolay N. Amelko, commanding the Pacific Fleet, led the *Sverdlov*-class cruiser *Dmitriy Pozharskiy* and two other ships to Madras and Bombay in 1968; the cruiser then visited Aden, Ceylon, Iraq, Pakistan, Somalia, and Yemen. Late that year the Kynda-class missile cruiser *Admiral Fokin* paid a visit to Mombasa while a submarine tender with two diesel submarines and an oiler visited Dar-es-Salaam. These visits led to an almost continuous Soviet naval presence in the Indian Ocean.

This naval presence was part of broader Soviet involvement in the region. First, Soviet logistic support for the Hanoi regime during the Vietnam War of the 1960s relied heavily upon merchant ships that sailed from the Baltic and Black Sea ports through the Suez Canal (until it was closed in June 1967, after which they steamed around Africa), and across the Indian Ocean to Haiphong and lesser ports of North Vietnam. Second, Soviet leaders helped to mediate the Indian-Pakistani conflict of 1965. India was a most desirable ally for the Soviets because of Pakistan's close relationship with both the United States and Communist China. This provided the basis for closer ties between Moscow and Delhi.

A series of Soviet warship calls to Indian Ocean ports and a visit to India by Admiral Gorshkov in February 1968 marked the beginning of intensive Soviet military assistance to that country, including the transfer of Soviet surface ships and submarines, and technical assistance in developing a large naval base at Vishakhapatnam. Indo-Soviet political relations reached a high point in August 1971, with the signing of a Treaty of Peace and Friendship, which included articles on military assistance. Four months later India invaded and overran

East Pakistan; Soviet-provided weapons were heavily employed by the Indians. On the naval side of the conflict, Soviet-provided surface warships and submarines helped the Indians to heavily damage the Pakistani Navy. Indian-manned Osa missile boats sank one Pakistani destroyer and damaged a second, sank several merchant ships, and fired their SS-N-2 Styx missiles against shore targets.

On the eve of that conflict both the Soviet Union and United States had heavily reinforced their naval forces in the Indian Ocean. While the Soviet buildup was slower and smaller than that of the United States—which was able to deploy rapidly a task force centered on the nuclear-propelled aircraft carrier *Enterprise* (CVAN 65)—the December 1971 conflict did demonstrate the readiness of the Soviets to confront the United States at sea.[19] Naval analyst Bruce Watson recorded, "The Soviet [Indian Ocean] squadron's presence increased from 1,200 ship days in 1968 (a daily average of approximately three ships) to 10,500 ship days in 1974 (a daily average of approximately 29 ships. . . .)."[20]

In this period the Soviets began to use the island of Socotra at the approaches to the Gulf of Aden and astride the southern entrance to the Red Sea as a fleet anchorage. Mauritius, too, became a favored Soviet port of call, and Soviet warships began to moor regularly to buoys in the Seychelle Islands and the Chagos Archipelago. The subsequent Soviet involvement in the continuing conflict between Ethiopia and Somalia, first on one side and then the other, saw Soviet naval and merchant ships in the ports of the ally—of the moment.

During this period the Soviet support of the Indian armed forces was considerable. Most significant, India became the sixth nation to operate nuclear-propelled submarines—after the United States, Soviet Union, Great Britain, France, and China—when Indian Navy leased the 20-year-old Charlie (Project 670) submarine *K-43*. Renamed *Chakra* (wheel), she raised the Indian colors on 4 January 1988, and was operated by that navy until returned to the Soviet Navy in January 1991. The *Chakra* served in a training role for some 150 Indian submariners, supervised by Soviet personnel. Also, in 2004 the Indian government purchased the retired Soviet aircraft carrier *Admiral Gorshkov*. In 2013, after extensive modifications the carrier became operational in the Indian Navy.[21] Admiral Gorshkov had been a prime participant in the massive support provided to the Indian armed forces.

At almost the same time as the increase of Soviet naval activity in the Indian Ocean, mostly with ships from the Pacific Fleet, naval units from the Northern and Black Sea Fleets began to steam farther into the Atlantic. There was no significant Soviet naval activity in the western Atlantic immediately following the aborted Soviet missile venture in Cuba in October 1962, when all four Soviet Foxtrot (Project 641) diesel-electric submarines in the Caribbean area were detected and identified by U.S. naval forces. That was the situation until in mid-June 1969, when two diesel attack submarines, a November (Project 627A) nuclear attack submarine, and a submarine tender departed from the Barents Sea, steamed around Norway's North Cape and down into the Atlantic; at the same time, a Kynda-class missile cruiser and two destroyers passed through the Turkish Straits, the length of the Mediterranean, and into the Atlantic. The two groups rendezvoused off the Azores on 3 July and fueled from two tankers; the nine ships then entered the Caribbean for almost a month of exercises. En route south the group was reported by a Pentagon spokesman to be within Shaddock cruise missile range of the eastern coast of the United States.

A year later, during the extensive *Ocean* exercises of April 1970, a pair of Tu-95 Bear naval reconnaissance aircraft took off from a Northern Fleet base, travelled around Norway, overflew Soviet ships operating in the Iceland–Faeroes gap, and then continued south to land in Cuba. This non-stop flight of more than 5,000 miles marked the first time that Bear aircraft had landed outside of the Soviet Bloc. Another pair of Bear reconnaissance aircraft flew into Cuba later in April, and a third pair made the flight in May.[22] Also that April, a Kresta-class cruiser and a destroyer broke away from the *Okean* exercises in the North Atlantic and joined en route by a nuclear-propelled Echo II (Project 675) cruise missile submarine, two diesel attack submarines, and a submarine tender, entered the Caribbean during May. This was the first visit of a Soviet nuclear submarine to a non-Bloc port. This also was the start of regular Soviet surface ship, submarine, and naval aircraft deployments to the Caribbean during the remainder of the Cold War. Also about this time, the Soviets began establishing a huge communications intercept installation at Lourdes, Cuba. The facility intercepted telephone, fax, and other communications relayed overseas from the U.S. mainland by satellite. At its peak the Lourdes facility was staffed by about 6,000 men and women.

Off the Atlantic coast of Africa in 1975–1976 Soviet naval forces supported revolutionaries in Angola. Soviet aircraft flew thousands of Cuban combat and support troops and advisors into Angola, while Soviet merchant ships—with a warship sometimes present—brought in weapons and supplies for the Cubans and for the Angolan revolutionaries. Soviet naval forces supported the latter: a destroyer, landing ship, and oiler were among the first Soviet forces to reach the area.[23] The Soviets transported an estimated 20,000 troops and advisors, plus tanks, other vehicles, and artillery to Angola.

Soviet naval ships had regularly transited the Pacific en route to and from the Indian Ocean, as well as for port calls to Indonesia when Moscow and Djakarta had cordial relations, but Soviet surface ships made the first long-range Pacific voyage in the fall of 1971. A Kresta-class missile cruiser, two missile-armed destroyers, a nuclear Echo II cruise missile submarine, two diesel-electric submarines, and a tanker steamed into Hawaiian waters, coming within sight of Oahu. A Pentagon spokesman said that the cruise demonstrated that the Soviet Fleet could operate in international waters—anywhere.[24]

Soviet warships had exercised in the Philippine Sea during the spring 1970 *Okean* exercises, in which the battle problem had moved northward into the Sea of Japan. This movement was simultaneous with a northward movement of the Atlantic portion of the exercise, through the Iceland–Faeroes gap and into the Norwegian Sea. The 1970 *Okean* exercises were—and remain—the largest peacetime naval exercise in history, conducted over several ocean areas by 84 surface warships; by about 80 submarines (including 15 nuclear-propelled); 45 naval auxiliary, surveying, and intelligence collection ships; and several hundred aircraft. As part of the exercises, hundreds of Soviet naval and strategic aircraft flew simulated strikes against warships in the Atlantic and Pacific—strikes thousands of miles apart *coordinated to within a few minutes of each other,* demonstrating the high level of coordination exercised by Admiral Gorshkov's headquarters in Moscow. Ironically, almost simultaneous with *Okean* the U.S. Navy cancelled a major exercise in the Pacific that was to involve some 50 ships and submarines. The exercise, named Ropeval 2-70, was according to Pentagon sources cancelled because of funding cutbacks.[25]

Soviet naval ships had avoided the Gulf of Tonkin and nearby waters during the conflict of the 1960s—with the notable exception of intelligence collection ships and nuclear-propelled submarines. The former kept watch—when they could—on U.S. carrier operations in the Gulf, possibly for lessons that could be applied to the growing Soviet carrier program. Subsequently, with the fall of South Vietnam to the communists, Soviet naval aircraft began flying from former U.S. airfields; communications facilities were established ashore, followed by regular calls of Soviet ships for replenishment and a run on the beach for their crews. This was particularly significant for Soviet warships deploying to and returning from the Indian Ocean.[26]

The Balance Sheet

The specific full impact of these forward operations by the Soviet Navy under Admiral Gorshkov's direction is difficult to determine. Without doubt, these ships have been used to counter U.S. political-military activities and to demonstrate to Third World states that the Soviet Union could and would provide them with military support. Writing of the transit in 1979 of the Soviet *Kiev*-class aircraft carrier *Minsk* around Africa en route to the Pacific Fleet, Dr. Watson noted, "The *Minsk*'s visit [to Angola] was probably calculated to indicate resolute Soviet support for Angola in its struggle with the South African government. Angola and South Africa had undergone a period of border conflict that threatened to escalate into more widespread hostilities. The visit to Luanda, coupled with the *Minsk* group's presence off the South African coast, conveyed the message that the USSR would honor its commitment to Angola and would not tolerate hostile South African action."[27]

These port visits were coupled with local official visits to the ships and, on occasion, underway demonstrations of Soviet naval capabilities. For example, in April 1970, the missile-helicopter carrier *Leningrad* hosted President Abdel Nasser of Egypt while cruising in the eastern Mediterranean, and a year later the *Leningrad* sailed the Black Sea with Party Secretary Leonid Brezhnev on board to entertain Communist Party leaders from Bulgaria, Czechoslovakia, East Germany, Mongolia, and Poland.

These operations, long described by Admiral Gorshkov as part of the role of navies in peacetime, fit well with the expansionist policies of the Soviet governments. In 1969, Foreign Minister A. A. Gromyko declared, "The Soviet Union, which, as a large world power, has widely developed international connections, cannot take a passive attitude toward those events that might be territorially remote but that touch on our security and also on the security of our friends."[28] Brezhnev, commenting on the military and naval [*Okean*] maneuvers of 1970, stated, "At the present time no question of any importance in the world can be resolved without our participation, without taking into account our economic and military might."[29]

The Soviet Navy provided a significant portion of the "military might" of the Soviet Union, an arm that could be employed in "territorially remote" areas. Further, the increase in Soviet naval activity—as well as strategic forces—came as the United States found itself bogged down in a seemingly endless conflict in the jungles of Vietnam. The British Institute for Strategic Studies observed, "The Soviet Union, unlike the United States, was not reacting to a sense of over-commitment abroad. On the contrary, its ambition seemed to be to wipe out the strategic advantages the United States had previously gained from a superior number of nuclear weapons and even more from command of the seas. Soviet policy sought to achieve parity, or more than parity, with the United States, in both respects."[30]

The American response to Admiral Gorshkov's buildup of the Soviet Navy was not unanimous. Veteran defense writer George Wilson posited,

> Hardly a week passes without some American admiral, defense official or politician sounding the alarm about the menacing Soviet navy....
>
> But all of the scare talk—including Adm. Elmo R. Zumwalt's recent warning that the Soviet navy threatens to "deny us use of the seas in support of our allies and our overseas forces"—fails to point out that the Russians are still a long way from matching the U.S. Navy.[31]

Still, Admiral Gorshkov's navy had arrived on the world scene.

CHAPTER 14

The Final Years

The Soviet Navy has been converted in the full sense
of the word into an offensive-type, long-range armed
force . . . which could exert a decisive influence on the
course of armed struggle in theaters of military
operations of vast extent.

—Admiral S. G. Gorshkov, *Morskoy Sbornik* (no. 2, 1967)

And nonetheless we managed to do it! Our Navy has
become such that a return to previous naval policy is
impossible. In fact, prior to us there wasn't any
(naval policy). . . .

—Admiral Gorshkov's last words to Rear Admiral
 Nikolay P. V'yunenko, a close colleague

I n 1975 Admiral Gorshkov reached the nominal Soviet military
retirement age of 65. There were some indications that he would
step down after almost two decades in command of the Soviet Navy.
Such predictions were premature.

Indeed, the Soviet Navy could be said to have been entering
still another phase of development under the admiral's direction: in
May of that year the *Kiev* was placed in commission—the first of a
series of 43,000-ton aircraft carriers. Although the ship's air group
of some 12 Yak-36 Forger VSTOL fighters and 24 Ka-25 Hormone

helicopters was far short of the 85-plane air wing of a larger U.S. carrier, the *Kiev* still represented a massive Soviet investment in technology, materials, and people. The ship was a step in the direction of overcoming what Gorshkov had long pointed out as one of the major shortfalls of the Soviet Navy: the lack of sea-based aviation.

New Ships and Exercises

Virtually all allocation of resources within the Soviet Union was based on centralized, five-year economic plans. In general, the resource allocations were decided before the plan began, and once a plan was under way there was very little opportunity for change, because of the intense interdependence of the various segments of the Soviet economy. Thus, the decision to build the *Kiev*-class aircraft carriers—the largest ships yet built in the country—was argued at the highest levels of the Navy, the military establishment, and the government. The technical requirements for the design were approved in October 1968.[1] Several years of lead time were required to prepare detailed plans, order components, and make ready the Nikolayev South shipyard on the Black Sea to construct the ship.

The *Kiev* was laid down on 21 July 1970, at the end of the five-year plan. The ship was launched two years later, in December 1972, corresponding with the promotion of General Ivan I. Borzov, head of Soviet Naval Aviation, to the rank of Marshal of Aviation, the first naval aviator to attain that rank.

The end of the 1966–1970 five-year economic plan, during April–May 1970, also saw the largest peacetime exercises ever conducted by any navy. Commemorating the 100th anniversary of the birth of V. I. Lenin, as noted in the previous chapter, the *Okean* exercises had phases in the North Atlantic, Mediterranean, Indian Ocean, and western Pacific as well as in seas adjacent to the Soviet Union.

Admiral Gorshkov personally directed the multi-ocean exercises. The four fleets were operating according to a preplanned exercise scenario, under the operational control of naval headquarters in Moscow. Gorshkov stated that *Okean* was an operational training program for all aspects and levels of the Navy, that "the *Okean* maneuvers demonstrated that the Soviet Navy is always ready to carry out its sacred duty to defend the state interests of the Soviet Union."[2] The Minister of Defense, Marshal A. A. Grechko, who was on board a cruiser during the concluding phases, declared: "The *Okean* maneuvers were evidence of the increased naval might of our socialist state, an index of the fact that our Navy has become so great and so strong that it is capable of executing missions in defense of our state interests over the broad expanses of the World Ocean."[3]

Thus, the *Okean* exercises were primarily a report to the Soviet leadership on the efficacy of the Navy, a service that continued to devour vast quantities of resources, facilities, and manpower. Impressed by the *Okean* exercises and Admiral Gorshkov's persuasive arguments, the Politburo supported the construction of additional aircraft carriers, as well as several other new warship classes. During the 1971–1975 five-year program four new classes of cruisers and destroyers were begun, among them the four 28,000-ton *Kirov* series of nuclear-propelled missile cruisers—the largest warships built since World War II by any nation except for aircraft carrier-type ships.[4]

Beyond their direct costs of construction and operation, these large ships disturbed the orderly flow of work in Soviet shipyards that facilitates series production and hence the much-sought workforce stability. If a shipyard is producing small- or even medium-sized ships in series, it can easily maintain a stable workforce. When a segment of that specialized force completes work on one hull there is always another of the same type waiting. "A much reduced number of large ships is quite another matter, as the character of the work at the yard changes radically over the life of the project," according to Dr. Norman Friedman, a warship historian and author.[5] "Thus, the larger the ship, the more it must be built outside the stable rate of work inherent in a tightly planned economy." Admiral Gorshkov's larger and still larger warships accordingly had a serious impact on Soviet shipbuilding and hence the carefully planned economy.

And Aircraft Carriers

In the late 1970s Western intelligence began reporting preparations under way at the Nikolayev shipyard for construction of a still larger aviation ship or aircraft carrier. By the early 1980s construction was definitely in progress of a giant carrier of perhaps 65,000 tons full-load displacement, a ship fitted with arresting wires and capable of operating some 60 to 70 conventional take-off and landing aircraft. The investment in such a ship, with completion envisioned about 1989–1990, could be seen as a new mark of support for the Navy by the Brezhnev-controlled Politburo. This ship, eventually named *Fleet Admiral of the Soviet Union Kuznetsov*, would be launched in 1985 and placed in commission in 1991.

In addition, several new submarine series were begun, among them the Typhoon (Project 941) ballistic missile submarine. With a submerged displacement of some 48,000 tons, these underwater giants were the world's largest submarines, with more than twice the displacement of the U.S. Trident strategic submarines. The Soviets already were operating at the U.S.-Soviet strategic arms limit of 62 modern SLBM submarines carrying more than 950 missiles. The submarine-launched ballistic missile had become a primary component of the Soviet strategic offensive force and, as probably the most survivable component, the basis for a "strategic reserve," as called for in Soviet military doctrine.

The Soviet submarine programs begun in the 1960s stressed not only size but quality and quantity. The submarine construction program and naval aircraft procurement continued apace; no reductions were necessitated by the massive investment in surface warships, another indication of the high level of support for Gorshkov's navy within the highest levels of the government. As a senior U.S. intelligence officer—and coauthor of this volume—wrote in 1984, "The Soviet navy is, and will remain, primarily a submarine navy."[6] (This viewpoint was to be echoed three decades later, in 2015, by Admiral Viktor Chirkov, then Commander-in-Chief of the Russian Navy: "The nuclear submarine fleet is the priority in the Navy shipbuilding program.")[7]

As final evidence of increasing emphasis on a balance of quantity and quality of ships, Admiral Gorshkov is said to have resisted new designs put forward simply for the sake of something new. Reportedly, Gorshkov had a sign in his office that declared: "Better Is the Enemy of Good Enough." Why build a better ship if the current design will do? This philosophy led to long-duration ship and aircraft production lines.[8] New designs were put into production when they provided *significant* increases in capability.

Admiral Gorshkov continued his close relationship with the national leadership—with Brezhnev, Kosygin, and Grechko. He was able to call their attention to how his far-sailing warships and their port visits were supporting Soviet foreign policies and, through exercises, "demonstrated" their potential combat effectiveness. In April 1975—at the conclusion of the Five-Year Plan—there was another multi-ocean series of exercises, *Okean*-75. Again there were large-scale maneuvers in the Atlantic and Pacific as well as in lesser seas; some 220 surface ships and submarines were involved. Naval and Air Forces strategic aircraft participating in *Okean*-75 flew some 700 sorties from bases inside of the Soviet Union and from overseas airfields: Bear-D reconnaissance aircraft used a field in Equatorial Guinea, Il-38 May anti-submarine aircraft and An-12 Cub electronic reconnaissance aircraft flew from Somalia, and An-12 Cubs operated out of Aden. Bear-D aircraft from bases in the Soviet Union exercised over the Indian Ocean, again demonstrating the remarkable range of this reconnaissance/targeting aircraft. Significantly, the missile cruiser-helicopter ships *Moskva* and *Leningrad*, which had had major roles five years earlier, were not at sea during *Okean-75*. (The *Leningrad* had operated two Mi-8 Hip helicopters in the mine clearance role at the southern entrance to the Suez Canal in 1973–1974 following the Arab-Israeli "Yom Kippur War."[9] That ship also operated for seven weeks in the Caribbean area in March–April 1984, as part of the periodic Soviet naval deployment to the Caribbean; she was the largest Soviet warship to operate in that area up to that time.)

Another major *Okean*-style exercise was expected to occur in the spring of 1980, as at the conclusion of the two previous five-year plans. That year there were several small exercises, as well as the significant Soviet naval presence in the Indian Ocean and the Mediterranean. There was no *Okean-80*. The reasons appear to have included the potential of a super-power confrontation because of the high state of U.S. military readiness owing to the Iranian hostage situation and the fear of further antagonizing the West in the wake of the Soviet invasion of Afghanistan, and during the continuing crisis in Poland.

However, the Soviet fleet was not idle. In July 1981, there was a large amphibious exercise in the eastern Mediterranean, a joint Soviet-Syrian operation in which 1,000 Soviet marines were landed. Also that summer, a combined Soviet–Polish–East German naval exercise was held in the Baltic; and that fall the massive, all-Soviet *Zapad*-81 amphibious landing exercise was carried out in the eastern Baltic. These smaller exercises were intended to impress the Poles with the contribution that the Soviet Navy could make to a Soviet invasion of Poland—if politically necessary. They may also have been intended to impress the Politburo that the Navy too could be of assistance in such "internal security operations."

Costs and Problems

The continued expansion of the Soviet Fleet was not achieved without great difficulty. As noted above, Admiral Gorshkov had faced opposition even from within the Navy as well as from without during his long tenure as commander-in-chief. By the 1970s he was losing some of his key political supporters. Premier Aleksey Kosygin, the political leader from Leningrad, died in 1980; Gorshkov's wartime colleague and Minister of Defense since 1967, A. A. Grechko, died in 1976. His replacement, Dmitriy Ustinov, was essentially a civilian, with a long career in armament production, who lacked close ties to the Navy.[10] There were reports in 1982 that Gorshkov and Ustinov had "had a serious disagreement over strategic matters . . . and, except for the personal intervention of President Leonid Brezhnev, Ustinov would have 'put Gorshkov out to pasture.'"[11] Gorshkov's Russian biographer (and friend) also has noted an even bigger differences in views between Gorshkov and the new Chief of the General Staff, Marshal Nikolai V. Ogarkov.[12] (Ogarkov served in that position from 1977 to 1984.)

Leonid Brezhnev passed from the scene in late 1982, replaced by Yuriy Andropov, who himself would be succeeded, upon his death a year later, by Konstantin Chernenko. Andropov, formerly head of the KGB, had no significant ties to the Navy, nor did Chernenko, a longtime Party worker and propagandist.

In an apparent move to demonstrate naval capabilities for his new political bosses, especially the ailing Andropov, Admiral Gorshkov organized a hasty naval operation in September 1983—actually a world-wide series of exercises, with 40 surface combatants and numerous submarines and land-based naval aircraft participating. Several ship classes that had entered service since the *Okean* of 1975 took part, including *Kiev*-class aircraft carriers. The impact on the new political leadership, however, probably was limited, in view of demands from the other services for larger allocations of resources, especially to support the on-going and frustrating combat operations in Afghanistan, and also of the chronic problems in the Soviet civilian economy.

Admiral Gorshkov's extended naval operations not without cost. A Soviet Golf (Project 629A) diesel-electric, ballistic missile submarine sank in the Pacific in 1968 with no survivors; near the end of the *Okean* exercises in 1970 a November (Project 627A) nuclear attack submarine was lost off the Atlantic coast of Spain (Cape Finisterre), most of her crew being rescued; a nuclear Hotel (Project 658) ballistic missile submarine had an engineering casualty in the North Atlantic in 1972 and had to be towed back to her Northern Fleet base; a Kashin-class missile destroyer blew up and sank in the Black Sea in 1974, the press reporting the deaths of at least 200 crewmen; in 1983 a nuclear Charlie (Project 670) cruise missile submarine sank near Petropavlovsk with loss of life; in 1984 a massive explosion at a missile-munitions facility in the Northern Fleet base area cost many lives and destroyed a large proportion of the fleet's weapons; and in 1986 a nuclear Yankee (Project 667A) ballistic missile submarine suffered a missile fuel explosion and sank some 680 miles northeast of Bermuda.[13] Except for the 1968 missile submarine loss, all of these casualties were widely reported in the international press; the loss of the Golf SSB *K-129* made worldwide headlines in the 1970s when it was revealed that the U.S. Central Intelligence Agency, using the heavy lift ship *Hughes Glomar Explorer*, had salvaged a portion of that submarine in a clandestine operation in the North Pacific.

Also, two events occurred that were politically embarrassing to the Soviet Navy. In 1975 a part of the crew of the Krivak-class frigate *Storozhevoy* mutinied and took the ship to sea from the Baltic port of Riga in an attempt to reach Swedish waters (the ship was attacked by Soviet aircraft and the mutineers surrendered). In 1981 a

Soviet Whiskey-class diesel submarine ran aground within Swedish territorial waters near the Karlskrona naval base.

Admiral Gorshkov survived all of these tribulations and disasters, as well as many lesser problems. Some of his flag officers may not have.

Naval Leadership

Admiral Gorshkov made several changes in leadership in this new phase of development of the Soviet Navy. In the mid-1970s most of the senior naval commands were shifted. Admiral V. A. Kasatonov, Gorshkov's classmate and friend, was replaced as First Deputy Commander-in-Chief, a position he had held from 1964 to 1974, by Nikolay I. Smirnov, previously the Pacific Fleet commander. The Pacific Fleet command thus changed in 1974, as did that of the Black Sea Fleet, followed in 1975 by the Baltic Fleet command and in 1977 by the Northern Fleet command. The command of naval aviation changed in 1974 because of the death of Marshal Borzov, a key architect in the development of Soviet sea-based aviation.

In 1977, Fleet Admiral Georgiy M. Yegorov moved from command of the Northern Fleet to Chief of the Main Naval Staff and became, like Smirnov, a likely successor to Admiral Gorshkov. That July the command of the large Northern Fleet passed into the hands of Vice Admiral Vladimir Nikolayevich Chernavin, at the time 50 years of age and one the youngest of the fleet commanders in the post–World War II period. A submariner, a year later he was promoted to full admiral; in 1981 he became a candidate member of the Central Committee.

It appeared that these men would guide the development and activities of the Soviet Navy well into the 1980s. However, the internationally publicized grounding of the Whiskey-class submarine in Swedish waters—carrying nuclear torpedoes, as was standard at the time—and an internal debate within the Soviet Navy would lead to further changes among Admiral Gorshkov's senior officers. The debate was sparked by a two-part article in *Morskoy Sbornik* by Vice Admiral K. A. Stalbo, "Some Issues of the Theory of the Development and Employment of the Navy" (April and May 1981 issues). Stalbo, a strong, longtime supporter of Gorshkov who was a member of the editorial board of *Morskoy Sbornik*, the Navy's professional journal, invited discussion of his views.

The response was rapid and sharp. Several flag officers challenged Stalbo's views as narrow and incomplete, overlooking combat employment, training, indoctrination, other technical areas, and ideology. The last-named objection, that Stalbo had inadequate knowledge of the fundamental position of Marxist-Leninist theory concerning the development and use of military forces, was a most serious charge in the Soviet society.

Remarkably, the critics included Admiral Chernavin, then the commander of the Northern Fleet; Admiral V. V. Sysoyev, former commander of the Black Sea Fleet and at the time head of the Marshal Grechko Naval Academy (i.e., the Naval War College); and Rear Admiral G. G. Kostev, head of the naval faculty of the Lenin Political-Military Academy—an impressive array of flag officers, that was joined by other admirals as well as lower-ranking officers.[14] The debate soon encompassed issues beyond those raised by Stalbo, indicating either a significant controversy within the Soviet Navy or the need to clear the air because of pressures being brought to bear by the General Staff. Admiral Gorshkov did not participate in the discussion in *Morskoy Sbornik*, or in some of the other military journals in which related articles appeared.

During the debate several senior naval officers were reassigned: Fleet Admiral Yegorov, Chief of the Main Naval Staff (and Chernavin's predecessor as head of the Northern Fleet), left that prestigious post and was reassigned as Chairman of the DOSAAF Central Committee.[15] While placing a senior admiral as head of DOSAAF may have had some long-term advantages for the Navy, the post was certainly not a promotion for the 64-year-old Yegorov. He had been involved with the Whiskey fiasco, and that event has been cited by some observers as the reason for his sudden departure.

Admiral Chernavin succeeded Yegorov in February 1982, having been commander of the Northern Fleet from 1977 to 1981. Chernavin not only rose to that key post at naval headquarters but became a First Deputy Commander-in-Chief, senior on the precedence list to the other first deputy, Fleet Admiral Smirnov, his nominal senior. This situation placed Chernavin as the most likely successor to Admiral Gorshkov . . . someday.

The significance of the Stalbo debate remains unclear. One interpretation of the controversy is that Stalbo had overstepped his prescribed bounds and appeared to be proposing a naval strategy independent of other military services and thus by definition strongly at odds with Soviet doctrine. At the time, Stalbo's writings were interpreted by some observers as an attack on Admiral Gorshkov and indications that the old admiral was about to be forced into retirement. Perhaps those writings also could have signaled a downgrading of the Navy's position and an indicator of reduced naval budgets to come. But subsequent events failed to support any of these hypotheses. Gorshkov remained in office for three more years, and there was no slackening of warship construction or forward-area deployments. Gorshkov's 1982–1985 writings contained no discernible *mea culpa*. Further discrediting the notion that Gorshkov had fallen out of favor with the Soviet leadership is the fact that Mikhail Gorbachev made no significant reductions in Soviet Navy allocations. The Navy continued to receive approximately one-fourth of the military budget— a total out of all proportion to its historical share and all the more noteworthy in a military system still dominated by Army officers. If the hostile response to Stalbo was somehow related to a plan (or actual effort) to remove Gorshkov it failed badly.

Indeed, during this same period the Soviet Navy acquired yet another important mission in support of Soviet national strategy and diplomacy. In response to the Soviet deployment of SS-20

Intermediate-Range Ballistic Missiles (IRBMs) in Warsaw Pact countries, the United States decided to deploy Pershing II IRBMs and Ground-Launched Cruise Missiles (GLCMs) in Western Europe.[16] The Soviet Union required an "analogous response" to be able to place U.S. targets at risk from nuclear weapons launched from somewhere other than Soviet soil. There was nowhere to turn besides the Soviet Navy, whose ballistic and cruise missile submarines could strike American targets from the sea. The analogous-response era was short-lived, and both sides removed their intermediate-range missiles from Western and Central Europe, but the importance of having a navy capable of attacking far-distant land targets from less than strategic platforms was reinforced in the collective minds of the Soviet leadership.

Mikhail Gorbachev became the General Secretary of the Central Committee—the head of the Soviet regime—in March 1985. Some nine months later, Admiral Gorshkov announced his retirement. Rumors abounded that Gorbachev had found Gorshkov too old and too inflexible, that he wanted a younger man to head the Navy. The Navy, the argument went, was devouring an extra-ordinary share of capital resources, and cutting its budget would simply be too difficult with Gorshkov still in command.

The rumor was not without logic, and in retrospect it may have contained an element of truth. Admiral Gorshkov was planning for the future of the Navy. As early as 1981 he had considered serious personnel changes that positioned Chernavin to be groomed to be the next CinC. At the same time, Gorshkov wished to propose his own retirement, due to his age and failing health. But the press of daily work kept him from acting on this plan. He may have chosen to wait to retire until 1986, his 30th anniversary as CinC. In any case, on 9 December 1985 he issued his last order, passing his position and authority to Fleet Admiral Vladimir N. Chernavin, who was at the time age 56. The other First Deputy CinC was Admiral Smirnov, age 67; he would remain in active service until 1992.

A U.S. intelligence appraisal of Admiral Gorshkov's probable successor earlier in 1985 had called attention to the implications of a turnover to a new CinC:

- A new commander would not be able to count on inheriting Gorshkov's clout and maintaining intact the Navy's position in internal disagreements concerning roles and missions or the allocation of resources. Although a younger naval commander may in fact find it easier to work with the new political and military leadership that has recently emerged, his success in defending the Navy's interests will have to be established over time.
- Both Chernavin and Smirnov are submarine officers, whereas Gorshkov's early operational experience was with surface ships. Either of these officers might promote submarine programs at the expense of large surface ships such as aircraft carriers and nuclear-propelled cruisers, which Gorshkov considers essential to the balanced development of the Soviet Navy.[17]

In 1988, shortly after Admiral Gorshkov stepped down, a book appeared that offered some tantalizing glimpses into the recent thinking of the Soviet Navy's leadership under Gorshkov, *The Navy: Its Role, Prospects for Development and Employment.* The 1985–1991 Five-Year Plan already had been decided, and *The Navy* sought to make a strong case to Gorbachev's civilian advisors and other important sectors of Soviet society concerning the future funding of naval programs and force levels.

The Navy was written by three naval officers, with a foreword by Admiral Gorshkov (who passed away the year that the book was published).[18] The book appeared as Gorbachev was restructuring the Soviet bureaucracy and shifting economic priorities. As U.S. intelligence analyst Theodore A. Neely wrote in his review of *The Navy,* "This book represents honestly pro-navy arguments in a nation that is now being forced to make difficult decisions about its national priorities."[19]

The book listed three principal missions for the Navy: first, "repelling enemy aerospace attacks"—destroying Western strategic missile submarines; second, "suppressing the enemy's military-economic potential"—strikes against land targets by ballistic and cruise missile submarines; and third "destroying enemy force groupings"—supporting the flanks of ground forces by destroying enemy anti-submarine forces, by executing amphibious landings to seize straits and islands, and by waging anti-carrier warfare.

Submarines would have key roles in all of these missions, and *The Navy* emphasized the continuing improvement in all aspects of undersea craft (albeit often referring to "the foreign press" as a data source, a common ploy of Soviet writers addressing classified or sensitive subjects). *The Navy* predicted "in the near future" for submarines:

- Operating depths of 6,560 feet (2,000 m) or greater
- Interconnected spherical pressure hulls for deeper operating depths[20]
- Major reductions in "physical fields" (i.e., detectable characteristics of the submarine)
- Speeds of 50 to 60 knots (and over 100 knots in the longer term)
- Increased reactor plant output with reduction in specific weight (e.g., with gas-cooled and single-loop reactors)
- Unified engine-propulsor units operating on the principle of hydrojet engines with a steam plant
- Decreasing water resistance through improved hydrodynamic properties, including the use of polymers
- Torpedo speeds of 200 to 300 knots
- Improved ballistic (strategic) and cruise (anti-ship) missiles
- Consideration of arming submarines with *manned aircraft* [emphasis in original]
- Increased automation.

The conclusion of this section of *The Navy* included this summary:

> The traditional name "submarine" hardly will be applicable to them. These will be formidable nuclear powered ships invulnerable to the action of other forces and capable of monitoring enormous ocean expanses, deploying covertly and rapidly to necessary sectors, and delivering surprise, powerful strikes from the ocean depth against a maritime and continental enemy. Their unlimited operating range in combination with high speed makes them an almost ideal means for military marine transportation and for accomplishing other missions.

While the strategic or tactical utility of some of these submarine characteristics could be questioned, all would have had some degree of military value—and some would change the nature of submarine/anti-submarine warfare. Could they be achieved? If one compares the start and service dates of such advanced submarines as the Alfa (Project 705) and of such weapons as the high-speed Shkval torpedo with contemporary Western undersea projects, the answer probably is *yes*. Admiral Gorshkov had created a fleet—with due emphasis on submarines—that could lead the world in many submarine parameters.

(Significantly, there were several omissions in submarine design goals in *The Navy*. Quieting was not mentioned, and neither were exotic propulsion plants or titanium hulls. The Soviets were already emphasizing quieting, and no major break-throughs were envisioned. But the Soviets were also pursuing with great emphasis non-acoustic detection means and non-acoustic quieting of their submarines.)

As one of the authors of this volume wrote in analyzing *The Navy,* "The most remarkable thing about this book is not that a book justifying the navy was written but that *this* book, justifying the Soviet navy in *this* manner, was written at *this* time. It is certain to have caused some discomfort in Moscow. It should be useful in the West in highlighting that 'defensive strategy' notwithstanding, the Soviet Navy still believes the best defense is a good offensive."[21]

Naval shipbuilding continued apace through the remainder of Gorbachev's tenure. In November 1988 the keel was laid at the Black Sea shipyard in Nikolayev for a ship to be named the *Ul'yanovsk*. Honoring the birthplace of V. I. Lenin, the *Ul'yanovsk* was to be a nuclear-propelled aircraft carrier, to displace approximately 75,000 tons—by a significant margin the largest warship to be constructed in the Soviet Union; she would be larger than any warship built outside of the United States.

The End of an Era

Early in his retirement Admiral Gorshkov apparently suffered a stroke. He partially recovered and was able to continue to write, but he died on 13 May 1988, in Moscow, less than 18 months into his retirement. His official obituary stated that he had suffered a "serious and prolonged illness."[22] In what some view as a final irony, Admiral Gorshkov's grave at Novodevichiy is next to that of his old nemesis—Nikita Khrushchev.

The Soviet Union collapsed in December 1991, and Admiral Chernavin—Gorshkov's successor as the last CinC of the Soviet Navy—became the first CinC of the Navy of the Commonwealth of Independent States, soon to evolve into the (new) Russian Navy. He skillfully led the Navy's transition as the nation went through traumatic and tumultuous times. He retired as CinC in August 1992, and the 1990 Five-Year Plan that he had helped to develop never reached fruition. The state's new leader, Boris Yeltsin, was forced to make huge military cutbacks generally and specific reductions in the Navy. But Admiral Gorshkov's legacy would remain.

CHAPTER 15

Summary and Conclusions

The Soviet Union, unlike the United States, was not reacting to a sense of over-commitment abroad. On the contrary, its ambition seemed to be to wipe out the strategic advantages the United States had previously gained from a superior number of nuclear weapons and even more from command of the seas. Soviet policy sought to achieve parity, or more than parity, with the United States, in both respects.

—International Institute for Strategic Studies, *Strategic Survey*, 1969 (1970)

Admiral Gorshkov was a loyal, talented, and determined communist and naval officer. These characteristics, aided by his wartime experiences and the political-military contacts made during a relatively short pre-1955 naval career, elevated him to command of the Soviet Navy. Once in command, he was able to create a fleet that in many respects could challenge the U.S. Navy.

Tenacity too should be listed among Admiral Gorshkov's characteristics. Consider that when he was called to Moscow in 1955 his orders—from the then all-powerful Nikita Khrushchev—were to discard surface warships, cut the size of the Navy, and produce only missile-armed submarines and land-based aircraft to defend Soviet shores from American aircraft carrier strikes and possible amphibious landings. He carried out those directives—*to some extent.*

But within a decade of his coming to Moscow, major surface warships, including "aviation ships." and submarines that were in some respects the world's most advanced, were being constructed in Soviet shipyards. Further, where previously Red warships had clung to the lengthy Soviet coastline and the seas bordering the country, a decade later they were ranging far and wide on the world's oceans, even to Cuba in the backyard of the United States. Those ships had established a permanent presence in the Mediterranean—previously a NATO-dominated sea—as well as in the Indian Ocean and western Pacific Ocean. The *Okean* exercises of 1970 remain the world's largest peacetime naval operations in terms of numbers of participating ships and aircraft and of geographic spread, across several seas and oceans.

Still, Admiral Gorshkov's major contribution lies not in ships or sailors or aircraft but in his ability to make the Soviet regime—whose military establishment had almost always been dominated by Army officers—understand the roles and value of naval forces to the Soviet state in both peace and war—roles and value that successors have extrapolated to the Russian state. Indeed, as Gorshkov wrote and as his fleet at times could demonstrate, the Navy was unique among the military services in its capability for peacetime as well as combat operations at great distances from Soviet territory.

On the Personal Side

Admiral Gorshkov's dominant personal attribute was his command presence: when he was in the room there was no question of who was in charge. It was clear that he was a man accustomed to power, although he was never described as possessing the egotistical traits that such men often display. He could be brusque, but he also was capable of being very affable and even grandfatherly, particularly toward junior officers. As a rule, he was rather aloof in public gatherings when there were foreigners present and seldom was effusive even to his closest associates. But he could become very responsive and animated if engaged in a conversation regarding naval history or strategy.

A former assistant U.S naval attaché in Moscow, Commander Steve Kime, described a conversation with Admiral Gorshkov during a reception in the 1970s:

> I elbowed my way through the crowd of surprised officers directly to him [Gorshkov]. He and his deputy, Fleet Admiral V. A. Kasatonov, standing next to him, were amused by this and waved off a panicked Soviet Foreign Liaison Officer about to intercede.
>
> I stuck out my hand and told Gorshkov what an honor it was to meet someone I had followed in *Morskoy Sbornik*, the Russian Naval Digest, though I noted that he hadn't written much since a major piece in 1967. He laughed at this, shook my hand, and asked me what interested me about his article. Admiral Kasatonov, his deputy and a former Pacific Fleet commander, enthusiastically joined in. I had read his stuff too. Gorshkov was flattered that I knew that his designation "Hero of the Soviet Union" was earned in Black Sea amphibious actions against the Germans.[1]

As Commander-in-Chief, Admiral Gorshkov probably could be characterized as an officer who was greatly respected and sometimes feared by his subordinates but seldom viewed with great affection. Captains 1st Rank Vladimir P. Kuzin and Vladislav N. Nikol'skiy, in their comprehensive and detailed history of the Soviet Navy from 1945 to 1991, are at best ambivalent in their treatment of Gorshkov, his role in developing the Soviet Navy, and his leadership traits.[2] They give him rather grudging credit for creating "The National Way" as a philosophy that emphasized the Navy's strategic role in fielding and protecting the Soviet strategic missile submarine force while simultaneously threatening Western nuclear attack forces. Selling this philosophy positioned the Navy as second only to the Strategic Rocket

Forces and gained for the Navy an unprecedented degree of prestige, as an important service no longer to be considered merely the loyal handmaiden of the Army.

Kuzin and Nikol'skiy recognize Admiral Gorshkov also as the architect of a true multi-purpose navy—what Gorshkov referred to as a "balanced fleet." But they characterize him as an "authoritative ideologue" and his leadership style as of the "people at the top know best" variety.[3] Having given Gorshkov credit for his accomplishments, in fact, Kuzin and Nikol'skiy go on to charge that he was wasteful in his expenditure of the generous funding that he was able to justify and was authoritative to the point of imperiousness, welcomed no dissenting opinions, and, above all, did not leave the Navy in a position to withstand the political fluctuations that would take place after his departure:

The model for the use of the Navy was raised by S. G. Gorshkov to the absolute and attempts to subject it to criticism or even doubts were mercilessly cut off. During such circumstances not only different thinking people but also those capable of making atypical decisions (they usually had the label of quarrelsome pinned to them) did not rise to the top command positions in the Navy. In fact . . . just like after the defeat of the "old school" in the 1930s, a stagnation which has not been broken to this day [1996] set in. The stagnation in theory led to the absence of new ideas among the leadership of the Navy for developing a new strategy at the end of the 1970s and beginning of the 1980s when changes took place in policy (the era of détente and limitations in strategic weapons) and in military technology (increasing of the "transparency" of the oceans and consequently the gradual loss by submarines of their main property—covertness). In the ideological regard, S. G. Gorshkov left behind only executors (extremely

inconsistent) of his designs. The thirty years of dominance in
the Navy by this leader is a whole era which cannot be eval-
uated unambiguously. However, the fact that after 1991 the
rapid destruction of our Navy started, even more intensively
than for the other branches of the armed forces, restrains us
from only a positive evaluation of it. S. G. Gorshkov was not
able to create the main thing—*the mechanism for protecting the
Navy against political fluctuations.*[4]

All of the Soviet Union's icons, political structure, and armed forces
were dismantled with the fall of the Soviet regime. If the Navy suffered more than the other military services that was most likely
because it was in most respects the most expensive to create and to
maintain, consuming an inordinate share of the resources allocated
to the armed forces.

Private Life and Personality

Admiral Gorshkov and his wife had three children—he considered
her son by a previous marriage as his own—and several grandchil-
dren. At least one of his sons, Petr Gorshkov, is known to have followed his father into the Navy.

Every morning the admiral was chauffeured from his Moscow
apartment to Naval Headquarters or, on occasion, to the Defense
Ministry.[5] In addition to his official quarters in Moscow, the family enjoyed a dacha on the outskirts of the city and a beach house
in Latvia on the Baltic coast, accommodations suitable for a senior
commander in the Soviet-era armed forces.

The admiral tended to minimize his appearances in public, leading a quiet, conservative, and respectable private life. The Gorshkovs
seldom entertained. In public gatherings he drank only moderately.
While there is no information to suggest that he embraced any reli-
gion, he was reported to be a man of strict moral principle.

Table 15-1. U.S. Navy Leadership, 1956–1985

Secretary of the Navy	Chief of Naval Operations
Charles S. Thomas May 1954–Mar. 1957	Arleigh A. Burke★ Aug. 1955–Aug. 1961
Thomas D. Gates Jr. Apr. 1957–June 1959	
William B. Franke June 1959–Jan. 1961	
John B. Connally Jan. 1961–Dec. 1961	George W. Anderson Aug. 1961–July 1963
Fred H. Korth Jan. 1962–Nov. 1963	David L. McDonald Aug. 1963–July 1967
Paul H. Nitze Nov. 1963–June 1967	
Paul R. Ignatius Sep. 1967–Jan. 1969	Thomas H. Moorer Aug. 1967–July 1970
John H. Chafee Jan. 1969–May 1972	Elmo R. Zumwalt July 1970–June 1974
John W. Warner May 1972–Apr. 1974	
J. William Middendorf II June 1974–Jan. 1977	James L. Holloway III June 1974–July 1978
W. Graham Claytor Jr. Jan. 1977–Oct. 1979	Thomas B. Hayward July 1978–June 1982
Edward Hidalgo Oct. 1979–Jan. 1981	
John H. Lehman Feb. 1981–Apr. 1987	James D. Watkins June 1982–June 1986

★ Admiral Burke was the U.S. Navy's longest-serving CNO.

Admiral Gorshkov had an informal side. He was sent as a senior government envoy on visits to several foreign countries, either as a member of a Ministry of Defense delegation or on his own as CinC of the Navy. These countries included Bulgaria, Cuba, North Vietnam, Algeria, Ethiopia, and India. Host country officers assigned to escort him reported that he was warm, friendly, and undemanding and that on occasion he displayed a sense of humor. He was seen at public gatherings only infrequently in his last years in office, giving rise to the speculation that he had health problems. If so, the nature of these problems was never revealed, but, as noted, his official obituary stated that he had suffered a "serious and prolonged" sickness. And, of course, he continued to have back issues following his jeep accident in World War II.

When he retired from active service in 1985, Admiral Gorshkov's almost three-decade tenure as CinC of the Soviet Navy had spanned the tours in the United States of 8 Chiefs of Naval Operations and 13 Secretaries of the Navy—the positions that most closely equated to that which Gorshkov held in the Soviet Navy (table 15-1). His ability to survive and to thrive in the face of the ever-changing Soviet political environment and military environments is further exemplified by his being able to increase his own status and that of the Soviet Navy through the tenure of five Communist Party First Secretaries.

Accomplishments and Legacy

Probably the easiest way to obtain an appreciation of Admiral Gorshkov's accomplishments during his almost three decades as Commander-in-Chief of the Soviet Navy is to peruse that navy's order of battle in 1956 and in 1985 (see table 15-2). In both periods there was a large navy, but the differences are immediately obvious. The 1956 fleet was a collection of ships either left over from World

Table 15-2. Soviet Navy Order of Battle, 1955 and 1985

	1955	1985
Submarines—nuclear propelled		
SSN torpedo attack	—	86
SSBN ballistic missile	—	63
SSGN cruise missile	—	50
Submarines—diesel-electric propelled		
SS modern	117	158
SS pre-1950	249	—
SSB ballistic missile	—	15
SSG cruise missile	—	16
TOTAL SUBMARINES	*366*	*388*
Surface Combatants		
VSTOL aircraft carriers (*Kiev*)	—	3★
Helicopter carriers (*Moskva*)	—	2
Battle cruisers (*Kirov*)	—	2★★
Battleships	2	—
Heavy cruisers	7	—
Light cruisers	21	—
Guided missile cruisers	—	27
Destroyers	115	48
Guided missile destroyers	—	35
Anti-submarine frigates	—	32
Light frigates, guardships	67	160
TOTAL SURFACE COMBATANTS	*212*	*309*
TOTAL FLEET	*578*	*697*

★ An additional aircraft carrier of the *Kiev* class was under construction.
★★ Nuclear-propelled; two additional nuclear-propelled ships of the *Kirov* class were under construction.
Note: Several of the ships in the 1955 order of battle were war reparations from Germany, Italy, or Japan; they were of little operational value.

War II or adaptations of World War II technology. There were no missile-firing or aviation-capable surface ships, and no nuclear submarines had yet entered service.

Looking at 1985, the order of battle reveals several classes of nuclear-propelled submarines with long-range ballistic missiles, a large fleet of nuclear attack and nuclear cruise missile–firing submarines, two classes of aviation ships and a third class under construction, and several classes of missile-capable cruisers and destroyers, among them nuclear-propelled "battle cruisers." More advanced, high-technology ships were under construction.

The orders-of-battle comparison reveals only part of the story. Very important in understanding his accomplishment and his legacy would be an examination of how Gorshkov was able to accomplish his successes. It should be noted that some of the decisions behind the construction of a modern Soviet Navy were taken before Gorshkov took command. He inherited from his predecessor, Admiral N. G. Kuznetsov, a nuclear submarine program that had been initiated in the closing days of Josef Stalin's tenure and strongly supported by Stalin's successor, Nikita Khrushchev. Similarly, the first missile-capable surface ships were already on the building ways, and experimentation with missiles on submarines was under way. Approval—at least in concept—already had been given for the construction of missile-capable cruisers, and the question of aircraft carriers was under discussion at the Main Naval Staff.[6]

It would be Admiral Gorshkov who would oversee the execution and expansion of these programs. To do so he had to justify them to the Army-dominated General Staff and Ministry of Defense, the massive military-industrial complex, and the senior political leadership. Gorshkov accomplished this by means of direct contact as well as extensive writings that examined historical and contemporary naval art and naval science and their applicability to the modern strategic needs of the Soviet Union. Most of these writings were unclassified and received broad dissemination in Soviet military journals.

They were widely read and debated within the Soviet Union. (They also were available in the West, where a small cadre of scholars and naval officers learned how to interpret the arcane language used in Soviet military writings and, in time, to discern and follow changes in Soviet strategy as it applied to the Navy.)

It was clear that Admiral Gorshkov was alert to any opportunity to improve the stature of the Navy and that he was articulate and persuasive in taking advantage of these opportunities. Particularly noteworthy among his writings was the series of 11 articles in *Morskoy Sbornik*, the official journal of the Soviet Navy, roughly equivalent to U.S. Naval Institute *Proceedings*.[7] His writings cleverly argued the need for a modern, large fleet and the capabilities that it should possess, given historical lessons, technological developments, the nature of the threat, and—*of course*—the imperatives of Marxist doctrine. Collections of Gorshkov's 1972 and 1973 writings were published as 11 monthly articles in the *Proceedings* during 1974, under the overall title of "Navies in War and Peace." Of course, as noted earlier, in 1979 an English-language translation of Gorshkov's *Seapower of the State* was published in the West.[8]

The admiral thus became a publicly recognized figure in the West, even appearing on the cover of *Time* magazine in 1968. The *Time* article in that issue began with the lead-in quoting Gorshkov: "The flag of the Soviet navy now proudly flies over the oceans of the world. Sooner or later, the U.S. will have to understand that it no longer has mastery of the seas."[9]

Noteworthy among the expressions of respect for Admiral Gorshkov in the Western press was an appreciation of *The Seapower of the State* by C. L. Sulzberger of the *New York Times* in February 1977, "Admiral of the World Ocean."[10] Drawing on an analysis of *The Seapower of the State* by the London-based International Institute of Strategic Studies, Sulzberger outlines the changes that Gorshkov had made or promised to make to develop the Soviet Navy "on a par with our own" (i.e., the U.S. Navy). In a bit of journalistic hyperbole that would have made Gorshkov smile—if not laugh out loud—Sulzberger opined that the admiral had earned for himself "an unparalleled reputation as a Russian seaman, far exceeding that of Catherine the Great's favorite, John Paul Jones."

All of this added to his prestige in within the Kremlin's hierarchy.

This does not imply that justifying a "balanced fleet" was either simple or quick for Admiral Gorshkov. It was neither; it came about incrementally, over a long period. In fact, debate regarding the future of the navy was still active the year Gorshkov died and continues in the post-Soviet era.

Admiral Kuznetsov, Gorshkov's predecessor as CinC, had been widely known as a proponent of the "Old School"—a high-seas fleet centered on major surface warships, a concept fully supported by Stalin. This was one of the reasons that Khrushchev replaced him with Gorshkov. Khrushchev was a strong proponent of a latter-day form of the "Young School" that would focus on submarines and land-based strike aircraft. He expected Gorshkov to move the Navy in that direction. Gorshkov was able to out-wait—some might say also out-wit—Khrushchev and, by various ploys, maintain support for his shipbuilding programs. But Gorshkov was *not* an "Old School" admiral and probably would have taken great umbrage at being characterized in that fashion. The Navy that he envisioned would be neither "Old School" nor "Young School": it would be what U.S. naval officer–intellect Robert Herrick described as the "Soviet School," and although to the knowledge of the authors of this work Gorshkov never used the term, he would likely be in full agreement with Herrick's definition of it:

An expedient synthesis of Old School and Young School tenets[,] . . . [t]he Soviet School modified the Old School full-command-of-the-sea concept to one of just limited "command of the sea."This limited command is to be gained initially just in regions of the key theaters of military action peripheral to the Soviet Union. This concept allows for expansion as more forces and forward bases become available. The ultimate aim is seen as gaining "strategic command" of entire key theaters of military action peripheral to the Soviet Union. From the Young School the Soviet School adapted the former's greater appreciation of submarines and planes. . . . The Navy was to have heterogeneous forces, that is, include both the light forces of the Young School and the capital ships, including aircraft, of the Old School. However, submarines were to represent the main striking forces and the capital ships were reduced from their Old School pre-eminence to merely providing combat support to the submarines.[11]

Commander Herrick traced the development of the "Soviet School" back to 1938, but, with minor modification, it can be seen as the overarching concept behind Gorshkov's "balanced fleet"—a fleet that could maintain sea control in limited areas adjacent to key theaters and could expand that control as required, from the near zone (100 nautical miles) to the mid-zone (up to 300 nautical miles) to the far zone—that is, beyond those distances. The balanced fleet would provide "combat stability" to the submarine force (most particularly the strategic missile force). Of course, the balanced fleet also would defend the Soviet Union from attack from Western naval forces and would continue to provide support for the seaward flanks of the Soviet Army. This also was a key factor in retaining support of Army marshals and generals.

Changes in technology and in the seaborne threats to the Soviet Union were expertly exploited by Gorshkov to justify his fleet buildup. To counter the nuclear strike aircraft on U.S. carriers he built up the force of submarines and aircraft armed with anti-ship missiles, later missile-armed surface ships as well. Subsequently, in response to Western submarines armed with ballistic missiles he built up a force of large anti-submarine ships, including aviation-capable ships, beginning with the innovative *Moskva* class. Also, of course, the Soviet Union required a large SSBN force to strike both strategic and military targets in the United States (the "main enemy"), as well as theater targets. The latter targets would specifically include ports, to prevent enemy use of them, as part of the mission of supporting the Soviet Army. And as expected, there would be the amphibious and other ships and craft—including the high-performance Wing-In-Ground (WIG) effect landing craft—required to support the Army's flanks.

The creation of the large SSBN force would, of course, demand additional surface and air forces to protect those missile submarines—again, to provide combat stability. This mission became particularly important when, in the early 1970s, the decision was taken that SSBNs with extended range missiles would operate in "bastions" near the Soviet Union, where they could be protected by Soviet naval forces, and also, if appropriate, under the polar ice. Those strategic missile submarines would become a strategic reserve that would be withheld from initial nuclear exchanges and used for war-termination or war-winning options. When both sides had launched all of their missiles, the "withheld" Soviet SSBN force would provide the balance of striking power required to ensure a favorable outcome for the Soviet Union. The Soviet SSBN force and the ships and aircraft required to ensure its combat stability took on an importance that the Navy had never previously enjoyed.

As U.S. naval analyst James McConnell observed, "Among the branches of the armed forces the navy [prior to the early-to-mid 1970s] still ranked last in combat capabilities but [by the mid-1970s] it ranked second, next to the Strategic Missile Troops in the contribution to national-defense capabilities. In the 1960s it was envisaged that the Navy could have only a 'serious' influence on a war's course and outcome. Now it was said it could have a 'decisive' influence."[12] Thus, the SSBN force in many respects became the single most important contributor to Admiral Gorshkov's subsequent justification of ever-increasing allocations for shipbuilding and aircraft procurement—for both the submarines and for the supporting forces to provide the well-articulated combat stability requirements.

A curious part of Admiral Gorshkov's justifications is that he tended to make only peripheral reference to the obvious—at least to Western observers—Soviet requirement to defend the homeland against attack by Western SSBNs. It was apparent that in time of rising tensions possibly leading to war, the Soviet Navy intended to station tattletale ships and attack submarines off Western SSBN bases in an attempt to trail egressing missile submarines prior to the outset of war. Clearly also, Soviet SSBN missiles—and possibly land-based intercontinental missiles—were targeted on the Allied bases themselves.

There also was the matter of the Western SSBNs at sea on "deterrent patrol." Admiral Gorshkov and his Navy continually explored methods for detecting missile submarines at sea. There were a number of references to "turning the seas transparent"—that is, detecting Western missile submarines at sea from space, aircraft, and by other non-acoustic means. Some of these references may have amounted to little more than hyperbole or wishful thinking, but they reveal an intense interest in this area—one that produced some results. Lacking the acoustic advantages long enjoyed by the U.S. submarine and anti-submarine forces, the Soviets are known to have dedicated significant assets to exploring non-acoustic anti-submarine warfare (ASW).[13] One U.S. naval officer, Harlan Ullman, astutely observed: "There can be no clear-cut conclusion as to the likely effectiveness of such measures, but for the advocates of a counter-deterrent strategy, the anti-Polaris tasks are perhaps not as *impossible* as conventional Western thinking tends to assume" (emphasis original).[14]

There is a final accomplishment of Admiral Gorshkov that should be mentioned. In his writings, Gorshkov made repeated references to the value of a navy to support Soviet foreign policy and to "protect the gains of socialism." There are clear, although often oblique references in his published work to the 1956 Suez crisis, the Cuban missile crisis of 1962, the 1967 and 1973 Arab-Israeli conflicts, and other crises and conflicts where having Soviet ships on the scene either made a difference or could have. Admiral Gorshkov argues the need for a Soviet Navy for high-seas naval presence well and persuasively, and the deployment of large numbers of Soviet ships in the Mediterranean and Indian Ocean/Red Sea during the Cold War provides evidence that this mission had taken hold within the senior Soviet leadership. It also lends substance to reports that Admiral Gorshkov had told the Navy to "go to sea and stay there." There apparently was no appeal for additional forces for the presence mission. The logic was more along the lines of demonstrating the wisdom of the investment in warships already made.

Western Perceptions

A number of articles appearing in the Western press in the 1960s and 1970s compared Admiral Gorshkov with such leading Western naval theorists as Captain Alfred Thayer Mahan and Admiral of the Fleet John (Jackie) Fisher.[15] The comparisons have usually been overdrawn. Although both Gorshkov and Mahan used history as the basis for establishing the importance of a navy and both wrote of new technology, Mahan expostulated a *universal* view of sea power, which he believed to be applicable to all maritime nations. Gorshkov's writings focused on naval strategy and doctrine that would be applicable primarily to the Soviet Union.

The comparison to Admiral Fisher was perhaps more valid, in that like Gorshkov, Fisher espoused a naval doctrine that was heavily based on new technological developments (e.g., the fast, all-big-gun dreadnought battleship) and the directions in which technological developments must take a navy. Like Gorshkov's, Fisher's frame of reference was more the needs of his own nation than creation of universal naval theory. But there is an important similarity among these three men: they all were writing in an attempt to impress upon reluctant national leadership the importance of a navy and the need to support the shipbuilding and new technology that a modern navy required.

Another factor to consider when comparing Gorshkov with Western naval personalities is that Gorshkov was an operational commander-in-chief, like Fisher (who served as First Sea Lord from 1904 to 1910, and again from 1914 to 1915). Mahan, in contrast, was primarily a scholar and held no operational positions after commanding the protected cruiser *Chicago* from 1893 to 1896.

Some Western commentators attempt to compare Admiral Gorshkov with Admiral Hyman G. Rickover, the head of the U.S. Navy's nuclear propulsion program from 1948 to 1981. Both Gorshkov and Rickover were innovators and pushed technology, although the latter, in retrospect, was highly conservative in his designs of nuclear-propelled surface ships and submarines. Rickover had no operational authority except what he could glean from the support of Congress, perceived authority that he sometimes used in direct opposition to the plans and efforts of the U.S. Navy's leadership as well as Department of Defense officials.[16]

Admiral Gorshkov was, then, both a theorist and a realist, an innovator and an operational commander. In his almost 30 years in command of the Soviet Navy he changed that body from a third-rate collection of almost impotent ships—some dating from the tsarist era—to a first-rate fleet. Indeed, some American naval leaders believed that in a nuclear war, the Gorshkov navy would be more capable of carrying out its missions than the U.S. Navy was capable of carrying out its own. This is a thesis that requires further examination.

The Bottom Lines

In the days of sailing ships it was relatively easy to compare navies by looking at numbers of ships, the numbers of guns they carried, and the weight (in terms of cannon balls) of their broadsides. In the age of steam it was essentially the same, with the number and caliber of guns substituted for weight of broadside. This methodology, with modification to allow for aircraft and aircraft carriers, was still in use well into the Cold War. Admiral Gorshkov's navy made this simplistic methodology obsolete.

Admiral Gorshkov himself wrote, "We have had to cease comparing the number of warships of one type or another and their total displacement (or number of guns in a salvo or the weight of this salvo), and turn to a more complex, but also more correct, appraisal of the striking and defensive power of ships, based on a mathematical analysis of their capabilities and qualitative characteristics."[17] In total numbers of ships, including major coastal craft, the Soviet Navy at the end of Admiral Gorshkov's career was the largest in the world. In terms of numbers of ocean-going warships, it was the second largest. In terms of total tonnage displacement, it trailed well behind the United States, because of the number and size of U.S. aircraft carriers. Further, it was well short of the combined number and displacement of NATO warships. But the numbers and tonnage reveal little and, in fact, can be quite misleading. The Soviet Navy was not designed for the same missions as the Western navies against which it was being compared.

Whatever the public strategy document of the moment may have stated, the U.S. Navy's strategy, doctrine, and force development during the Cold War centered on two missions: first, nuclear strike against the Soviet homeland—in early Cold War years with aircraft carriers and cruise missile submarines, later with ballistic missile submarines—and second, protection of the Atlantic sea-lanes against an anticipated Third Battle of the Atlantic with Red submarines seeking to sever the sea-lanes between the Americas and Western Europe, *which the Soviets never planned to conduct.* The fleet that these missions created was constantly used to provide presence in distant areas in support of U.S. foreign policy and occasionally was called upon to fight in distant wars (e.g., Korea, Vietnam, Afghanistan, Iraq, Syria). Other than in the area of potential anti-submarine warfare against Soviet SSBNs, nowhere in the litany of U.S. naval missions actually conducted was the Soviet Navy a major factor.

Soviet ships would be encountered on the high seas while the U.S. Navy was operating in forward areas, but there was confidence that the Soviet Navy would present a relatively minor threat to the U.S. Navy, one that its superior aircraft carriers could easily defeat. Indeed, the Soviet naval threat had little impact on U.S. ship construction or deployment. *But*, Admiral Gorshkov's surface ships and submarines served well to justify naval expenditures before Congress. The United States had a need for a large high-seas fleet quite independent of the size and capabilities of the Soviet Navy.

In contrast, Admiral Gorshkov's Soviet Navy was designed *primarily* to counter the U.S. Navy. Other than the SSB/SSBN force, with its obvious strategic nuclear strike mission, Soviet naval strategy was essentially defensive and designed to counter U.S. Navy offensive capabilities: anti-carrier, anti-SSBN, support of Soviet SSBNs against Western anti-submarine forces, anti-amphibious assault, and, of course, supporting the seaward flanks of the Soviet Army.

Thus, it is not possible to compare navies in a conventional "Which navy is better?" fashion. There were missions that the U.S. Navy was more capable of executing, and there were missions at which the Soviet Navy was better. The real question to be asked is which navy was better capable of performing *its own* missions in the face of opposition from the other. This question is complex and really answerable only through war gaming and careful net assessment. Arguably, even these techniques would yield different answers depending on the assumptions made.

It is obvious that the Soviet Navy had conducted a very careful assessment of U.S. Navy strengths and weaknesses and designed weapons systems, strategy, and tactics with these in mind. It is not obvious that the U.S. Navy had conducted as careful an intellectual analysis of Soviet strengths and weaknesses and designed weapons and tactics accordingly. The *peacetime* U.S. Navy was continually called on to deal with other adversaries, to serve in a political-military role, and to develop weapons and tactics designed for other uses. For its part, Admiral Gorshkov's navy had in particular a more fully developed strategy for nuclear war and an arsenal far better suited to fighting in that environment. It war-gamed nuclear war at sea extensively and practiced it in exercises. The U.S. Navy seldom did either.

In a war that was nuclear at the outset, the Soviet Navy would undoubtedly have had the advantage. In a conventional war the advantage would likely have accrued to the U.S./NATO forces, although to a degree highly dependent on the time, location, and manner of the start of hostilities. A war that began as a conventional war and then "went nuclear" would be a more difficult scenario to analyze and would involve such variables as how long the war had remained conventional, how well U.S./NATO anti-submarine forces had been able to cope with the very serious Soviet submarine threat, how long European ports had been available to receive reinforcements, and a host of others. Clearly, a thoughtful comparison of the Soviet and U.S./NATO navies would reveal that Admiral Gorshkov had designed a navy that was quite capable of inflicting great damage and was to be taken very seriously—perhaps more seriously than it was at the time. In his writings Gorshkov continually stressed the importance of surprise and "the battle for the first salvo" to help ensure Soviet victory at sea.

The Ultimate Legacy

Admiral Gorshkov's ultimate legacy is clear: a Soviet Navy recognized as a critical component of Soviet war-fighting strategy, second only to the Strategic Rocket Forces; a Soviet Navy seen by the West as large, potent, and capable; a Soviet Navy acknowledged by senior Soviet/Russian political leadership as a significant contributor to the achievement of foreign policy goals. In sum, he bequeathed to the Soviet state a navy that was important to the state on its own merits and not solely a supporting arm for the Soviet Army.

Admiral Gorshkov built a Soviet Navy that could challenge unfettered American use of the sea. He accomplished this despite traditional Russian and Soviet emphasis on land power, with limited historical effectiveness at sea—indeed at times having no sea-going navy at all. Importantly, the reflection of the navy that Gorshkov built sails on today. It is far smaller. But it is still a far-reaching navy, one that continues to push advanced technologies, and it continues to provide Russia's political leaders with important diplomatic and military tools. To senior Russian leadership it is still an *important* navy.

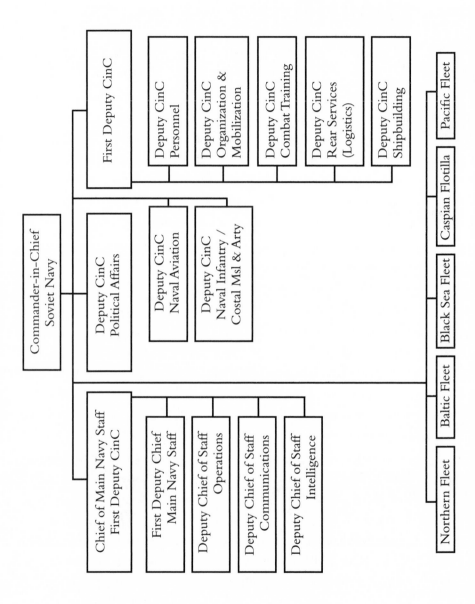

Figure 15-1. Soviet Navy Organization

CHAPTER 16

From Soviet Navy to Russian Navy

At last Russia has returned to the world arena as a strong state—a country which others heed and that can stand up for itself.

—President Vladimir Putin (2008)

The collapse of the Soviet Union in December 1991 was one of the most traumatic events in Russia's long history. It cost the central regime not only the loss of the Baltic republics and the Ukraine, but also Byelorussia, the Transcaucasian republics of Georgia and Armenia, and all of the Moslem republics of Central Asia. The Russian-Soviet Empire, built over three centuries, ceased to exist within days. With it went critical industries, including major shipyards, as well as raw materials, manpower, and economic capacity that had supported the vast military establishment of the Soviet regime.

Millions of Russian people now found themselves living in "foreign" countries. The further diminution of financial capability meant that Boris Yeltsin, the "new" Russia's first president, would have to accelerate the reductions in the armed forces begun by his predecessor, Mikhail Gorbachev. Under Gorbachev the reductions to the Soviet Navy had been relatively modest. Many old, inactive surface ships and submarines had been towed away for scrapping. This had given the immediate appearance of a major reduction in the Navy's order of battle, but the preponderance of the scrapped ships had been little more than floating—and sometimes barely floating—hulks. Their loss had had little impact on the operational capability of the fleet. Soviet Navy ships continued to deploy out of area, although at a somewhat diminished pace, and the budget of the Soviet Navy, to all appearances, suffered little or no reduction early in new-Russia era.

But all of this would have to change. Navies are very expensive: warships are not only expensive to build but costly to maintain, man, and operate. A large shipbuilding program requires the dedication of extensive capital investment and places a great strain on a nation's pool of engineers and technically capable workers. Historically, nations have cut back on investments in their navies when economic times are tough and there is no immediate threat from seaward approaches. This had been true for tsarist Russia and for the Soviet Union. For Boris Yeltsin, naval expenditures were a logical place to look for some of the savings required to offset the financial impact of the dissolution of the Soviet Empire.

The reductions came quickly, and they were draconian—far beyond what Western observers had anticipated. The impact on the operational capability of the Navy was compounded by the mass exodus of trained naval personnel to their newly independent native lands, in particular to the Baltic States. Added to this, many Russian conscripts simply deserted their ships and posts.

The situation was so horrific that even patrols by strategic missile submarines—probably the Navy's number-one priority—were curtailed. In some years there were no SSBN patrols, in others only one, two, or three, until well into the 21st Century. (It should be noted that the Soviet Navy had normally kept only 10 to 15 percent of its strategic missile submarines at sea at any given time—compared to some 50 percent for the U.S. Navy. At the same time the Soviet and new Russian Navy had many SSBNs in port in a high state of readiness for going to sea. Also, Soviet/Russian strategic missile submarines could launch their long-range ballistic missiles while in port—a procedure that was exercised.)

Under the new fiscal realities surface ships and submarines had to be placed in reserve or discarded because they could not be adequately manned. Often the admirals had difficulty in coming up with even the 25 percent manning required to keep a ship in "active reserve" status. The new Russian Navy could not afford to man or to operate some ships that were relatively new, such as the four *Kiev*-class aircraft carriers, the two *Kuznetsov*-class carriers (one operational, one just launched and unfinished), and the *Ul'yanovsk*, Russia's unfinished nuclear-propelled carrier, very early in her construction. Three of the *Kievs* were sold for scrap, one was sold to India for operational service; the unfinished *Kuznetsov* was sold by Ukraine for completion in China; and the *Ul'yanovsk* was scrapped on the ways. Only the *Admiral Kuznetsov*, of some 55,000 tons full load and completed in 1990, was retained in Russian service—the nation's only surviving aviation ship.

Shipbuilding ground to a virtual halt. One-half of the Soviet shipyards that had built surface naval ships were not in the "new" Russia. The Nikolayev shipyard, which had built all the Soviet aviation ships, beginning with the *Moskva*, was now in the independent country of Ukraine. The factory that had built gas turbines for most Soviet surface combatants also was in Ukraine (and in later years, after the Russian seizure of the Crimea and its support of dissidents in the eastern Ukraine, the factory ceased to provide gas turbines for Russian warships, inflicting additional delays in warship construction).

When the Cold War ended there were in Russia five yards building nuclear-propelled submarines: Krasnoye Sormovo (in Gor'kiy), Admiralty (St. Petersburg), Sudomekh (St. Petersburg), Komsomol'sk-on-Amur, and Severodvinsk. (The Admiralty and the adjacent Sudomekh yards had been consolidated into a single administrative entity—the United Admiralty Association—in 1972.) All nuclear submarine construction was now consolidated at Severodvinsk, and the Admiralty complex concentrated on conventional submarines for

Russia and foreign customers. The submarine-building program that had in the Soviet era produced eight or nine submarines per year in the 1980s now completed one or two—every once in a while. Submarines and surface ships entering a shipyard for overhaul could expect to remain there for several years.[1]

Within the shipyards, beyond the loss of skilled workers (who sought other employment that actually *paid* them, even part-time), component suppliers ceased providing material, because they, too, were not being paid; periodically shipyards "went dark," the government being in arrears in its electric bills. The ship and submarine design bureaus—collectively a key component of the military-industrial complex—continued working, but with far fewer naval architects and engineers, as hundreds of members of their staffs sought other work. For example, the Malachite submarine design bureau in St. Petersburg (no longer Leningrad) declined in the 1990s from some 2,500 employees to 1,200.[2] Engineers still at the design bureaus sought part-time work of almost any kind to continue earning rubles for food and rent.

By the end of 2015 the Russian Navy was less than one-fourth the size of the Soviet Navy of 1985, the year Admiral Gorshkov retired, and the average age of the fleet was now in excess of 20 years.[3] The submarine force was now only about one-fourth the size of the 1991 force. The surface force of 2017 was roughly the same size as in 1991, but only because of the large number of small combatants built or retained. In terms of larger combatants, ASW frigates and larger, the fleet had shrunk significantly. Beyond the discarding of aircraft carriers, most of the Gorshkov-built cruisers and destroyers were gone. One could almost hear the echo of Nikita Khrushchev's demand: "Scrap the cruisers!"

About 2005 a decision appears to have been made under President Vladimir Putin to begin rebuilding the Russian Navy and to deploy it once again on the high seas in support of foreign policy. A ship-building program was announced that went through the year 2020. In 2008, reports surfaced that Russia would again build nuclear-propelled aircraft carriers; subsequent statements by Russian Navy officials indicated that preliminary design work had begun. But loss of the Nikolayev shipyard in the Ukraine meant that a ship that large could be constructed only at the SEVMASH yard (the Northern Machine-Building Enterprise, in Severodvinsk). It is at least possi-ble to construct a carrier in sections and then combine them—as recently done in Britain. But all Russian facilities involved would require major modifications to build a carrier. (The single operational Russian carrier, the *Admiral Kuznetsov*, entered the SEVMASH yard in 2017 for a multi-year modernization and life-extension program.)

Meanwhile, as the carrier program continued to be delayed, the government announced plans to build a class of large, 15,000-ton destroyers of the Lider (Leader) class—to be nuclear propelled. That program also was encountering delays. The construction of small combatants—small frigates and corvettes—was, however, continu-ing, and those ships were far more heavily armed than their Western counterparts (see below).

Back to Sea
Periodic long-range operations by Russian Navy continued, albeit at a far lower rate than during the latter years of the Gorshkov era. In 2008 there was a visit to the Mediterranean by a task force led by the aircraft carrier *Admiral Kuznetzov* and the nuclear-propelled battle cruiser *Petr Velikiy* (Peter the Great). The cruiser then proceeded across the Atlantic to make a port call in Venezuela before crossing the Atlantic again for visits in South Africa and returning home via the Indian Ocean and Mediterranean. The November port call in Venezuela coincided with a visit there of the Russian president, Dmitry Medvedev.

In 2012, Defense Minister Sergey Shoygu announced that Russia would maintain up to ten ships in the Mediterranean.[4] In separate

comments, Admiral Viktor Chirkov, the Commander-in-Chief of
the Russian Navy (2012–2016), stated in 2013 that 80 Russian warships and support ships were then "offshore in various parts of the
global ocean" and pointed out that time spent forward deployed in
2013 was 15 percent higher than in 2012.[5] Both totals comprised
small numbers of combatant ships relative to the number of auxiliary and support ships.

Perhaps the most dramatic example of Russia's use of the Navy
to further foreign policy goals occurred on 7 October 2015, when
a Russian Navy *Gepard*-class frigate and three smaller, 950-ton,
Sviyazhsk-class patrol ships launched 26 Kalibr land-attack cruise
missiles from the Caspian Sea against targets in Syria, a distance
of more than 900 miles.[6] Subsequently, more Kalibr missiles were
launched from a Kilo (Project 636)–class diesel-electric submarine
and a frigate into Syria from the eastern Mediterranean Sea in support of Russian ally Bashar Assad, the Syrian dictator.

The carrier *Admiral Kuznetsov* sailed from the Northern Fleet to
the Mediterranean in the fall of 2016 carrying an austere air group
on board and accompanied by several surface combatants.[7] Her contribution to the Russia air campaign over Syria was limited and brief.
Still, like the Kalibr missile strikes, the carrier demonstrated that the
Russian Navy could provide direct—and highly publicized—support of the nation's foreign policy goals.

At the same time, Russian landing ships and merchant ships were
transporting troops, tanks, weapons, and aviation supplies to Syria
to support the Assad government. Naval Infantry was also brought
into Syria, as revealed when a Russian aircraft was shot down by
Turkey and naval helicopters carrying marines rescued the surviving crewman.

Ambitious Plans

In 2013 the Russian government announced a several-fold increase
in its shipbuilding budget over previous years. Highly significantly, it

now accounted for a quarter of the acquisition budget of the armed forces; in fact, the Russian Navy was second only to the Strategic Rocket Forces in the size of its overall budget allocation. President Putin announced that by 2020 this program would produce 16 nuclear-propelled submarines, 8 diesel-electric submarines, and 51 surface combatants.[8] Beyond that, some existing ships would be overhauled and placed back in active service. Among these would be the *Kirov*-class nuclear battle cruiser *Admiral Nakhimov.*

As further evidence of a rehabilitation of the Navy, the first *Dolgorukiy* (Project 935/Borey)–class strategic missile submarine entered service in 2013, with additional units following; the first *Severodvinsk* (Project 885)–class cruise missile submarine was completed in 2014, again with more following. Both of these lead submarines had been long on the building ways, but in their long gestation periods—16 and 20 years, respectively—they had been extensively (some would say "completely") redesigned and updated. Russia continues to construct improved Kilo-class diesel-electric boats, both for its own use and for foreign transfer. Air-Independent Propulsion (AIP) submarines are said to be under development.

As this volume went to press it appeared that the Russian Navy may have passed its low point and was on its way back, albeit with many "bumps" along the course ahead. It is clear that President Putin, in his determination to reestablish Russia as a great power, has placed considerable importance on an ocean-going navy, to assert Russia's status as a great power, to provide for the forward defense of the nation, and to support Russian foreign policy. This was reflected in the 2009 document *National Security Strategy of the Russian Federation*: "Russia believes that the maintenance of strategic stability and equitable strategic partnership can be supported by the presence of contingents of the armed forces of the Russian Federation in conflict zones, on the basis of norms of international law, with the goals of resolving political, economic, and other challenges by non-military means."[9] On 20 July 2017, President Putin issued a decree "On confirming the Basis of Russian Federation state policy in the area of naval activity through 2030":

> The basic goals of Russian naval activity includes: maintaining naval potential at a level guaranteeing deterrence of aggression against Russia from maritime directions and the capability to cause unacceptable damage on any potential adversary; maintenance of strategic stability and international order at sea including the effective use of the Navy as one of the basic instruments of Russian foreign policy; and maintenance of conditions conducive to the exploitation and rational use of maritime natural resources in the interest of the country's socio-economic development.[10]

Many of the points made by Admiral Gorshkov during his long tenure as commander-in-chief regarding the peacetime value of a strong navy find expression in the documents and statements of today's Russian leadership. Russia has endured some difficult times since Admiral Gorshkov retired and the Soviet regime ended, but now its borders are secure, and its economy, although weak, is relatively stable. Vladimir Putin is a strong "tsar."

Russian shipbuilding has shown signs of a slow resurgence, and Russian Navy ships are once again seen on the high seas, particularly in the Mediterranean. If, however, it appears that the pendulum has begun to swing back—toward a more viable navy—just how far back it will swing cannot be predicted. It can safely be said that the Russian Navy of the foreseeable future will not attain the size, stature, or relative capabilities of Admiral Gorshkov's navy, which most likely represented a high point. To restore the order of battle to something approaching the Gorshkov fleet would require a very expensive, long-term shipbuilding program. Even if Russia were able to afford such a program, Putin's stated goal of "reasonable sufficiency and effectiveness at a cost the country can afford" would seem to preclude such expenditures. Today's Russian fleet, however, although much smaller than in the later years of the Gorshkov era, is still based on his drive for quality and for capabilities to carry out peacetime as well as wartime missions in the interests of the state.

Whatever the strength and composition of the Russian Navy of the foreseeable future, one factor appears certain—that it still will bear the imprint of Admiral Sergey Georgiyevich Gorshkov.

APPENDIX A

Admiral Gorshkov Chronology

26 February 1910*	born in Kamenets–Podolskiy, Ukraine
1927	attended M.V. Frunze Naval Academy
1931	navigator on destroyer *Frunze* (Black Sea)
1932	flag navigator of minesweeping and harbor defense brigade (Pacific)
1934	commanding officer, escort ship *Burun* (Pacific)
1937	destroyer commanding officer course (Pacific)
1938	commanding officer, destroyer (Pacific)
1939	chief of staff, destroyer brigade (Pacific)
1939	commander, destroyer brigade (Pacific)
June 1940	commander, cruiser brigade (Black Sea)
November 1940	command course, Voroshilov Naval Academy
1941	returned to command, cruiser brigade (Black Sea)
September 1941	promoted to rear admiral
October 1941	commander, Azov Flotilla
August 1942	membership in Communist Party
August 1942	deputy commander, Novorossiysk defense region
September 1942	acting commander, 47th Army (until October 1942)
February 1943	commander, Azov Flotilla
December 1943	suffers concussion and spinal damage in vehicle accident
February 1944	returns to active service
April 1944	commander, Danube Flotilla
September 1944	promoted to vice admiral

January 1945	commander of squadron (*eskadra*) (Black Sea)
November 1948	chief of staff, Black Sea Fleet
August 1952	commander, Black Sea Fleet
August 1953	promoted to admiral
July 1955	First Deputy Commander-in-Chief of Navy; acting Commander-in-Chief
January 1956	Commander-in-Chief of Navy and First Deputy Minister of Defense★★
February 1956	Candidate Member, Central Committee of the Communist Party of the Soviet Union
October 1961	Full Member, Central Committee CPSU
April 1962	promoted to admiral of the fleet
May 1965	awarded Hero of the Soviet Union
October 1967	promoted to fleet admiral of the Soviet Union
December 1985	retired from active service
13 May 1988	passed away in Moscow

★ New style calendar; 13 February in old style calendar.

★★ Subsequently Deputy Minister of Defense vice First Deputy.

APPENDIX B

Admiral Gorshkov's Awards and Honors

Soviet Awards

- Hero of the Soviet Union, twice awarded (1965, 1982)
- Order of Lenin, seven times awarded (1953, 1960, 1963, 1965, 1970, 1978, 1982)
- Order of the October Revolution (1968)
- Order of the Red Banner, four times awarded (1942, 1943, 1947, 1959)
- Order of Ushakov, 1st and 2nd Classes
- Order of Kutuzov
- Order of the Patriotic War, 1st Class (1985)
- Order of the Red Star
- Order for Service to the Homeland in the Armed Forces of the USSR, 3rd Class (1975)
- USSR State Prize (1980)
- Lenin Prize (1985)
- Honorary Citizenship of Sevastopol, Vladivostok, Berdyansk, Eisk, and Severodvinsk
- Jubilee Medal, "In Commemoration of the 100th Anniversary since the Birth of Vladimir Il'ich Lenin"
- Medal, "For the Defence of Odessa"
- Medal, "For the Defence of the Caucasus"
- Medal, "For the Victory over Germany in the Great Patriotic War 1941–1945"
- Jubilee Medal, "20 Years of Victory in the Great Patriotic War 1941–1945"
- Jubilee Medal, "30 Years of Victory in the Great Patriotic War 1941–1945"
- Jubilee Medal, "40 Years of Victory in the Great Patriotic War 1941–1945"
- Medal, "For the Capture of Budapest"
- Medal, "For the Liberation of Belgrade"
- Medal, "Veteran of the Armed Forces of the USSR"

- Jubilee Medal, "30 Years of the Soviet Army and Navy"
- Jubilee Medal, "40 Years of the Armed Forces of the USSR"
- Jubilee Medal, "50 Years of the Armed Forces of the USSR"
- Jubilee Medal, "60 Years of the Armed Forces of the USSR"
- Medal, "In Commemoration of the 250th Anniversary of Leningrad"

Foreign Awards
- Gold Patriotic Order of Merit (East Germany)
- Scharnhorst Order (East Germany)
- Gold Order of the Partisan Star (Yugoslavia)
- Order of Sukhbaatar (Mongolia)
- Order of the Hungarian People's Republic, 1st Class (Hungary)
- Order of the People's Republic of Bulgaria, 1st Class (Bulgaria)
- Grand Cross of the Order of St. Alexander, with Swords (Bulgaria)

Monuments and Namings
- Monuments erected in Kolomna and Novorossiysk
- Memorial plaque on the former Russian Navy Headquarters building in Moscow
- Memorial plaque on the headquarters building of the Black Sea Fleet
- Central Hospital of the Navy
- School Number 9 in Kolomna, from which he graduated in 1926
- Railway station Kupavna, Moscow Oblast
- Neighborhood of Novorossiysk
- Central Sports Club of the Navy
- The Admiral Gorshkov Award (Russian Navy, 2006)
- *Kiev*-class aircraft carrier completed in 1987 as the *Baku* renamed the *Admiral Flota Sovetskogo Soyuza Gorshkov* in 1991 (would be sold to India in 2013 and renamed *Vikramaditya*)
- Frigate named *Admiral Gorshkov*, completed in 2017

APPENDIX C

Heads of the Soviet Navy, 1918–1991

October 1918–April 1919	Vasili Mikhailovich Altfater
April 1919–February 1920	Yevgeny Andreyevich Berens
February 1920–November 1921	Aleksandr Vasiliyevich Nemits
November 1921–December 1924	Eduard Samoilovich Pantserzhansky
December 1924–August 1926	Vyacheslav Ivanovich Zof
August 1926–June 1931	Romuald Adamovich Muklevich
June 1931–August 1937	Vladimir Mitrofanovich Orlov
July–August 1937	Lev Mikhailovich Galler
August 1937–December 1937	Mikhail Vladimirovich Viktorov
December 1937–November 1938	Pyotr Alexandrovich Smirnov
November 1938–March 1939	Mikhail Petrovich Frinovsky
April 1939–January 1947	Nikolai Gerasimovich Kuznetsov
January 1947–July 1951	Ivan Stepanovich Yumashev
July 1951–January 1956	Nikolai Gerasimovich Kuznetsov★
January 1956–December 1985	Sergey Georgyevich Gorshkov
December 1985–December 1991	Vladimir Nikolayevich Chernavin★★

★ Second term as Commander-in-Chief/Navy Minister.
★★ Subsequently the Commander-in-Chief of the Navy of the Commonwealth of Independent States, through August 1992.

APPENDIX D

Soviet/Russian Officer Ranks

Line officers of the Soviet and now Russian Navies have traditional naval ranks but historically with seven grades of commissioned rank below flag grades, compared with six in the U.S. Navy. This rank structure reflects the early German naval influence on the Russian Navy.

The title of "admiral" fell into disuse at the start of the Soviet regime, because of its tsarist antecedents. Admiral ranks were not re-introduced until May 1940, when seven Soviet officers were given the title. Many more officers were appointed to flag rank during World War II. The rank of Admiral of the Fleet (*Admiral Flota*) was introduced in May 1940, to be abolished in 1955 with the establishment of the rank of Admiral of the Fleet of the Soviet Union (*Admiral Flota Sovetskogo Soyuza*) but re-established in 1962. The fleet admiral rank is the equivalent of the rank of marshal, and Admiral of the Fleet of the Soviet Union was equivalent to Marshal of the Soviet Union.

Exact comparisons with U.S. ranks are difficult and can be confusing. For example, a Soviet/Russian Navy captain first rank wears the broad sleeve stripe of a commodore or rear admiral (lower half) in Western navies yet wears the shoulder insignia of a colonel, his nominal Army equivalent. The issue is further complicated by the fact that the Soviet/Russian armed forces do not have a brigadier general rank: their one-star military rank is major general.

During most of the Cold War the U.S. Navy had only one rear admiral rank (two stars), and the Soviet rank of rear admiral could easily be equated. During the last five years of Admiral Gorshkov's tenure, the U.S. Navy introduced the one-star rank of rear admiral (lower half). Then the Soviet Navy rank of rear admiral could best be equated to *both* U.S. rear admiral ranks. The Soviet-era rank of fleet admiral would then equate to the U.S. Navy rank of fleet admiral (five stars), which was created during World War II but has not been awarded since. The Soviet rank of Admiral of the Fleet of the Soviet Union has no Western equivalent.

Admiral Gorshkov was the last officer to hold the rank of Admiral of the Fleet of the Soviet Union. There were several fleet admirals on active duty at the time of the collapse of the Soviet Union in 1991, but the rank of neither fleet admiral nor Admiral of the Fleet of the Soviet Union/Russia was in use by the modern Russian Navy when this volume went to press.

In the post-Soviet naval structure the rank of midshipman (*michman*) has been deleted.

Table D-1. Soviet/Russian Officer Ranks

Soviet Navy	Soviet Military and Specialized Naval Branches	U.S. Navy
Michman	Ensign	Warrant officer
Lieutenant	Lieutenant	Ensign
Senior Lieutenant	Senior Lieutenant	Lieutenant (junior grade)
Captain Lieutenant	Captain	Lieutenant
Captain 3rd Rank	Major	Lieutenant Commander
Captain 2nd Rank	Lieutenant Colonel	Commander
Captain 1st Rank	Colonel	Captain
Rear Admiral	Major General	Rear Admiral
Vice Admiral	Lieutenant General	Vice Admiral
Admiral	Colonel General	Admiral
Fleet Admiral	General of the Army Marshal	Fleet Admiral
(none)	Chief Marshal	(none)
Admiral of the Fleet	Marshal of the Soviet Union	Fleet Admiral of the Soviet Union
(none)	Generalissimus★	(none)

★ Rank assumed by Josef Stalin in 1945.

NOTES

Perspective

1. N. Polmar discussions with Adm. Chernavin in Washington, D.C., 6 November 1991, and in Moscow, 10 and 12 November 1992.
2. Adm. S. G. Gorshkov, *Vo Flotskom Stroyu* [In Naval Ranks] (St. Petersburg: Logos, 1996).
3. Capt. 1/R M. S. Monakov, *GLAVKOM: Zhizn' i rabota flota admirala Sovetskogo Soyuza S. G. Gorshkova* [Commander-in-Chief: The Life and Work of Fleet Admiral of the Soviet Union S. G. Gorshkov] (Moscow: Kuchkovo Polye, 2008).
4. Capt. 1/R V. P. Kuzin and Capt. 1/R N. I. Nikol'skiy, *Voyenno-Morskoy Flot SSSR 1945–1991* [The Soviet Navy, 1945–1991] (St. Petersburg: Historical Naval Society, 1996).
5. Adm. Brooks served as Director of Naval Intelligence from July 1988 to August 1991.

Chapter Two. Growing Up in the New World Order, 1910–1927

1. Monakov, *GLAVKOM*, 9–13.
2. The monarchies of Russia, Germany, Austria-Hungary, and Turkey fell as a result of World War I.
3. The British *Dreadnought,* launched in 1906, was a revolutionary design— an "all-big-gun" battleship—with firepower and speed that outclassed all previous battleships. Her appearance initiated a dreadnought-building race among the European naval powers, primarily Britain, Germany, and Russia.
4. Later, during the Russian Civil War, Adm. Kolchak rose to be the Supreme Commander of the White—anti-Bolshevik—forces in Siberia. See Peter Fleming, *The Fate of Admiral Kolchak* (New York: Harcourt, Brace & World, 1963).
5. Born Lev Davidovich Bronstein in the Ukraine, Trotsky became a revolutionary at an early age.
6. Russia changed from the old (Julian) calendar to the new (Gregorian) on 1 February 1918. At that time the difference was 13 days.
7. See E. M. Halliday, *The Ignorant Armies* (New York: Harper & Brothers, 1958); and John Bradley, *Allied Intervention in Russia 1917–1920* (New York: Basic Books, 1968).

8. W. Bruce Lincoln, *Red Victory: A History of the Russian Civil War* (New York: Simon & Schuster, 1989), 73.

9. Adm. S. G. Gorshkov, *The Seapower of the State* (Oxford, U.K.: Pergamon, 1979), 130.

10. Gorshkov, *Vo Flotskom Stroyu*, 15.

Chapter Three. The Education of an Admiral, 1927–1941

1. Kolomna subsequently re-named the school in honor of the admiral, who is counted as one of the city's "five notable people."

2. The Order of Lenin, Red Banner, Order of Ushakov, M.V. Frunze Higher Naval School—the direct successor of the naval officer commissioning school founded by Peter the Great and the functional equivalent of the U.S. Naval Academy at Annapolis, Md.

3. Gorshkov, *Vo Flotskom Stroyu,* 16.

4. These ships were designated Project 26; full load displacement in long tons is provided for warships throughout the text.

5. John Erickson, *The Soviet High Command 1918–1941* (London: Macmillan, 1962), 392.

6. Project 23. Details of these programs are provided in Jürgen Rohwer and Capt. 1/R Mikhail S. Monakov, *Stalin's Ocean-Going Fleet: Soviet Naval Strategy and Shipbuilding Programmes 1935–1953* (London: Frank Cass, 2001).

7. The machinations of aircraft carrier programs in the Stalin era are described in Robert Waring Herrick, *Soviet Naval Theory and Policy: Gorshkov's Inheritance* (Annapolis, Md.: Naval Institute Press, 1998), especially 86–93. Also see N. Polmar, *Aircraft Carriers: A History of Carrier Aviation and Its Influence on World Events*, vol. 2, *1946–2006* (Washington, D.C.: Potomac Books, 2008), 339–362.

8. President Roosevelt recognized and established diplomatic relations with the Soviet Union on 16 November 1933, ending almost 16 years of American non-recognition of the Soviet regime.

9. This was the German *Lützow*, launched in July 1939 and transferred to the Soviet Union in April 1940. She was unfinished, with only half of her main battery of eight 8-inch (203-mm) guns installed. She was sunk at Leningrad by German forces in 1942 and salvaged by the Soviet Navy the same year. Renamed first *Petropavlovsk* (1940), then *Tallinn* (1944), and finally *Dniepr* (1953), she was scrapped having never been completed as a cruiser.

10. See Robert Conquest, *The Great Terror* (London: Macmillan, 1968); his chapter "Assault on the Army" (pp. 201–235) is particularly instructive.

11. Seweryn Bialer, *Stalin and His Generals* (London: Souvenir, 1970), 75.

12. Ibid., 63.

13. Monakov, *GLAVKOM,* 155. *Flagman* was the highest "rank" in the Soviet Navy; the term "admiral" was in desuetude from the Civil War until mid-1940.

14. Adm. N. G. Kuznetsov, *Memoirs of the Wartime Minister of the Navy* (Moscow: Progress, 1990), 97. Kuznetsov also described the circumstances of his appointment in "Before the War," *Oktyabr'* (no. 9, 1965), 174–182. This is reprinted in Bialer, *Stalin and His Generals,* 90–98.

15. Monakov, *GLAVKOM,* 112.

16. See Stuart D. Goldman, *Nomonhan, 1939: The Red Army's Victory That Shaped World War II* (Annapolis, Md.: Naval Institute Press, 2012).

17. Monakov, *GLAVKOM,* 134–147.

18. Ibid., 185.

Chapter Four. Gorshkov at War, 1941

1. The six Type IIB U-boats operated in the Black Sea from the Rumanian port of Constanza from October 1942 to October 1944. Three of the U-boats were lost during the war, and three were scuttled on 10–11 September 1944; two of the latter were salvaged by the Soviets and placed in service from 1947 to 1960. See N. Polmar and Jurrien Noot, *Submarines of the Russian and Soviet Navies, 1718–1990* (Annapolis, Md.: Naval Institute Press, 1991), 316–317.

2. David E. Murphy, *What Stalin Knew: The Enigma of Barbarossa* (New Haven, Conn.: Yale University Press, 2005), xv.

3. Monakov, *GLAVKOM,* 192.

4. Ibid., 196.

5. The bizarre events surrounding the start of the war were described from the naval perspective by Adm. N. G. Kuznetsov in "The Navy on the Eve of the Great Fatherland War," *Voyenno-istoricheskiy Zhurnal* (no. 9, 1965), 73–74, and "On the Eve," *Oktyabr'* (no. 11, 1965), reprinted in Bialer, *Stalin and His Generals,* 189–200.

6. Adm. Gorshkov, "Navies in War and in Peace," *Morskoy Sbornik* (no. 10, 1972), 13.

7. Monakov, *GLAVKOM,* 195.

8. Capt. 1st Rank K. F. Fakeyev, "The Landing at Grigorevka," *Morskoy Sbornik* (no. 9, 1971), 58.

9. Ibid., 59.

10. This may be true in the context that the admiral ranks were established in the Soviet Navy in May 1940. However, when A. G. Golovko took the post of commander of the Northern Fleet in July 1940, at age 32, he was a

rear admiral (being promoted to vice admiral in September 1941); he possibly held flag rank (i.e., *flagman*) in his earlier positions of commander of the Amur River and then the Caspian Flotillas.

Chapter Five. The Sea of Azov, 1942

1. Mariupol was known as Zhdanov from 1948 to 1989.
2. Monakov, *GLAVKOM,* 227.
3. Adm. Gorshkov, "The Black Sea Fleet in the Battle of the Caucasus," *Voyenno-Istoricheskiy Zhurnal,* no. 3 (1976), 14.
4. Monakov, *GLAVKOM,* 250.
5. Adm. Gorshkov, unpublished manuscript of book *Yug* [The South], chapter 2: "In the Sea of Azov," 16–17; referenced in Monakov, *GLAVKOM,* 246.
6. Monakov, *GLAVKOM,* 250–251.
7. Ibid., 252–253.
8. The dreadnought *Parizhkaya Kommuna* (completed in 1914 as *Sevastopol,* renamed *Parizhkaya Kommuna* in 1921, *Sevastopol* again in 1943), saw no further service during the war. After the war she was partially rehabilitated and served as a training ship until 1954, after which she was scrapped. Some reports state that her main battery guns were replaced at Poti, but this is doubtful—it is highly unlikely that replacement barrels were available at the port or that there were proper facilities or technicians available for the work.
9. Werner Baumbach, *The Life and Death of the Luftwaffe* (New York: Ballantine, 1960), 140–141. The Junkers Ju 88 was a twin-engine bomber and one of the most versatile aircraft of World War II.
10. Monakov, *GLAVKOM,* 272 .
11. I. D. Kirin, *Chernomorskiy Flot v Bitve za Kavkaz* [The Black Sea Fleet in the Battle for the Caucasus] (Moscow: Voyenizdat, 1958), 58–59.
12. A short time before Grechko had been promoted to major general, the Soviet one-star rank, by the end of the war he had advanced two more grades, to colonel-general.
13. See Gorshkov, "Black Sea Fleet in the Battle of the Caucasus," 26; and *Bolshaya Sovetskaya Entsiklopediya* [Large Soviet Encyclopedia] (Moscow: 1972), vol. 7, 136.
14. Monakov, *GLAVKOM,* 275.
15. Ibid., 285.
16. Robert G. Poirier and Albert Z. Conner, *The Red Army Order of Battle in the Great Patriotic War* (Novato, Calif.: Presidio, 1985), 7.
17. Monakov, *GLAVKOM,* 286–288.

18. These German divisions were: 18 panzer, 13 motorized infantry, 78 infantry, and 8 mountain/light infantry. Subsequently, Italian, Hungarian, Rumanian, Spanish, and Russian anti-Soviet (mostly Cossack) troops joined the German forces fighting in Russia.

19. The city was named Volgograd from 1589 to 1925 and again from 1961. Soviet sources contend that the Germans lost 147,200 killed and over 91,000 captured; few of the latter survived internment. The Luftwaffe had flown 30,000 wounded men out of Stalingrad before the battle ended. The Russians have not published official data on their own casualties. See for example Marshal Vasiliy I. Chuikov, *The Battle for Stalingrad* (New York: Holt, Rinehart and Winston, 1964), 263, and Earl F. Ziemke, *Stalingrad to Berlin: The German Defeat in the East* (Washington, D.C.: Department of the Army, 1967), 79.

Chapter Six. On the Offensive, 1943–1945

1. For details of this campaign see Marshal A. A. Grechko, *Bitva za Kavkaz* [The Battle for the Caucasus] (Moscow: Voyenizdat, 1969).

2. Capt. 1st Rank A. Sverdlov, "The Azov Flotilla on the Offensive (August–September 1943)," *Morskoy Sbornik* (no. 9, 1973), 65.

3. Kholostyakov had with Leonid Brezhnev a close association that continued until the Soviet leader's death in 1982. Kholostyakov, who retired as a vice admiral, was bludgeoned to death in Moscow on 21 July 1984, amidst reports of his involvement with the black market and political intrigue.

4. Monakov, *GLAVKOM*, 304. Vasilevsky had coordinated the Soviet offensives on the upper Don River near Voronezh and Ostrogozhsk in January 1943, leading to decisive encirclements of several German divisions. In mid-January he was promoted to the rank of General of the Army and 29 days later, on 16 February 1943, to Marshal of the Soviet Union.

5. Ibid., 318.

6. The troops were 177,355 German soldiers, 50,139 other Axis solders, and 28,486 Russian auxiliaries.

7. Capt. R. C. S. Garwood, Royal Navy, "The Russians as Naval Allies," in *The Soviet Navy*, ed. M. G. Saunders (New York: Praeger, 1958), 81.

8. Monakov, *GLAVKOM*, 322.

9. Garwood, "Russians as Naval Allies," 81. MTB = motor torpedo boat; MGB = motor gunboat.

10. Capt. 1st Rank K. Vorobyev, "In the Rush of Combat," *Morskoy Sbornik* (no. 2, 1980), 60.

11. Vice Adm. Friedrich Ruge (Federal German Navy), *Der Seekrieg: The German Navy's Story 1939–1945* (Annapolis, Md.: U.S. Naval Institute, 1957), 291.

12. P. N. Pospelov, ed., *Istoriya Velikoy Otechestvennoy Voyny Sovetskogo Soyuza 1941–1945* [History of the Great Patriotic War of the Soviet Union 1941–1945] (Moscow: Voyenizdat, 1961), 3:427.

13. Rear Adm. K. A. Stalbo, "The Naval Art in the Landings of the Great Patriotic War," *Morskoy Sbornik* (no. 3, 1970), 29.

14. Gorshkov, "Navies in War and in Peace," 18.

Chapter Seven. Rebuilding a Nation and a Navy, 1945–1953

1. Milovan Djilas, *Conversations with Stalin* (New York: Harcourt, Brace and World, 1962), 182.

2. For details of this program and its several iterations see Rohwer and Monakov, *Stalin's Ocean-Going Fleet.*

3. The Baltic Fleet was divided into the Fourth and Eighth Fleets from February 1946 to January 1956; the Pacific Fleet was divided into the Fifth and Seventh Fleets from January 1947 to January 1953.

4. The technical Krylov Academy and the command-and-staff Voroshilov Academy existed separately from 1945 through 1960, when they were combined into the K. Ye. Voroshilov Naval Academy, precursor of today's N. G. Kuznetsov Naval Academy.

5. Sergey Zonin, "An Unjust Trial," *Morskoy Sbornik* (no. 2, 1989), 78–84.

6. "The Admirals' Affair" (in Russian), http://www.rgavmf.ru/lib/cherniavsky_admiral.pdf, accessed 15 October 2014.

7. Ibid.

8. Monakov, *GLAVKOM*, 396.

9. In the post-war period Soviet submarine classes have been assigned letter code designations by U.S.-NATO intelligence, the phonetic "Whiskey" being used for the designation *W.* The designations were assigned in random order.

10. These Army officers were Marshals A. M. Vasilevskiy, I. S. Konev, V. D. Sokolovskiy, and Colonel-General B. L. Vannikov, respectively.

11. Nicholas Shadrin (Nicholas Artamonov), "Development of Soviet Maritime Power" (unpublished PhD dissertation, September 1972), 84.

12. The dreadnought was the former Italian battleship *Giulio Cesare*, ceded to the Soviet Union after Italy surrendered to the Allies in September 1943 but not delivered to the Red Navy until 1949. Although completed in 1914, she had been extensively modernized in the 1930s.

Chapter Eight. After Stalin

1. Zhdanov had died in 1948 (at age 52).

2. When dismissed in 1946, Zhukov held the important position of Commander-in-Chief of Ground Forces. In June 1946, he took command

of the Odessa Military District, far from Moscow and lacking in strategic significance and small in assigned troops.

3. Malenkov, quoted in *Pravda* (13 March 1954).

4. Marshal Zhukov, quoted in *Pravda* (13 February 1955).

5. Ministry of Defense, *Pamyatka Soldatu i Serzhantu po Zashchite ot Atomnogo Oruzhiya* [Handbook for Soldiers and Sergeants on Protection from Atomic Ordnance] (Moscow, 1954), 1.

6. Beria, longtime head of Stalin's secret police apparatus, head of the atomic bomb project, and deputy premier since 1946, was arrested on a charge of treason, and, on 23 December 1953, executed.

7. The huge shipbuilding "halls" (covered shipways) at Severodvinsk and Komsomol'sk were erected at Stalin's direction in the 1930s to construct battleships. The city of Severodvinsk, founded as Sudostroy, was renamed Molotovsk from 1938 to 1957, for Stalin's lieutenant Vyacheslav Molotov; for convenience the name Severodvinsk is used throughout this text.

8. N. Korshunova in *Pravda*, 26 June 1964. The capitalist countries were Denmark, Finland, Italy, Japan, and Sweden; the Bloc countries were East Germany, Hungary, Poland, and Yugoslavia.

9. Gorshkov, "The Development of Naval Science," *Morskoy Sbornik* (no. 2, 1967), 20.

10. Nikita Khrushchev, *Khrushchev Remembers: The Last Testament* (Boston: Little, Brown, 1974), 25.

11. Nikita Khrushchev, *Khrushchev Remembers: The Last Testament*, 26.

12. Monakov, *GLAVKOM*, 428–429.

13. Nikita Khrushchev, *Khrushchev Remembers: The Last Testament*, 29.

14. Monakov, *GLAVKOM*, 427. Parkhomenko was relieved as fleet commander in December 1955, having been in command only since July 1955, and apparently was retired from the Navy at that time. Kulakov was assigned as political officer of the Khronstadt Fortress and then of naval educational institutions in the Leningrad area from 1956 to 1971, being promoted to vice admiral in 1961; he also received major decorations, including Hero of the Soviet Union.

15. Michael Parrish, letter to N. Polmar, 8 July 1991.

Chapter Nine. Gorshkov, Zhukov, and the Stalingrad Group

1. Among Adm. Gorshkov's contemporaries in the U.S. Navy, Adm. Elmo R. Zumwalt became Chief of Naval Operations at age 49; Adm. James L. Holloway III, at age 52; Admirals Arleigh Burke and John Hayward at age 54; Admirals George W. Anderson, Thomas Moorer, and James Watkins at age 55; and Adm. David MacDonald at age 57.

2. Nikita Khrushchev, *Khrushchev Remembers: The Last Testament*, 28.

3. Ibid., 31. Also see chapter 2, "The Navy," 19–34; it has the sub-chapters "The Fall of Admiral Kuznetsov" and "The Rise of Admiral Gorshkov."

4. *Slovar Biograficheskoy Morskoy* [Naval Biographic Dictionary] (St. Petersburg: LOGOS, 2001), 166.

5. Rear Adm. Kemp Tolley, *Caviar and Commissars: The Experiences of a U.S. Naval Officer in Stalin's Russia* (Annapolis, Md.: Naval Institute Press, 1983), 133–134.

6. The Stalingrad Group relationships are developed extensively by Roman Kolkowicz in *The Soviet Military and the Communist Party* (Princeton, N.J.: Princeton University Press, 1967).

7. Marshal Zhukov quoted in *Krasnaya Zvezda* and *Sovetskiy Flot* (12 May 1957).

8. In 1988 a Soviet nuclear-propelled cruise missile submarine—the *K-43* of the Charlie (Project 670) type—was transferred on loan to India; that marked the first time that a nuclear ship had been transferred to another nation. A second nuclear submarine later was exchanged for that first unit. Subsequently, India has constructed nuclear submarines.

9. *Pravda* (27 October 1957).

10. Eight years later—and seven months after Khrushchev's dismissal—Marshal Zhukov appeared in an honored position at the Moscow Victory Day celebrations on 9 May 1965. That was the start of his second rehabilitation process, the first having begun at the end of Stalin's reign.

11. Marshal Malinovskiy quoted in *Krasnaya Zvezda* (25 October 1962).

12. Col. Oleg Penkovskiy, *The Penkovskiy Papers* (New York: Doubleday, 1965), 232.

13. Tu-16 was the Soviet military designation for this (Tupolev) aircraft; Badger was the NATO code name for the aircraft. NATO code names for Soviet bombers began with the letter *B*, for fighters with the letter *F* (Fitter, Foxbat, Flanker), and the letter *M* for maritime patrol/ASW aircraft (Madge, May, Mail).

Chapter Ten. Building a Revolutionary Fleet

1. See N. Polmar and K. J. Moore, *Cold War Submarines: The Design and Construction of U.S. and Soviet Submarines* (Washington, D.C.: Brassey's, 2004), 11–38, et seq. Published in Russian as *Podvodnyye Lodki Kholodnoy Voyny: Proyektirovaniye i Stroitel'stvo Podvodnykh Lodok SSHA i SSSR* (St. Petersburg [Russia]: Malachite, 2011).

2. This missile had the NATO code name Scrubber, although U.S. intelligence agencies tended to use the name Strela. The NATO designation SS-N-(–) indicates a surface-to-surface naval weapon; such weapons had

S letter names assigned by NATO. Most if not all Soviet post-war missile development initially were based on German technology and technicians; the Germans successfully used air-to-surface missiles (glide bombs) in 1943–1945 to sink the Italian battleship *Roma* and to sink or damage several U.S. and British warships. See Martin J. Bollinger, *Warriors and Wizards: The Development and Defeat of Radio Controlled Glide Bombs of the Third Reich* (Annapolis, Md.: Naval Institute Press, 2010).

3. Gorshkov, "The Development of Soviet Naval Science," *Morskoy Sbornik* (no. 2, 1967), 20.

4. See Vice Adm. Jerry [Gerald E.] Miller, *Nuclear Weapons and Aircraft Carriers: How the Bomb Saved Naval Aviation* (Washington, D.C.: Smithson Institution Press, 2001); and Polmar, *Aircraft Carriers,* vol. 2, *1946–2006,* especially chapter 3, "Atomic Bombs Aboard Ship," 37–52.

5. The Regulus I cruise missile, operational on surface ships and submarines from 1959 to 1964, had a range of some 500 miles; the follow-on Regulus II, which did not become operational, was a 1,200-mile missile. The Regulus was launched from aircraft carriers, cruisers, and from surfaced submarines. Also see N. Polmar and Capt. John O'Connell, USN (Ret.), *Strike from the Sea* (Annapolis, Md.: Naval Institute Press, 2019).

6. Nikita Khrushchev, *Khrushchev Remembers: The Last Testament,* 31.

7. The *K-3* later received the honorific name *Leninskiy Komsomol*—the (communist) youth group, named for Lenin.

8. The SS-NX-13 became operational in 1975, but had a limited deployment in ballistic missile submarines because of the Strategic Arms Limitation Talks (SALT) agreements. See Polmar and Moore, *Cold War Submarines,* 180–181; and N. Polmar, "Antiship Ballistic Missiles . . . Again," U.S. Naval Institute *Proceedings* (July 2005), 86–87.

9. Major crew reduction was made possible, in part, by providing the world's first integrated combat information–control system fitted in a submarine. The system integrated navigation, tactical maneuvering, and weapons employment; it automatically developed optimum decisions and recommended them to the commanding officer. The original crew goal was 12; subsequent studies and direction by Adm. Gorshkov led to the increase in personnel.

10. Radiy A. Shmakov, "Ahead of Their Time," *Morskoy Sbornik* (no. 7, 1996), 57–61. Also, Shmakov discussions with N. Polmar, St. Petersburg, 6 December 1996, and 7 May 1997.

11. Nikita Khrushchev, *Khrushchev Remembers: The Last Testament,* 30.

12. While the *Ordzhonikidze* was in Portsmouth Harbor during Khrushchev's visit to England in April 1956, the Royal Navy attempted to carry out

underwater surveillance of the ship's hull. A veteran British diver—Lionel (Buster) Crabb—undertook the mission; he disappeared. Not until almost 14 months later was his body found, at sea—missing head and hands.

13. Khrushchev, quoted in *New York Times* (22 September 1959).

14. Gorshkov, "Navies in War and Peace," *Morskoy Sbornik* (no. 2, 1973), 19.

15. Khrushchev, quoted in *Izvestiya* (15 January 1960).

16. Gorshkov, "Faithful Guard Over the Security of the Homeland," *Sovetskiy Flot* (23 February 1960).

17. Sergey N. Khrushchev, *Nikita Khrushchev and the Creation of a Superpower* (University Park: Penn State University Press, 2000), 77. The younger Khrushchev was an aerospace engineer who had worked for missile designer Vladimir Chelomei. He wrote the book while at Brown University, having become an American citizen in 1999.

18. Ibid.

19. Nikita Khrushchev, *Khrushchev Remembers: The Last Testament*, 33.

20. Lt. (jg) Richard M. Basoco, USNR, and Lt. (jg) Richard H. Webber, USNR, "Kynda-Class Missile Frigates," U.S. Naval Institute *Proceedings* (September 1964), 140. The term "frigate" was used by the U.S. Navy from 1951 to 1975 to designate large destroyer-type ships and small cruisers; the Kyndas subsequently were identified as cruisers by the U.S. Navy, while the Soviets had always designated the type as a *raketnyy kreyser*—missile cruiser.

21. Soviet/Russian naval aviation officers are specialists and use air/army ranks. They do not serve on board ship as do U.S. naval aviators, nor do they hold "naval" commands.

22. John Erickson, "The Soviet Naval High Command," U.S. Naval Institute *Proceedings* (May 1973), 69.

Chapter Eleven. New Directions

1. Adm. Igor Kasatonov, Soviet Navy (Ret.), *The Fleet Goes Out to the Ocean: The Story of Fleet Admiral V. A. Kasatonov* (St. Petersburg: Astra-Luxe, 1995), 268.

2. These missiles had the NATO designation SS-N-2 Styx; they were used by the Egyptian Navy in 1967 to sink the Israeli destroyer *Eilat*. See chapter 10.

3. The Royal Navy initiated the development of a nuclear mine to be carried by X-craft midget submarines into Soviet ports (Operation Cudgel); however, the project was halted before the mines were produced.

4. Soviet plans for deployments to Cuba from Anatoli I. Gribkov [Lt. Gen., Soviet Army] and William Y. Smith [Gen., USAF (Ret.)], *Operation Anadyr: U.S. and Soviet Generals Recount the Cuban Missile Crisis* (Chicago: Edition q, 1994), 27–28 ff; N. Polmar discussions with Cuban military historians, Havana, 1–5 September 2002.

5. Some Soviet sources—and Western intelligence evaluations—indicated that the SS-N-14 was designed for the anti-ship as well as the anti-submarine role.

6. Gorshkov, quoted in *Krasnaya Zvezda* (5 February 1963). See James Cable, *Gunboat Diplomacy* (New York: Praeger, 1971), esp. chap. 5, "The Soviet Naval Enigma," 130–156.

7. Adm. Gorshkov, "Navies in War and in Peace," *Morskoy Sbornik* (no. 2, 1972), 20.

8. The U.S. Polaris A3 missile that became operational in submarines in 1964 had a range of 2,500 nautical miles. The missile could be carried in all 41 Polaris submarines.

9. William Beecher, "Soviet Missile Sub on Atlantic Post," *New York Times* (24 April 1970), 1.

10. N. Polmar and Edward Whitman, *Hunters and Killers: Anti-Submarine Warfare since 1943* (Annapolis, Md.: Naval Institute Press, 2016), vol. 2, esp. chapter 9, "Strategic ASW: The United States," 155–168.

11. Vice Adm. H. G. Rickover, "The Soviet Naval Program," *New York Times,* 13 November 1970, 36.

12. Adm. V. A. Alafuzov, "On the Appearance of the Work 'Military Strategy,'" *Morskoy Sbornik* (no. 1, 1963), 92.

13. P. Ye. Melnikov and Yu. I. Chernov, *Sovetskaya Voyennaya Entsiklopediya* [Soviet Military Encyclopedia] (Moscow: Voyenizdat, 1978), 5:403. Maj. Gen. Melnikov was the commander of the Naval Infantry at that time.

14. Gorshkov, "Development of Naval Science."

Chapter Twelve. Selling a Balanced Navy

1. Adm. Gorshkov, "The Development of the Soviet Naval Service," *Morskoy Sbornik* (no. 2, 1967), 19.

2. Copies of these articles were passed to the West by Col. Oleg Penkovskiy before his arrest by the KGB in October 1962. See Penkovskiy, *Penkovskiy Papers*, 227–228.

3. Marshal Malinovskiy, "The Revolution in Military Affairs and the Task of the Military Press," *Kommunist Vooruzhennykh Sil* (November 1963), 9.

4. Marshal of the Soviet Union V. D. Sokolovskiy, *Soviet Military Strategy* (London: Macdonald and Jane's, 1975). This edition, which compares the three editions of the Soviet work, offers excellent editing, analysis, and commentary by Mrs. Harriet Fast Scott. Sokolovskiy had been Marshal Zhukov's chief of staff during World War II. He served in the important position of Chief of the General Staff (and a First Deputy Minister of Defense) from June 1952 until May 1960, thus becoming one of the last officers not of the Stalingrad group to hold a senior military position during the Khrushchev era.

5. Marshal Sokolovskiy et al., eds., *Voyennaya Strategiya* (Moscow:Voyenizdat, 1962), 335.

6. Ibid., 340.

7. Adm.V. A. Alafuzov, "On the Appearance of the Work 'Military Strategy,'" *Morskoy Sbornik* (no. 1, 1963), 94.

8. Marshal Sokolovskiy et al., eds., *Voyennaya Strategiya*, 2nd ed. (Moscow: Voyenizdat, 1963), 399.

9. This Soviet Shipyard No. 190 was established in St. Petersburg specifically to construct naval ships. Between 1935 and 1989 it was known as Zhdanov Shipyard. Subsequently it has been the SevernayaVerf (Northern Shipyard).

10. Rear Adm. K. A. Stalbo, "On Some Categories of Naval Art in Their Contemporary Manifestation," *Morskoy Sbornik* (no. 1, 1961).

11. Monakov, *GLAVKOM*, 526.

12. Gorshkov, "Navies in War and in Peace," 23.

13. Adm. Gorshkov, *Silovaya Derzhava Gosudarstva* [The Seapower of the State] (Moscow: Voenizdat, 1976); trans. and repr. in English, Annapolis, Md.: Naval Institute Press, 1979.

14. Adm. Gorshkov, *Red Star Rising at Sea* (Annapolis, Md.: U.S. Naval Institute, 1974).

15. Adm. Elmo R. Zumwalt Jr., in *Red Star Rising at Sea,* vi.

16. James M. McConnell, *The Gorshkov Articles, the New Gorshkov Book and Their Relation to Policy* (Arlington,Va.: Center for Naval Analyses, July 1976), 3–4.

17. Unlike Mahan, Gorshkov was neither a historian nor a theoretician. Perhaps his role in shaping the Soviet Navy might be better compared to that of von Tirpitz with the German Navy or Fisher with the British Royal Navy.

18. Rear Adm. George H. Miller, USN (Ret.), in *Red Star Rising at Sea,* 9.

19. Gorshkov, "Navies in War and in Peace," 13.

20. Rear Adm.V. S. Belli, "Theoretical Principles of Conducting Operations," 1938 Synopsis-Thesis at the Naval Academy, St. Petersburg; quoted in Gorshkov, "Navies in War and Peace," *Morskoy Sbornik* (no. 8, 1973), 21.

Chapter Thirteen. To the World's Oceans

Epigraph from James Cable, essay in *The Soviet Union in Europe and the Near East: Her Capabilities and Intentions* (report of a seminar sponsored jointly by Southampton University and the Royal United Services Institution, Milford-on-Sea, 23–25 March 1970).This essay was based in part on Cable's classic work *Gunboat Diplomacy.*

1. Rear Adm. George H. Miller, USN (Ret.), "Sea Power as an Instrument of National Strategy," lecture at the Naval War College, Newport, R.I. (8 January 1970).

2. Nikita Khrushchev, *Khrushchev Remembers: The Last Testament*, 431.

3. Gorshkov, "Navies in War and Peace," 16.

4. Central Intelligence Agency, *Soviet Naval Policy and Programs*, NIE 11–15–74 (Washington, D.C.: 23 December 1974), 7.

5. Gorshkov, "Navies in War and Peace," 17.

6. Ibid., 21.

7. Gorshkov, "Naval Cruises Play Role in Training, International Relations," *Bloknot Agitatora* (no. 8, April 1973), 6.

8. Percentages are rounded; see Robert G. Weinland, *Soviet Naval Operations: Ten Years of Change*, PP 125 (Arlington, Va.: Center for Naval Analyses, August 1974), and Bruce W. Watson, Red Navy at Sea: Soviet Naval Operations on the High Seas, 1956–1980 (Boulder, Colo.: Westview, 1982).

9. The Soviets lost their base rights in Egypt in 1972, shortly before the outbreak of the Arab-Israeli conflict of 1973.

10. Rear Adm. N. Navoytsev, in *Moscow News* (17 May 1969). Navoytsev, later admiral, served as Deputy CinC of the Navy for Operations from 1976 to 1986.

11. Most Soviet surface warships and auxiliaries in the Mediterranean were rotated from the Black Sea Fleet. Because of 1936 Montreux Convention restrictions on submarine passage through the Dardanelles, which required the craft to visit a dockyard before returning to the Black Sea, Soviet submarines in the Mediterranean were rotated from the Baltic or Northern Fleet, with all nuclear-propelled boats from the latter.

12. Gorshkov, *Red Star Rising at Sea*, 131–132.

13. Cdr. Robert Waring Herrick, USN (Ret.), *Soviet Naval Theory and Practice* (Newport, R.I.: Naval War College Press, 1988), 120, 129.

14. Lyle J. Goldstein and Y. M. Zhukov, "A Tale of Two Fleets: A Russian Perspective on the 1973 Naval Standoff in the Mediterranean," *Naval War College Review* (Spring 2004), 27–63.

15. An interesting commentary and potential responses is Lt. Cdr. William H. Gregory, USN, "Their Tattletales (Our Problems)," U.S. Naval Institute *Proceedings* (February 1984), 97–99.

16. Elmo R. Zumwalt Jr., *On Watch* (New York: Quadrangle, 1976), 446–447.

17. Vice Adm. Daniel Murphy, quoted in ibid., 447.

18. Portugal did make the airfield in the Azores available for U.S. aircraft flying to Israel.

19. See Watson, *Red Navy at Sea*, 150–151. This volume is the best published overview of Soviet naval operations for that period.

20. Ibid., 148.

21. Originally completed in 1987 as the *Baku*, the carrier was renamed the *Admiral Flota Sovetskogo Soyuza Gorshkov*; the ship was retired from the Russian Navy in 1996.

22. The large, four-turboprop, swept-wing Bear was developed as a strategic bomber for the Air Forces; subsequent variants were cruise missile carrier, reconnaissance, and naval recon/targeting. Originally given the military designation Tu-20 and the NATO name Bear, the aircraft primarily was known by the Tupolev bureau designation Tu-95 and the later variants as Tu-142.

23. George C. Wilson, "Two Soviet Warships Head for Angola," *Washington Post* (7 January 1975), A1, A12; Peter Osnos, "Soviets Deny Moving Warships toward Angola," *Washington Post* (9 January 1976), A7.

24. Dana Adams Schmidt, "Soviet Naval Force Sails among Hawaiian Islands," *New York Times* (18 September 1971), 15.

25. "Navy Cancels Maneuvers as Russians Planned Theirs," *Baltimore Sun* (21 April 1970), 1.

26. The relationship with Vietnam survived the demise of the Soviet regime: a submarine training center was established at Cam Ranh Bay for training Vietnamese submariners, followed by the transfer to Vietnam of six Russian-built Kilo (Project 636) submarines, beginning in 2014.

27. Watson, *Red Navy at Sea*, 67.

28. A. A. Gromyko, quoted in *Pravda* (11 July 1969).

29. Quoted in Ambassador Foy D. Kohler, "The New Role of the Soviet Navy as a Political Instrument in Foreign Affairs" (paper, University of Miami, Miami, Fla., 1973), 6.

30. Institute for Strategic Studies, *Strategic Survey 1969* (London: 1970), 6.

31. George C. Wilson, "Soviet Navy Still Far behind U.S. Sea Power," *Washington Post* (31 May 1971), A13.

Chapter Fourteen. The Final Years

The admiral's last words as given in the second epigraph are from Monakov, *GLAVKOM*, 636. V'yunenko was a naval theoretician and author.

1. V. N. Burov, *Otechestvennoye Voennoye Korablestroeniye* [Domestic Military Shipbuilding] (St. Petersburg: Sudostroeniye, 1995), 517.

2. Gorshkov, "Ocean Cruises: School of Combat Training" in *"Okean": Manevry Voyenno-Morskogo Flota SSSR, Provedenyye v Aprele–Maye 1970 Goda* [*Okean*: Maneuvers of the USSR Navy Conducted in April–May 1970], ed. Rear Adm. N. I. Shablikov et al. (Moscow: Military Publishing House, 1970), 15.

3. Marshal Grechko, "Always Be Prepared to Defend the Socialist Fatherland," in Shablikov, *"Okean,"* 7.

4. These exceptions include the U.S. Navy's large, full-deck amphibious assault ships designated LHA/LHD.

5. Dr. Norman Friedman, "The Soviet Fleet in Transition," U.S. Naval Institute *Proceedings* (May 1983), 173.

6. Capt. Thomas A. Brooks, USN, "Their Submarines," U.S. Naval Institute *Proceedings* (January 1984), 48. Brooks, a career intelligence officer, served as Director of Naval Intelligence from July 1988 to August 1991.

7. Office of Naval Intelligence, *The Russian Navy: A Historic Transition* (Washington, D.C.: December 2015), 17; available online at www.oni.navy.mil.

8. The most significant example being the Tu-20/Tu-95/Tu-142 Bear bomber aircraft, which has been in almost continuous production in many variants since the early 1950s; see chapter 13, note 22.

9. In addition to the two large Mi-8 helicopters, the *Leningrad* carried four Ka-25 Hormone helicopters during the Suez mine-clearing operation. In that period the carrier also operated in the northwest Indian Ocean before returning to the Black Sea.

10. Ustinov's first professional position was as a Navy artillery engineer.

11. "Father of the Red Navy to Get Pink Slip?," *Sea Power* [U.S. Navy League] (February 1983), 19. This story was widely told at the time, but was made without public documentation.

12. Manokav, *GLAVKOM,* 627.

13. See N. Polmar and Michael White, *Project Azorian: The CIA and the Raising of the K-129* (Annapolis, Md.: Naval Institute Press, 2010).

14. The debate is discussed by Dr. Robert C. Suggs, "The Soviet Navy: Changing of the Guard?," U.S. Naval Institute *Proceedings* (April 1983), 36–42.

15. DOSAAF—the Voluntary Society for Cooperation with the Army, Aviation, and Fleet—provided para-military training for boys, including specialized re-induction training for draftees.

16. These Gryphon GLCMs were the land-transported/launched version of the U.S. Navy's Tomahawk ship/submarine-launched land-attack missile.

17. Central Intelligence Agency, *The Gorshkov Succession: Implications for the Soviet Navy,* SOV-M-85-10176 (Washington, D.C.: 27 September 1985), 2.

18. Rear Adm. Nikolay V'yunenko, Capt. 1st Rank Boris N. Makeyev, and Capt. 1st Rank Valentin D. Skugarev, *The Navy: Its Role, Prospects for Deployment and Employment* (Moscow: Military Publishing House, 1988).

19. Theodore A. Neely Jr., review of *The Navy: Its Role, Prospects for Development and Employment,* by V'yunenko Makeyev, and Skugarev, U.S. Naval Institute *Proceedings* (January 1989), 124.

20. A similar concept was that used, on a much smaller scale, in the U.S. Navy's two Deep Submergence Rescue Vehicles (DSRVs), which had a maximum operating depth of 5,000 feet. Subsequently the concept was used with the Russian research submarine Project 1830 (given the "popular" name *Losharik*).

21. Rear Adm. Thomas A. Brooks, "A Nuclear War-Fighting Treatise," U.S. Naval Institute *Proceeedings* (May 1989), 138.

22. Manokav, *GLAVKOM*, 632, 636.

Chapter Fifteen. Summary and Conclusions

1. Cdr. Steve Kime, USN (Ret.), *An Officer's Story: A Politico-Military Journey* (Bloomington, Ind.: AuthorHouse, 2015), 135.

2. Kuzin and Nikol'skiy, *Voyenno-Morskoy Flot SSSR*, 16.

3. Ibid., 25.

4. Ibid., 29 [emphasis original].

5. Russian Navy Headquarters was moved from Moscow to the Admiralty complex in St. Petersburg in October 2012.

6. Discussions of aircraft carrier procurement in the Soviet Navy can be traced back to the 1930s.

7. The U.S. Naval Institute—despite its name and location on the grounds of the Naval Academy in Annapolis, Maryland, and the active and retired naval personnel on its boards—is a private, professional society. It was established in 1873.

8. Gorshkov, *Seapower of the State*.

9. "Russia: Power Play on the Oceans," *Time* (23 February 1968), 23–28.

10. C. L. Sulzberger, "Admiral of the World Ocean," *New York Times* (26 February 1977), 19.

11. Herrick, *Soviet Naval Theory and Policy*, 282.

12. James M. McConnell, *The Soviet Naval Mission Structure*, CNA 85-1865 (Alexandria, Va.: Center for Naval Analyses, 1985), 19.

13. Polmar and Whitman, *Hunters and Killers*, vol. 2, esp. chapter 9, "Strategic ASW: The United States," 147–154.

14. Lt. Cdr. Harlan Ullman, USN, "The Counter-Polaris Task," in *Soviet Naval Policy: Objectives and Constraints,* ed. Michael MccGwire, Ken Booth, and John McDonnell (New York: Praeger, 1975), 597.

15. In 1906, after his retirement, Mahan was promoted to rear admiral in recognition of his service in the American Civil War.

16. For example, Rickover strongly opposed gas turbine propulsion for surface warships; see Norman Polmar and Thomas B. Allen, *Rickover: Controversy and Genius* (New York: Doubleday, 1982), 228–229, 233–236.

17. Gorshkov, "Navies in War and Peace."

Chapter Sixteen. From Soviet Navy to Russian Navy

1. See N. Polmar, "Beneath the Waves," U.S. Naval Institute *Proceedings* (June 2012), 88–89; and "Shipyards: Can They Build a New Fleet?" *Proceedings* (April 2017), 72–73.

2. Malachite was responsible primarily for the design of nuclear-propelled attack submarines, including the November, Alfa, Victor, Akula, and *Severodvinsk* classes.

3. Office of Naval Intelligence, *Russian Navy*, 16.

4. Thomas Fedyszyn, "Russia's Navy Rising," *National Interest* (28 December 2013), online at http://nationalinterest.org/commentary/russias-navy-new-red-storm-rising-9616.

5. "Russia to Expand Mediterranean Fleet to 10 Warships—Navy Chief," *Russia Today* (13 September 2013), 1.

6. See N. Polmar, "Putin's 'Fleet in Being,'" U.S. Naval Institute *Proceedings* (December 2015), 86.

7. The air group consisted of ten Su-33 Flanker-D, five newer MiG-29 Fulcrum fighters, and an assortment of helicopters: Ka-27 Hormone anti-submarine, Ka-31 Helix airborne early warning, and Ka-52K Hokum-B attack/gunship variants.

8. "Russia Significantly Boosts Nuclear Fleet," *Russia Today* (31 July 2012), 1.

9. *Russia's National Security Strategy to 2020*, Decree of the President of the Russian Federation, Nr. 537 (12 May 2009).

10. Decree of the President of the Russian Federation on approval of the fundamentals of the state policy of the Russian Federation in the field of naval activities for the period until 2030, Nr. 327 (20 July 2017), online at Kremlin.ru/media/acts/files/0001201707200015.pdf.

SELECTED BIBLIOGRAPHY

Books—Russian

Abramonov, P. F. *Admiral: O Dvazhdi Geroye Sovetskogo Soyuza S. G. Gorshkov* [Admiral: Twice Hero of the Soviet Union S. G. Gorshkov]. Moscow: Politizdat, 1986.

Bolshaya Sovetskaya Entsiklopediya [Large Soviet Encyclopedia]. Vol. 7. Moscow: 1972.

Burov, V. N. *Otechestvennoye Voennoye Korablestroyeniye* [Domestic Military Shipbuilding]. St. Petersburg: Sudostroyeniye, 1995.

Gorshkov, S. G. *Morskaya Moshch Gosudarstva* [The Seapower of the State]. Moscow: Voyenizdat, 1976; reprinted in English by the Naval Institute Press, 1979.

————. *Vo Flotskom Stroyu* [In Naval Ranks]. St. Petersburg: LOGOS, 1996.

Grechko, A. A. *Bitva za Kavkaz* [Battle for the Caucasus]. Moscow: Voyenizdat, 1989.

Kasatonov, I. *Flot Vykhodit v Okean: Povest' ob admirale flota V. A. Kasatonove* [The Fleet Goes Out to the Ocean: The Story of Fleet Admiral V. A. Kasatonov]. St. Petersburg: Astra-Luxe, 1995.

Kirin, I. D. *Chernomorskiy Flot v Bitve za Kavkaz* [The Black Sea Fleet in the Battle for the Caucasus]. Moscow: Voyenizdat, 1958.

Kuzin, V. P., and N. I. Nikol'skiy. *Voyenno-Morskoy Flot SSSR 1945–1991* [The USSR Navy 1945–1991]. St. Petersburg: Historical Naval Society, 1996. English translation by the Defense Intelligence Agency, LN54–98, 1998.

Monakov, M. S. *GLAVKOM: Zhizn' i Rabota Admirala Flota Sovetskogo Soyuza S. G. Gorshkova* [Commander-in-Chief: The Life and Work of Fleet Admiral of the Soviet Union S. G. Gorshkov]. Moscow: Kuchkovo Polye, 2008.

Polmar, Norman, and K. J. Moore. *Podvodnyye Lodki Kholodnoy Voyny: Proyektirovaniye i Stroitel'stvo Podvodnykh Lodok SShA i SSSR* [Cold War Submarines: The Design and Construction of U.S. and Soviet Submarines]. St. Petersburg: Malachite, 2011.

Pospelov, P. N. *Istoriya Velikoy Otechestvennoy Voyny Sovetskogo Soyuza 1941–1945* [History of the Great Patriotic War of the Soviet Union 1941–1945]. Vol. 3. Moscow: Voyenizdat, 1961.

Shablikov, N. I., et al. *Okean: Manevry Voyenno-Morskogo Flota SSSR Provedenyye v Aprele–Maye 1970 Goda* [Okean: Maneuvers Conducted by the Soviet Navy in April–May 1970]. Moscow: Military Publishing House, 1970.

Sokolovskiy, V. D., et al., eds. *Voyennaya Strategiya* [Military Strategy]. Moscow: Voyenizdat, 1st edition 1962; 2nd edition 1963; 3rd edition 1968.

Sorokin, A. I. *My s Atomnykh Podvodnykh Lodok* [We Are from the Nuclear Submarines]. Moscow: DOSAAF, 1969.

Spassky, I. D., ed. *Istoriya Otechestvennogo Sudostryoeniya.* Vol. 5, *1946–1991* [History of Indigenous Shipbuilding]. St. Petersburg: Sudostroyeniye, 1996.

V'yunenko, Nikolay P., Boris N. Makeyev, and Valentin D. Skugarev. *Flot: Yego Rol', Perspektivy Razvertyvaniya i Zanyatnosti* [The Navy: Its Role, Prospects for Deployment and Employment]. Moscow: Military Publishing House, 1988.

Books—English

Bathurst, R. B. *Understanding the Soviet Navy: A Handbook.* Newport, R.I.: Naval War College Press, 1979.

Baumbach, Werner. *The Life and Death of the Luftwaffe.* New York: Ballantine, 1960.

Bialer, Seweryn. *Stalin and His Generals.* London: Souvenir, 1970.

Bollinger, Martin J. *Warriors and Wizards: The Development and Defeat of Radio-Controlled Glide Bombs of the Third Reich.* Annapolis, Md.: Naval Institute Press, 2000.

Bradley, John. *Allied Intervention in Russia, 1919–1920.* New York: Basic Books, 1968.

Brown, Archie, et al. *The Cambridge Encyclopedia of Russia and the Soviet Union.* Cambridge. Cambridge University Press, 1982.

Cable, James. *Gunboat Diplomacy.* New York: Praeger, 1971.

Chuikov, V. I. *The Battle for Stalingrad.* New York: Holt, Rinehart, and Winston, 1964.

Conquest, Robert. *The Great Terror.* London: Macmillan, 1968.

Dismukes, Bradford, and James McConnell, eds. *Soviet Naval Diplomacy.* New York: Pergamon, 1979.

Djilas, Milovan. *Conversations with Stalin.* New York: Harcourt, Brace, and World, 1962.

Erickson, John. *The Soviet High Command 1918–1941.* London: Macmillan, 1962.

Fleming, Peter. *The Fate of Admiral Kolchak.* New York: Harcourt, Brace, and World, 1963.

Goldman, Stuart D. *Nomonhan, 1939: The Red Army's Victory That Shaped World War II.* Annapolis, Md.: Naval Institute Press, 2012.

Gorshkov, S. G. *Red Star Rising at Sea*. Annapolis, Md.: Naval Institute Press, 1974.

————. *The Seapower of the State*. Oxford [U.K.]: Pergamon, 1979.

Gribkov, Anatoli I., and William Y. Smith. *Operation Anadyr: U.S. and Soviet Generals Recount the Cuban Missile Crisis*. Chicago: Edition q, 1994.

Halliday, E. M. *The Ignorant Armies*. New York: Harper Brothers, 1958.

Herrick, Robert Waring. *Soviet Naval Strategy*. Annapolis, Md.: U.S. Naval Institute, 1968.

————. *Soviet Naval Theory and Practice*. Newport, R.I.: Naval War College Press, 1988.

————. *Soviet Naval Theory and Policy: Gorshkov's Inheritance*. Annapolis, Md.: Naval Institute Press, 1998.

Khrushchev, Nikita S. *Khrushchev Remembers*. Boston: Little, Brown, 1970.

————. *Khrushchev Remembers: The Last Testament*. Boston: Little, Brown, 1974.

Khrushchev, Sergey N. *Nikita Khrushchev and the Creation of a Superpower*. University Park: Penn State University Press, 2000.

Kime, Steve. *An Officer's Story: A Politico-Military Journey*. Bloomington, Ind.: AuthorHouse, 2015.

Kolkowicz, Roman. *The Soviet Military and the Communist Party*. Princeton, N.J.: Princeton University Press, 1967.

Kuznetzov, N. G. *Memoirs of the Wartime Minister of the Navy*. Moscow: Progress, 1970.

Lincoln, W. Bruce. *Red Victory: A History of the Russian Civil War*. New York: Simon and Schuster, 1989.

Luckett, Richard. *The White Generals: An Account of the White Movement and the Russian Civil War*. New York: Viking, 1971.

MccGwire, Michael., ed. *Soviet Naval Developments: Capability and Context*. New York: Praeger, 1973.

————, Ken Booth, and John McDonnell, eds. *Soviet Naval Policy: Objectives and Constraints*. New York: Praeger, 1975.

———— and John McDonnell, eds. *Soviet Naval Influence: Domestic and Foreign Dimensions*. New York: Praeger, 1977.

McGruther, Kenneth R. *The Evolving Soviet Navy*. Newport, R.I.: Naval War College Press, 1978.

Meister, Jurg. *Soviet Warships of the Second World War*. London: Macdonald and Jane's, 1977.

Miller, Jerry [Gerald E.]. *Nuclear Weapons and Aircraft Carriers: How the Bomb Saved Naval Aviation*. Washington, D.C.: Smithsonian Institution Press, 2001.

Mitchell, Donald W. *A History of Russian and Soviet Sea Power*. New York: Macmillan, 1974.

Murphy, David E. *What Stalin Knew: The Enigma of Barbarossa.* New Haven, Conn.: Yale University Press, 2005.

Nguyen, Hung P. *Submarine Detection from Space: A Study of Russian Capabilities.* Annapolis, Md.: Naval Institute Press, 1993.

Penkovskiy, Oleg. *The Penkovskiy Papers.* New York: Doubleday, 1965.

Pipes, Richard. *Russia under the Old Regime.* New York: Charles Scribner's Sons, 1974.

Podvig, Pavel. *Russian Strategic Nuclear Forces.* Cambridge, Mass.: MIT Press, 2001.

Poirier, Robert G., and Albert Z. Conner. *The Red Army Order of Battle in the Great Patriotic War.* Novato, Calif.: Presidio, 1985.

Polmar, Norman. *Aircraft Carriers: A History of Carrier Aviation and Its Influence on World Events.* Vol. 2, *1946–2006.* Washington, D.C.: Potomac Books, 2008.

———— and K. J. Moore. *Cold War Submarines: The Design and Construction of U.S. and Soviet Submarines.* Washington D.C.: Brassey's, 2004.

———— and Jurrien Noot. *Submarines of the Russian and Soviet Navies, 1718–1990.* Annapolis, Md.: Naval Institute Press, 1991.

———— and John O'Connell. *Strike from the Sea.* Annapolis, Md.: Naval Institute Press, 2018.

————, Eric Wertheim, and Mark Warren. *Chronology of the Cold War at Sea 1945–1991.* Annapolis, Md.: Naval Institute Press, 1998.

———— and Michael White. *Project Azorian: The CIA and the Raising of the K-129.* Annapolis, Md.: Naval Institute Press, 2010.

———— and Edward Whitman. *Hunters and Killers: Anti-Submarine Warfare since 1943.* Vol. 2. Annapolis, Md.: Naval Institute Press, 2016.

Rohwer, Jürgen, and Gerhard Hummelchen. *Chronology of the War at Sea.* London: Ian Allan, 1972.

———— and Mikhail S. Monakov. *Stalin's Ocean-Going Fleet: Soviet Naval Strategy and Shipbuilding Programmes 1935–1953.* London: Frank Cass, 2001.

Ruge, Friedrich. *Der Seekrieg: The German Navy's Story 1939–1945.* Annapolis, Md.: U.S. Naval Institute, 1957.

Saunders, M. G., ed. *The Soviet Navy.* New York: Praeger, 1958.

Serge, Victor. *Year One of the Russian Revolution.* New York: Holt, Rinehart and Winston, 1972.

Smith, Frederic N. *Biographical Directory of Flag Rank Soviet & Russian Naval Officers 1917–1999.* Arlington, Va.: Newcomb, 2000.

Sokolovskiy, V. D. *Soviet Military Strategy.* London: Macdonald and Jane's, 1975.

Tolley, Kemp. *Caviar and Commissars: The Experience of a U.S. Naval Officer in Stalin's Russia.* Annapolis, Md.: Naval Institute Press, 1983.

Watson, Bruce W. *Red Navy at Sea: Soviet Naval Operations on the High Seas, 1956–1980.* Boulder, Colo.: Westview, 1982.

Ziemke, Earl F. *Stalingrad to Berlin: The German Defeat in the East.* Washington, D.C.: Department of the Army, 1967.

Zumwalt, Elmo R. *On Watch.* New York: Quadrangle, 1976.

Articles—Russian

(Most of these articles were read in English-language translations, hence page numbers for the original articles are not provided here.)

Alafuzov, V. A. "On the Appearance of the Work 'Military Strategy.'" *Morskoy Sbornik* (no. 1, 1963).

Fakayev, K. F. "The Landing at Grigorevka." *Morskoy Sbornik* (no. 9, 1971).

Gorshkov, S. G. "The Black Sea Fleet in the Battle of the Caucasus." *Voyenno-Istoricheskiy Zhurnal* (no. 3, 1976).

———. "The Development of Naval Science." *Morskoy Sbornik* (no. 2, 1967).

———. "Faithful Guard over the Security of the Homeland." *Sovetskiy Flot* (23 February 1960).

———. "Navies in War and Peace." *Morskoy Sbornik* (no. 5, 1972); (no. 10, 1972); (no. 12, 1972); (no. 2, 1973); (no. 8, 1973).

———. "The Oceanic Guard of the Homeland." *Agitator* (July 1974).

Kuznetsov, N. G. "The Navy on the Eve of the Great Fatherland War." *Voyenno-Istoricheskiy Zhurnal* (no. 9, 1965).

———. "On the Eve." *Oktyabr'* (no. 11, 1965); reprinted in Bialer, *Stalin and His Generals,* 189–200.

Malinovskiy, Rodion Ya. "The Revolution in Military Affairs and the Task of the Military Press." *Kommunist Vooruzhennykh Sil* (November 1963).

Shmakov, R. A. "Ahead of Their Time." *Morskoy Sbornik* (no. 7, 1996).

Stalbo, K. A. "The Naval Art in the Landings of the Great Patriotic War." *Morskoy Sbornik* (no. 3, 1970).

———. "On Some Categories of Naval Art in Their Contemporary Manifestation." *Morskoy Sbornik* (no. 1, 1961).

———. "Some Issues of the Theory of the Development and Employment of the Navy." *Morskoy Sbornik* (no. 4, 1981); (no. 5, 1981).

Sverdlov, A. "The Azov Flotilla on the Offensive (August–September 1943)." *Morskoy Sbornik* (no. 9, 1973).

Vorobyev, K. "In the Rush of Combat." *Morskoy Sbornik* (no. 2, 1980).

Zonin, Sergey. "An Unjust Trial." *Morskoy Sbornik* (no. 2, 1989).

Articles—English

(USNIP = U.S. Naval Institute *Proceedings*)

Baritz, Joseph J. "Soviet Military Theory: Politics and War," *Military Review* (September 1966): 310.

Basoco, Richard M., and Richard H. Webber. "Kynda-Class Missile Frigates." USNIP (September 1964): 140–142.

Beecher, William. "Soviet Missile Sub on Atlantic Post." *New York Times* (24 April 1970): 1.

Brooks, Thomas A. "Soviet Navy Perspective." USNIP (May 1989): 224–231. (This is an abridged version of Rear Adm. Brooks' 22 February 1989 statement before the Seapower Strategic, and Critical Materials Subcommittee on Intelligence, House of Representatives.)

———. "Their Submarines." USNIP (January 1984): 48–50.

———. "A U.S. View: Still Cautious." USNIP (May 1991): 183–187.

———. "Whither the Soviet Navy?." USNIP (February 1980): 103–104.

Erickson, John. "The Soviet Naval High Command." USNIP (May 1973): 66–87.

"Father of the Red Navy to Get Pink Slip?." *Sea Power* (February 1983): 19.

Fedyszyn, Thomas R. "Putin's Potemkin-Plus Navy." USNIP (May 2016): 42–47.

———. "Renaissance of the Russian Navy?." USNIP (March 2012): 30–35.

———. "Russia's Rising Navy." *National Interest*, 28 December 2013, online at http://nationalinterest.org/commentary/russias-navy-new-red-storm-rising-9616.

Friedman, Norman. "The Soviet Fleet in Transition." USNIP (May 1983): 156–173.

Goldstein, Lyle J., and Y. M. Zhukov. "A Tale of Two Fleets: A Russian Perspective on the 1973 Naval Standoff in the Mediterranean." *Naval War College Review* (Spring 2004): 27–63.

Gregory, William H. "Their Tattletales (Our Problems)." USNIP (February 1984): 97–99.

Kime, Steve F., et al. "Gorshkov's Final Words: What Do They Mean?." USNIP (May 1989): 131–148.

Manthorpe, William H. J., Jr. "The Influence of Being Russian on the Officers and Men of the Soviet Navy." USNIP (May 1978): 128–143.

———. "The Soviet View: Changing in 1990." USNIP (May 1991): 187–190.

———. "What the Soviets Are Saying." USNIP (May 1989): 218–222.

MccGwire, Michael. "Gorshkov's Navy," Part I. USNIP (August 1989): 44–51.

———. "Gorshkov's Navy," Part II. USNIP (September 1989): 42–47.

"Navy Cancels Maneuvers as Russians Planned Theirs." *Baltimore Sun* (21 April 1970): 1.

Neely, Theodore A. Review of *The Navy: Its Role, Prospects for Development and Employment,* by Nikolay P., V'yunenko, Boris N. Makeyev, and Valentin D. Skugarev. USNIP (January 1989): 124.

Osnos, Peter. "Soviets Deny Moving Warships Toward Angola." *Washington Post,* 9 January 1976, A7.

Polmar, Norman. "Antiship Ballistic Missiles ... Again." USNIP (July 2005): 86–87.

———. "Beneath the Waves." USNIP (June 2012): 88–89.

———. "A Continuing Interest . . . in Submarines." USNIP (November 1994): 103–105.

———. "Nuclear War at Sea." USNIP (July 1986): 111–113.

———. "Putin's Fleet in Being." USNIP (December 2015): 86–87.

———. "The Quest for the Quiet Submarine." USNIP (October 1995): 119–121.

———. "Shipyards: Can They Build a New Fleet?" USNIP (April 2017): 72–73.

———. "Strike from the Sea." USNIP (June 2006): 86–87.

———. "Submarines: All Ahead—Very, Very Slowly." USNIP (December 1998): 87–88.

———. "Trying to Get a Handle on Strategy." USNIP (July 1990): 101–102.

——— and Norman Friedman. "Their Missions and Tactics." USNIP (October 1982): 34–44.

———et al. "The Soviet Navy: An Update." USNIP (December 1985): 38–53.

———et al. "Their Navy's Future." USNIP (January 1984): 47–56.

Rickover, H. G. "The Soviet Naval Program." *New York Times* (13 November 1970): 36.

Rohwer, Jürgen. "Admiral Gorshkov and the Influence of History upon Sea Power." USNIP (May 1981): 150–173.

"Russia Significantly Boosts Nuclear Fleet." *Russia Today* (31 July 2012).

"Russia to Expand Mediterranean Fleet to 10 Warships—Navy Chief." *Russia Today* (13 September 2013).

"Russia: Power Play on the Oceans." *Time* (3 February 1968): 23–28.

Schmidt, Dana Adams. "Soviet Naval Force Sails among Hawaiian Islands." *New York Times* (18 September 1971): 15.

Suggs, Robert C. "The Soviet Navy: Changing of the Guard?" USNIP (April 1983): 36–42.

Sulzberger, C. L. "Admiral of the World Ocean." *New York Times* (26 February 1977): 19.

Whelan, Matthew J. "The Growing Soviet Amphibious Warfare Capability." USNIP (August 1979): 111–115.

Wilson, George C. Wilson. "Soviet Navy Still Far behind U.S. Sea Power." *Washington Post* (31 May 1971): A13.

———. "Two Soviet Warships Head For Angola." *Washington Post* (7 January 1975): A1, A12.

General Reference Works

Bolshaya Sovetskaya Entsiklopediya [Great Soviet Encyclopedia]. Moscow: 1972.

Combat Fleets of the World. Annapolis, Md.: Naval Institute Press, various editions.

Meister, Jurig. *Soviet Warships of the Second World War.* London: Macdonald and Jane's, 1977.

Polmar, Norman. *Guide to the Soviet Navy.* Annapolis, Md.: Naval Institute Press, various editions 1977–1991.

Slovar' Biograficheskoy Morskoy [Naval Biographical Dictionary]. St. Petersburg: LOGOS, 2001.

Miscellaneous

Belli, V. S. *Theoretical Principles of Conducting Naval Operations.* Lecture at the Naval Academy, St. Petersburg, 1938; quoted in Gorshkov, "Navies in War and Peace," *Morskoy Sbornik* (no. 8, 1973).

Cable, James. Essay published in *The Soviet Union in Europe and the Near East: Her Capabilities and Intentions*—a report of a seminar sponsored jointly by Southampton University and the Royal United Services Institution, Milford-on-Sea, 23–25 March 1970.

Central Intelligence Agency. *The Gorshkov Succession: Implications for the Soviet Navy.* SOV-M-85-10176. Washington, D.C., 27 September 1985.

———. *Soviet General Purpose Deployments outside Home Waters: Characteristics and Trends.* Washington, D.C., June 1972.

———. *Soviet Naval Policy and Programs.* NIE 11-15-74. Washington, D.C., 23 December 1974.

———. *Soviet Naval Writings: A Framework for Antisubmarine Warfare Strategy.* SR IR 71-12. Washington, D.C., July 1971.

———. *The Soviet Navy: Strategy, Growth, and Capabilities.* SR QP 72-2. Washington, D.C., June 1972.

Defense Intelligence Agency. *Soviet Maritime Expansion.* Washington, D.C., 1971.

———. *Soviet Naval Shipbuilding.* Washington, D.C., July 1976.

Gorshkov, S. G. Manuscript of *Yug,* chapter 2, "In the Sea of Azov."

Hoppe, Herbert, Norman Polmar, and A. C. Trapold. *Measures and Trends: US and USSR Strategic Force Effectiveness.* Alexandria, Va.: Santa Fe Corp., March 1978.

International Institute for Strategic Studies. *Military Balance*. London, various editions.

_____. *Strategic Survey 1969*. London, 1970.

Kohler, Foy D. "The New Role of the Soviet Navy as a Political Instrument in Foreign Affairs." Paper, University of Miami, Fla., 1973.

McConnell, James M. *The Gorshkov Articles, the New Gorshkov Book and Their Relation to Policy*. Arlington, Va.: Center for Naval Analyses, July 1976.

Melnikov, P. Ye., and Yu. I. Chernov. *Sovetskaya Voyenaya Entsiklopediya* [Soviet Military Encyclopedia]. Vol. 5. Moscow: Voyenizdat, 1978.

Miller, George H. "Sea Power as an Instrument of National Strategy." Lecture, Naval War College, Newport, R.I., 8 January 1970.

Ministry of Defense. *Pamyatka Soldatu Serzhantu po Zashchiteot Atomnogo Oruzhiya* [Handbook for Soldiers and Sergeants on Protection against Atomic Ordnance]. Moscow, 1954.

Office of Naval Intelligence, U.S. Navy. *The Russian Navy: A Historic Transition*. Washington, D.C., December 2015. Available at: www.oni.navy.mil.

———. *Understanding Soviet Naval Developments*. Washington, D.C., 1976.

Russia's National Security Strategy to 2020. Decree of the President of the Russian Federation, no. 537, 12 May 2009.

Shadrin, Nicholas [Nicholas Artamonov]. "Development of Soviet Maritime Power." Unpublished PhD dissertation, George Washington University, Washington, D.C., September 1972.

Weinland, Robert G. *Soviet Naval Operations: Ten Years of Change*. PP 125. Arlington, Va.: Center for Naval Analyses, August 1974.

———, Michael K. MccGwire, and James M. McConnell. *Admiral Gorshkov on Navies in War and Peace*. Arlington, Va.: Center for Naval Analyses, September 1974.

Websites

www.cia.gov
www.dtic.mil
www.oni.navy.mil

GENERAL INDEX

NATO code names are provided for Soviet/Russian aircraft.

SHIP AND SUBMARINE INDEX

All ships are Soviet/Russian unless otherwise indicated. NATO code names are shown in Roman type.

AS	submarine tender	DD	destroyer
BB	battleship	DDG	guided missile destroyer★
CA	heavy cruiser	DL	destroyer leader
CB	battle cruiser	FFG	guided missile frigate
CG	guided missile cruiser★	MGB	motor gunboat
CL	light cruiser	MTB	motor torpedo boat
CV	aircraft carrier	PC	patrol ship
CVA	attack aircraft carrier★	PCG	guided missile patrol ship
CVA	heavy aircraft carrier★★	PTG	guided missile craft
CVG	guided missile aircraft carrier	SS	submarine★
		SSB	ballistic missile submarine★
CVHG	guided missile helicopter carrier	SSG	guided missile submarine★

★ The suffix letter "N" indicates nuclear propulsion.

★★ Only assigned to the never-built *United States* (CVA 58).

ABOUT THE AUTHORS

Norman Polmar is an analyst, author, and consultant, specializing in naval, aviation, and technology subjects. He has directed studies related to the Soviet/Russian navies for various government organizations and industry, and has been a consultant or advisor on related issues to three U.S. Senators, the Speaker of the House, the Deputy Counselor to the President, and three Secretaries of the Navy. He has visited the Soviet Union/Russia several times as a guest of the Navy commander-in-chief, the submarine design bureaus, and the Institute of U.S. Studies. He has written or coauthored more than 50 published books.

Thomas A. Brooks, a retired rear admiral, was a career naval intelligence officer, serving in assignments afloat and ashore, including in Vietnam. He served as Director of Naval Intelligence from 1988 to 1991. Following his retirement from the Navy, he began a second career with AT&T, holding a senior position with the firm until 2001. Subsequently he was a faculty member at the National Defense Intelligence College for nine years, where he taught courses on intelligence history, warning, and industry-intelligence relationships. He has written extensively on intelligence-related subjects.

George E. Fedoroff is the Senior Intelligence Officer for Russia matters within the Office of Naval Intelligence, where he has
served since 1971. He has visited the Soviet Union/Russia on numerous occasions; since 1976 he has been a member of the U.S.
Navy delegation to annual U.S.-Soviet/Russian Navy Incidents at
Sea Agreement compliance reviews, and from 1991 through 2013 he
participated in the annual multi-national meetings and at-sea exercises involving the Russian Navy. Fluent in Russian, he has acted
as interpreter for the chairman of the U.S. Joint Chiefs of Staff, and
has participated in visit exchanges between senior U.S. and Soviet/
Russian naval officials, numerous ship visits, meetings, and sympo-
sia on naval issues.